# Contemporary Anti-Natalism

Given the pain, discomfort, anxiety, heartbreak, and boredom that most humans experience in their lives, is it morally permissible to create them? Some philosophers lately have answered 'No', contending that it is wrong to create a new human life when one could avoid doing so, because it would be bad for the one created. This view is known as 'anti-natalism'. Some contributors to this volume argue that anti-natalism is true because: agents have a *prima facie* duty to prevent suffering; it is immoral to violate another's right not to be harmed without having consented to it; and it is a serious wrong to exploit the weakness of a poorly off being to become a biological parent. Others here argue against anti-natalism on the ground, for instance, that many of our lives are not so bad and in fact are quite good and that the logic of anti-natalism absurdly entails pro-mortalism, the view that we should kill off as many people as possible. This book explores these and related issues concerning the evaluative question of how to judge the worthwhileness of lives and the normative question of what basic duties entail for the creation of new lives. Excepting one, all the chapters in this book were originally published in the *South African Journal of Philosophy*.

**Thaddeus Metz**, Professor of Philosophy at the University of Pretoria, South Africa, is particularly known for his work on philosophical approaches to the meaning of life. His books on the topic include: *Meaning in Life*; *God, Soul and the Meaning of Life*; and *What Makes a Life Meaningful? A Debate* (with Joshua Seachris, Routledge 2023).

# Contemporary Anti-Natalism

*Edited by*
**Thaddeus Metz**

LONDON AND NEW YORK

First published 2023
by Routledge
4 Park Square, Milton Park, Abingdon, Oxon OX14 4RN

and by Routledge
605 Third Avenue, New York, NY 10158

*Routledge is an imprint of the Taylor & Francis Group, an informa business*

*British Library Cataloguing in Publication Data*
A catalogue record for this book is available from the British Library

ISBN13: 978-1-032-35033-2 (hbk)
ISBN13: 978-1-032-35034-9 (pbk)
ISBN13: 978-1-003-32495-9 (ebk)

DOI: 10.4324/9781003324959

Typeset in Times New Roman
by Newgen Publishing UK

**Publisher's Note**
The publisher accepts responsibility for any inconsistencies that may have arisen during the conversion of this book from journal articles to book chapters, namely the inclusion of journal terminology.

**Disclaimer**
Every effort has been made to contact copyright holders for their permission to reprint material in this book. The publishers would be grateful to hear from any copyright holder who is not here acknowledged and will undertake to rectify any errors or omissions in future editions of this book.

# Contents

# Citation Information

Twelve of the thirteen chapters in this book were originally published in the *South African Journal of Philosophy*. The remaining one chapter was first published in the journal *Philosophical Papers*. When citing this material, please use the original page numbering for each article, as follows:

**Chapter 1**
*Contemporary Anti-Natalism, Featuring Benatar's* Better Never to Have Been
Thaddeus Metz
*South African Journal of Philosophy,* volume 31, issue 1 (2012), pp. 1–9

**Chapter 2**
*Hooray for Babies*
David Spurrett
*South African Journal of Philosophy,* volume 30, issue 2 (2011), pp. 197–206

**Chapter 3**
*Are Lives Worth Creating?*
Thaddeus Metz
*Philosophical Papers,* volume 40, issue 2 (2011), pp. 233–255

**Chapter 4**
*Better to Be*
David Boonin
*South African Journal of Philosophy,* volume 31, issue 1 (2012), pp. 10–25

**Chapter 5**
*Is Having Children Always Wrong?*
Rivka Weinberg
*South African Journal of Philosophy,* volume 31, issue 1 (2012), pp. 26–37

**Chapter 6**
*Sick and Healthy: Benatar on the Logic of Value*
Skott Brill
*South African Journal of Philosophy,* volume 31, issue 1 (2012), pp. 38–54

For any permission-related enquiries please visit:
www.tandfonline.com/page/help/permissions

# Notes on Contributors

**Christopher Belshaw**, The Open University, England, UK.

**David Benatar**, Department of Philosophy, University of Cape Town, South Africa.

**David Boonin**, Department of Philosophy, University of Colorado, USA.

**Skott Brill**, Department of Philosophy, Frostburg State University, Maryland, USA.

**Gerald Harrison**, College of Humanities and Social Sciences, Massey University, New Zealand.

**Rafe McGregor**, Department of Law and Criminology, Edge Hill University, Ormskirk, UK.

**Thaddeus Metz**, Department of Philosophy, University of Pretoria, South Africa.

**Asheel Singh**, Department of Philosophy, University of Johannesburg, South Africa.

**Saul Smilansky**, Department of Philosophy, University of Haifa, Israel.

**David Spurrett**, Department of Philosophy, University of KwaZulu-Natal, South Africa.

**Ema Sullivan-Bissett**, School of Philosophy, Theology and Religion, University of Birmingham, England, UK.

**Brooke Alan Trisel**, Independent Scholar, Columbus, USA.

**Rivka Weinberg**, Department of Philosophy, Scripps College, Claremont, CA, USA.

# Contemporary Anti-Natalism, Featuring Benatar's *Better Never to Have Been*

## Thaddeus Metz

## 1. Introduction

Anti-natalism is the view that procreation is invariably wrong to some degree and is often all things considered impermissible. The variant of anti-natalism that has interested philosophers in the past 25 years or so includes a claim about why it is morally problematic, namely, that potential procreators owe a duty *to the individual who would have been created* not to create her, as opposed to already existent people who would be wronged by her creation.[1] Contemporary anti-natalism is fascinating and important for requiring sophisticated reflection on the evaluative question of how to judge the worthwhileness of lives and on the normative question of what basic duties entail for the creation of new lives.[2]

Before the mid-1970s, English-speaking philosophers by and large accepted utilitarian answers to these questions, maintaining that a worthwhile life is one with a large net sum of (perhaps, higher) pleasures relative to pains, and that, roughly, one morally ought to promote such lives. Contemporary anti-natalists reject at least one of these utilitarian implications; their views should be seen as part of the flowering of anti-utilitarian value theory. First, contemporary anti-natalists often maintain that whether a life is worthwhile is not merely a function of a sufficiently high aggregate of positive and negative magnitudes. Some of them maintain that a single episode of badness, if it were large enough in absolute terms, would render life not worth living, regardless of the amount of goodness exhibited elsewhere in the life[3]; others hold that the value of well-being is personal, rather than impersonal, in the sense that pleasure provides a reason for one who already exists to experience it, but does not provide a reason to create a 'container person', in John Rawls' influential phrase, who would then experience it. Second, contemporary anti-natalists tend to hold a deontological conception of morality, according to which agents, say, must observe the rights of individuals to control their own lives or may not treat others' dignity merely as a means to a procreative end.

Notice that these kinds of principles transcend utilitarianism not merely in its positive variant, but also in its negative one. Negative utilitarianism is the view that one's sole basic duty is to minimize pain, where positive goods such as pleasure have no moral weight. Negative utilitarianism is well-known for entailing anti-natalism as well

---

1  For an instance of the latter view, see Paul Ehrlich, *The Population Bomb* (New York: Ballantine Books, 1968).

2  Note that the latter question, of how to act, is not for all anti-natalists based on how one answers the former question, of how to evaluate the quality of a life.

3  Where the prospect of death might be such a bad!

as pro-mortalism,[4] the view that it is often prudent for individuals to kill themselves and often right for them to kill others, even without their consent. It pretty clearly has these implications if one can kill oneself or others painlessly, but probably does so even if there would be terror beforehand; for there would likely be terror regardless of when death comes, and if death were to come sooner rather than later, then additional bads that would have been expected in the course of a life would be nipped in the bud. As counter-intuitive as the doctrine of anti-natalism might *itself* be, contemporary anti-natalists typically seek to defend it without appealing to principles, such as negative utilitarianism, that have (otherwise) absurd implications such as pro-mortalism. They aim to show that, although it is wrong to procreate, perhaps because it would be better never to create new lives, it does not follow either that, once a person exists, it would be better for her to die, or that one may rightly end others' (perhaps undesirable) existence against their will.

In short, contemporary anti-natalists aim to show that the balance of what is currently deemed moral common-sense amongst professional philosophers goes in their favour. They claim to be teasing out the unexpected anti-natal implications of principles that are widely held by academic ethicists, who tend not to be utilitarian these days. Roughly, then, I view the challenge posed by contemporary anti-natalists this way: if you are not a utilitarian (or at least if you are a deontologist), then you must, on pain of unreasonableness, hold the view that it is nearly always all things considered impermissible to procreate.

In the rest of this essay, I discuss several salient and philosophically interesting respects in which anti-natalists, including several contributors to this book, have sought to execute this general argumentative strategy and ways they have been questioned. I aim to provide a bird's-eye view of some of the recent debate and some of the directions in which it should go.

## 2. Benatar and His Critics

The most influential anti-natalist currently writing is David Benatar, a South African moral philosopher who published his first anti-natal statement in 1997,[5] and then followed it up with a book-length defence in 2006.[6] Several of the contributors to this book address Benatar's argumentation, to which Benatar replies at the end. As has become fairly well known by the field, Benatar makes two distinct arguments for contemporary anti-natalism, an 'extreme' rationale according to which procreation would wrong the one created if and because she were expected to suffer as little as a pin-prick, regardless of the amount of good she would have in her life, and a more 'moderate' rationale according to which, given a more familiar aggregative approach to evaluating life, the expected amount of good is not sufficiently high when compared to the expected amount of bad. I discuss these in turn.

The extreme position is called the 'asymmetry argument' because it appeals to purported differences in the way we evaluate desirable and undesirable conditions, depending on whether we are dealing with someone who already exists or someone

---

4   R. N. Smart, 'Negative Utilitarianism', *Mind* (1958) 67: 542–543. See also the first major part of Christopher Belshaw's essay in this book.

5   David Benatar, 'Why It Is Better Never to Come into Existence', *American Philosophical Quarterly* (1997) 34: 345–355.

6   David Benatar, *Better Never to Have Been* (New York: Oxford University Press, 2006).

who merely could. If someone exists, then, uncontroversially, it is *bad* for her to experience pain, where the reference to pain is for Benatar a synecdoche, standing for anything undesirable with regard to a person's quality of life, e.g., frustrated desires and shameful ways of being. Similarly, it is uncontestedly *good* for an existent person to experience pleasure, similarly a placeholder for ways in which her life could go well. However, pains and pleasures (and the respective un/desirables that they signify) should be evaluated in a different manner in the case of one who does not and never will exist. According to Benatar, the absence of pain is *good*, i.e., better than its presence, with regard to one who could have existed but in fact never will. In addition, the absence of pleasure is *not bad*, in the sense of no worse than its presence, unless there is someone who exists and would have been deprived of it.

Now, given these particular judgements of goodness and badness, the verdict that life is bad on the whole appears to follow straightaway. Regarding pain, it is bad to exist and better not to exist. And with respect to pleasure, while that is good to have if and when one exists, not having pleasure is no worse if one does not exist; it simply does not count if there is no one to be deprived of it. Therefore, non-existence is better in relation to existence; indeed, existence is downright harmful by comparison. And since it would treat others merely as a means to harm them in order to benefit oneself in the form of being a biological parent, it is wrong to procreate.

Part of what motivates Benatar to believe the asymmetric premises about well-being that do the work of underwriting the anti-natalist conclusion is his belief that they best explain four other, uncontroversial judgments, including the key intuition that while it would be *wrong* for one to *create* someone who one knows would suffer a torturous existence, it would *not* be wrong for one *not* to create someone who one knows would enjoy a wonderful existence. The former would be wrong and the latter would not be wrong because, for Benatar, no pain in non-existence is *better* than pain in existence, and because no pleasure in non-existence is *no worse* than pleasure in existence.

Recently, critics have done the difficult, intricate work of evaluating this central line of reasoning from Benatar. For instance, in his contribution to this book, David Boonin contends that there is another promising and more attractive explanation of why it would be impermissible to create what he calls a 'Cursed Child' and why it would be permissible not to create a 'Blessed Child'. For Boonin, *contra* Benatar, a Blessed Child would be better off being created, but one would do no wrong in failing to create him, since, in the absence of creation, there would be no actual person harmed. Rivka Weinberg makes a similar move against Benatar, contending that duties apply only ever to those who do or will exist, which principle, she contends, explains the existence of a duty not to create a Cursed Child and the absence of a duty to create a Blessed Child. Readers wanting to get at the heart of Benatar's asymmetry argument should read Boonin's and Weinberg's chapters as well as the deep replies to them Benatar makes here[7]; these critical discussions advance the field's thinking about the logic of not only procreational duties, but also duties more generally.

Benatar can be read as appealing to another kind of premise in support of the crucial parts of his asymmetry argument, namely, an analogy. He considers two individuals, Sick, who is prone to illness but can recover quickly, and Healthy, who never gets sick

---

7    For different attempts to question asymmetry, see my chapter as well as aspects of Skott Brill's, both of which Benatar replies to in the concluding chapter.

but also lacks the ability to heal speedily. Of these two, Benatar claims that Sick has no 'real advantage' over Healthy, since the latter, by virtue of not getting sick in the first place, is not deprived by the absence of the ability to recuperate with ease. By analogy, Benatar suggests, the pleasures of those who exist are not a real advantage over the absent pleasures of those who do not exist, because the absence of those pleasures is not bad, i.e., not a deprivation, for those who do not exist.

In his contribution, Skott Brill principally questions whether Benatar may rightly invoke the Sick/Healthy analogy to defend key aspects of the asymmetry argument. In particular, Brill notes that the analogy appeals to the instrumental good of the ability to recover from illness, but that the asymmetry rationale involves a final good of pleasure. Brill provides *prima facie* reason to think that this difference makes the analogy weak; it is to be expected that an instrumental good lacks value, or has 'no real advantage', when not needed to bring about a certain state of affairs, whereas final goods are often expected to have a dissimilar structure, roughly, to be good regardless of the circumstances, as in the case of pleasure.

Recall that the asymmetry rationale for anti-natalism is only one of Benatar's major arguments, the one that is extreme for entailing that, no matter how much pleasure or other goods one has in a life, they count for nothing in comparison to non-existence, since there is no one to be deprived of them. His other major argument for anti-natalism is more moderate for claiming that, supposing for the sake of argument that the pleasures of existence do count in its favour relative to non-existence, there are not so many of them as to make existence attractive. The bads of life, including pain, ill-health, and even death, typically outweigh its goods, and even when they do not, the amount of goodness overall is slight. According to Benatar, people routinely fail to apprehend just how bad life is because of 'Pollyannaism' that is deeply rooted in our species due to natural selection. Following Benatar's phrasing, let us call this the 'procreational Russian roulette' argument[8]; although a given child might get lucky and face an empty chamber, most children will suffer the bullet of a cruddy existence, making it wrong to pull the trigger by creating them.

It is particularly (but not solely) in the light of this argument that Rafe McGregor and Ema Sullivan-Bissett in their joint contribution question the coherence of Benatar's combination of anti-natalism and pro-mortalism.[9] They contend that, if most people's quality of life is so poor, as per Benatar, then it must be prudent for them to commit suicide and morally praiseworthy for them to help others do so when they cannot on their own. However, Benatar denies that people *typically* have reason to be killed, at least at the present moment. One intriguing element of Benatar's reasoning is a distinction he draws between a life worth starting, on the one hand, and a life worth continuing, on the other. The standards for the former, for Benatar, are different from those for the latter. So, for example, it could be the case that knowing a person would face a severe harm would be enough to forbid creating that individual, but, once that individual exists, she ought to continue to live as long as possible if that harm has already occurred or up to the point at which it would occur. Ultimately, the dispute between Benatar and his critics about whether anti-natalism and pro-mortalism are consistent might turn on *when* it

---

8     Benatar, *Better Never to Have Been*, p. 92.
9     Christopher Belshaw expresses similar concerns in his chapter.

becomes unreasonable to continue staying alive, supposing, with Benatar, that most lives are very bad.

There are of course those who deny this last claim. In particular, Saul Smilansky and Brooke Alan Trisel, in their respective essays in this symposium, try to argue that life is instead on the whole pretty good, at least for large segments of humanity. According to Smilansky, reports of happiness are on a par with reports of pain, viz., they are first-person accounts of one's mental states that are difficult for others to refute. That purported epistemic fact, combined with Benatar's own acknowledgement that many people report being happy, provides strong reason to believe that people are indeed happy. In addition, Smilansky notes that reports of happiness tend to co-vary with the conditions that one would reasonably think produce happiness, such as economic security and political stability, suggesting, *contra* Benatar, that it is not the illusoriness of Pollyannaism that is generating the reports, but rather the tracking of real features of people's lives. Finally, Smilansky contends that the relative infrequency of suicide is best explained by the fact that life is generally good, and, in large part, by virtue of the fact that it is often meaningful, even if it also painful or even unhappy on occasion.

At one stage Smilansky furthermore suggests that what is apparently bad in life is often instrumentally quite good, a point that Trisel explores in some depth. Trisel appeals to scientific evidence indicating that pain, while admittedly finally disvaluable, is extremely useful for avoiding even worse conditions such as death, disfigurement, and greater pain. Our quality of life would be much lower if we did not experience pain, and similar remarks would seem to apply to other day-to-day conditions that are bad in themselves, such as failure and loss.

In reply to Trisel, Benatar accepts the last point, but notes that it does not follow that life is typically on the whole good. Just because things could be worse does not mean that they are not very bad, Benatar suggests. Benatar's ultimate reply to Smilansky is similar: people can in fact be mistaken about whether their lives are good ones, and, even if people's reports of happiness and meaningfulness vary according to circumstances of their lives, their judgements could be, and in fact are, systematically overshooting the mark. Pollyannaism is one reason to think that is so, for Benatar, but another important reason is the standard he invokes to evaluate the quality of life, namely, perfection. Trisel argues that any standard for evaluating our lives other than what is nomologically possible for us is arbitrary (and Weinberg finds herself unable to find any standard at all that is not arbitrary), but Benatar replies here that perfection, 'the highest (logically) possible standard', is not. And given how far the quality of human life is from perfection, we ought to judge it to be lowly indeed.

Even if Benatar has shown that perfection is not arbitrary, in a narrow sense, readers should consider whether he has given enough reason to appraise human life in the light of it. He points out in his work that, just as an individual's life clearly should be not judged merely by her own standard, but from a more external one, so too should human life in general be evaluated from an objective perspective.[10] Depending on what is meant by a 'human standpoint', one could plausibly accept this point while denying that perfection is the relevant standpoint to invoke.[11] In any event, there is much more debate to

---

10  Benatar, *Better Never to Have Been*, pp. 82-84.

11  For instance, I have argued that the relevant perspective is the maximum value physically available to a being that was born human (even if it is no longer human), in Thaddeus Metz, 'Imperfection as Sufficient for a Meaningful Life: How Much Is Enough?', in Yujin Nagasawa and Erik Wielenberg (eds), *New Waves in Philosophy of Religion* (New York: Palgrave Macmillan, 2009), pp. 192–214.

be had about the nature and relevance of 'external', 'objective', or 'perfect' standpoints for appraising the quality of human life, an important issue to which the disputes in these pages are some contribution.

### 3. Fresh and Under-explored Versions of Anti-Natalism

The remaining discussions in this book focus less on Benatar's version of anti-natalism and more on articulating and defending other forms, including two that are utterly new to the field. Like Benatar's asymmetry argument, they start from fairly weak, non-utilitarian premises and end up with strong, anti-natal conclusions.

Gerald Harrison's argument for anti-natalism differs from Benatar's most strikingly in not being based on any judgements about whether life is worth living or not. Whereas Benatar argues that it is wrong to create a new person's life because it is never (or almost never) worth starting, Harrison grants that most people's lives might well be worth starting, but, despite that, denies that it is permissible to create them. According to Harrison, there are what he calls, in the deontological tradition of W. D. Ross, '*prima facie* duties' to improve people's well-being and to prevent suffering, amongst other things. These are obligations that have some, not necessarily conclusive weight, and Harrison maintains that they entail anti-natalism when combined with a plausible principle about duties, namely, that a duty to perform a certain act truly exists only if there would be a victim were the act not done.[12] Creating a new life is not necessary to fulfil the duty to promote happiness, since if one refrained from procreation no victim would exist. However, refraining from creating a new life is necessary to fulfil the duty to prevent harm, since every new life can expect to incur some harm and hence to be victimized.

Notice that Harrison's rationale for anti-natalism apparently avoids pro-mortalism, and he contends that it does so with more ease than Benatar's. For one, Harrison's argument is not based on judgements about the generally poor quality of life human beings have. For another, the *prima facie* duty to improve people's quality of life forbids killing those who already exist and instead requires helping them, as failure to do the latter would mean that there would be a victim.

Fascinating questions arise such as: what exactly does the central *prima facie* duty to prevent suffering involve?; for instance, might it be best understood as an obligation for one not to *impose* harm on others, an obligation that would allow one to *expose* others to (unforeseeable) harms that others might impose on them?[13]; what does it mean for there to be a 'victim' in the event a duty is not performed?; are there duties that lack victims in the event of non-performance?; should one think that instead of duties requiring victims, duties exist 'only if there is a *beneficiary* in the event that the purported duty *is* performed'?[14] This is another place where anti-natalism requires sorting out fundamental issues in deontological moral thought.

---

12    Cf. Boonin's and Weinberg's critical discussions of Benatar, which invoke a similar principle to make a different point.

13    A line that David DeGrazia suggests in the fifth chapter of his *Creation Ethics: Reproduction, Genetics, and Quality of Life* (Oxford: Oxford University Press, 2012).

14    As Benatar suggests in his reply to Harrison.

Beyond invoking the *prima facie* duty not to cause suffering to support anti-natalism, Harrison also appeals to the *prima facie* duty not to seriously affect someone, particularly negatively, without her consent. Seana Shiffrin has written an important paper that develops the latter line of argument in some detail,[15] on which argument Asheel Singh focuses in his contribution to this volume. According to Shiffrin and Singh, it is wrong to some extent, because it is an infringement of another's right, to impose harm on another without her consent, at least where such harm is not expected to prevent a greater harm to her, e.g., where one shoves another out of the way of an oncoming vehicle. Since one obviously can never obtain a person's consent to create her, since persons are invariably harmed by existence, and since procreation never serves the function of preventing a greater harm to the one created, procreation is always wrong, at least to some degree.

There is of course interesting debate to be had about whether, if this rights-based line of argument were true, procreation would be all things considered impermissible. Singh does not focus on that issue (though Harrison addresses it briefly), and instead raises and replies to an intuitive objection to the argument, namely, that its account of when one may impose harm on others is overly narrow. More specifically, Singh takes up the view that one may harm others in serious ways if one reasonably expects them afterwards to endorse one's having done so. Such a view would appear to support pro-natalism, since most people are glad to be alive or otherwise appear to endorse their existence.

Singh distinguishes between different senses of 'endorse' and argues against what he takes to be the most defensible version, in two ways. First, he argues that it does not entail that procreation is justified, since people rarely 'endorse' their having been created in the relevant sense. Second, he contends that the appeal to endorsement is misplaced, in part because it is vulnerable to counterexamples, and in part because it lacks a philosophical mooring—neither standard consequentialist nor deontological moral theories, he contends, can make sense of why endorsement should make harm permissible to impose without a person's consent. Singh concludes that the friend of the consent-based rationale for anti-natalism can successfully rebut the objection from endorsement.

Whereas Harrison appeals to the *prima facie* duty not to cause suffering, and both Singh and Harrison invoke the right not to be harmed without one's consent, Christopher Belshaw suggests that anti-natalism follows from the principle that is wrong to exploit the misfortunes of others, specifically, human babies. The lives of babies, Belshaw argues, are not qualitatively different from those of animals such as rabbits and sheep, where these beings lack an awareness of themselves over time (or at least a very sophisticated one). Instead, they tend to be 'caught in the moment', meaning that, for them, a later pleasure cannot compensate for a present pain. Although *we* might want to keep an animal alive and hence be willing to let it suffer now in the expectation that it will be happy down the road, Belshaw maintains that, from the perspective of the animal's welfare, it would be better for it to die painlessly than to undergo the burden. And if it would be better for such an animal to die painlessly rather than face any harm, the same is true for human babies, whose mental states are more or less the same and who are bound to suffer from hunger, colic, gastrointestinal discomfort, emotional distress, etc.

---

15    Seana Shiffrin, 'Wrongful Life, Procreative Responsibility, and the Significance of Harm', *Legal Theory* (1999) 5: 117–148.

Now, for Belshaw, if the lives of babies are not worth continuing, then it would have been better had they never been born in the first place and it is wrong to create such lives. Those who intentionally make a baby are taking advantage of its weakness and suffering, so that they will eventually have a biologically related person, in the sense of a deliberative agent aware of itself over time, in their lives.

As with Harrison and Benatar, Belshaw is keen to demonstrate that his rationale for anti-natalism does not entail pro-mortalism. On this score, Belshaw points out that, although a future good cannot make up for a present bad for a being unaware of its future, it can do so for a being that is aware of its future, namely, a person. People's lives are often worth living, as later benefits can make it rational from the standpoint of an individual's well-being to suffer current harms. Hence, the respect in which it would not be bad for babies to die, and even good for them to do so, does not apply to those who have emerged from babies, us. In contrast, Belshaw argues, it is difficult for Benatar to avoid pro-mortalism, on the face of it, since Benatar contends that the lives of *persons* are not worth starting and are very bad once begun.

Controversy abounds, but obvious falsity does not. Is it true that it would not be bad, and rather good for, say, a rabbit to die, supposing it had to suffer pain otherwise? If so, is the same true for human babies? And, if so, does it follow that we are wrong to create them? One might reasonably think that if one had to choose between saving the life of a person and allowing an animal to be tortured, one should do the former. However, does the logic of this position mean that it would be permissible to torture an animal, let alone a human baby, in order to create a person in the first place? Belshaw's new rationale for anti-natalism, like Harrison's, raises important questions for the field.

## 4. Conclusion

I have suggested that an anti-utilitarian value-theoretic perspective largely drives contemporary anti-natalism. The major advocates of the view that procreation wrongs the one created tend to hold premises about what makes a life worthwhile and about our duties that are at variance with dominant versions of consequentialism. With respect to worthwhileness, readers have encountered the view that a life worth starting is one that would encounter no pain or other negative condition at all since any pleasure or positive condition does not count in comparison to non-existence, in which there is no one to be deprived of it (Benatar). They have also considered the view that for the life of a human baby to be worth starting it must also encounter no pain, since it lacks the psychological connectedness over time necessary for a later pleasure to compensate for it (Belshaw). In terms of our duties, readers have addressed the non-consequentialist principles that agents have a *prima facie* duty to prevent suffering (Harrison), that it would be immoral to some degree for them to violate another's right not to be harmed without having consented to it (Shiffrin/Singh), and that it is a serious moral wrong to exploit the weakness of a poorly off being in order to become a biological parent (Benatar and Belshaw).

Although anti-utilitarian value theory is at the ground of contemporary anti-natalism, there are reasons to doubt the hypothesis, proffered at the beginning of this chapter, that one can escape anti-natalism only if one is a utilitarian or at least not a deontologist. In particular, there is a strand of deontology that is in this book underexplored in its application to the anti-natalism debate, namely, that aspect of Kant's moral theory (and

Catholic ethical thought) according to which rational nature (or human life) as such has a dignity. Even where anti-natalist arguments are not grounded on judgements that life is not worthwhile, as per Harrison and Shiffrin/Singh most clearly, they invoke moral principles in which the avoidance of pain is paramount. The duties not to cause suffering, not to harm without consent, and not to take advantage of another's misery all take welfare to be the focal point. However, a dignity-based approach to ethics does not, or at least need not, and it might provide theoretical resources in the deontological tradition to defend natalism, something explored by David Spurrett in his chapter.[16] Kantians routinely emphasize that deeming persons to have a dignity, viz., a superlative final value in virtue of what they are, does not mean that one ought to procreate as much as possible; respecting a being is not the same as promoting it, they rightly note. However, it is worth considering what an ethic of respect for human dignity might entail for the extinction of the human race. Even if respect does not require maximizing the number of beings with dignity, it would arguably forbid letting them go out of existence altogether, and might, moreover, require ensuring they are populated to some sort of adequate degree. Such an argumentative strategy would, amongst several others explored in this overview, be worth exploring all the more as the debate about anti-natalism continues.

---

16 See also Asheel Singh, *Life, Procreation, and Transcendence*, unpublished Doctoral thesis, University of Johannesburg (2018), http://hdl.handle.net/10210/495410.

# Hooray for Babies[1]

## David Spurrett

**Abstract**

David Benatar has argued that the coming into existence of a sentient being is always a harm, and consequently that people who have children always do wrong. The most natural objection maintains that in many lives (at least) while there is some pain, there are also goods (including pleasures) that can outweigh the suffering. From Benatar's perspective this move, while possibly useful in assessing the lives of those who actually exist, is not an effective defence of procreation. In the case of people who do not yet exist, he maintains that there is a crucial asymmetry arising from the putative fact that the absence of pain is good even if that good is not enjoyed by anyone, whereas absence of pleasure is not bad unless there is somebody for whom that absence is a deprivation. For the potentially existing, he concludes, preventing the pain of existence is justified, but not so facilitating enjoyment of its pleasures. I argue that the asymmetry is insufficiently motivated. I also sketch two additional lines of argument against the asymmetry. First, it may not include all relevant factors. Second, plausible duties to prevent pain require possible sufferers, but do not apply straightforwardly when extended to include preventing the sufferers themselves.

> 'Maybe the earth would be better off without us.
> Safe and clean and perfect ...
> ...like a toy nobody ever played with.'
> – E Horne & J Comeau

## 1. Introduction

David Benatar argues that the coming into existence of a sentient being is always a harm to that being no matter how good the life as long as it contains *some* pain, and consequently that people who have children always do wrong (1997, and 2006). If human beings did the right thing in this respect, which means refraining entirely from procreation, the consequence would be the extinction of the human species. Consistently, Benatar maintains that this would be a morally desirable outcome – a world

---

1   After I had chosen this title it found it was already the title of two books, one about children and one for them. The title was not intended as a nod in the direction of either book. I am indebted to Adriano Palma for thoughtful and detailed comments on an earlier draft, as well as to Patrick Lenta, Julia Clare and an anonymous reviewer for their feedback. Thad Metz, Andrea Hurst, Elisa Galgut and Olga Yurkivska made useful comments and criticisms on presentation of this paper at the January 2011 meeting of the PSSA. I have not done full justice to their contributions in this brief paper, but hope to in ongoing work.

without human beings is indeed preferable to one containing them. A hypothetical "last generation" persuaded of this view, and seeking a final solution would, Benatar concedes, live out its last years of dreadful suffering in a world where social order had collapsed, but should nonetheless be admired for their supererogatory heroism (354).[2]

These are very strong claims, and it is surely worth evaluating the arguments putatively in their favour before rushing off and trying to bring about the end of humanity.[3] In what follows I outline Benatar's argument (as stated in his 1997), then critically discuss his defence of some key premises. I find the defence he offers wanting, and identify additional reasons for suspicion that the premises are true, or that they can bear the weight he wishes to place on them. The very preliminary and brief evaluation I offer here is broadly 'internal' in the sense that the framework of Benatar's position, especially the identification of pains and pleasures as paradigmatic benefits and harms, is not subject to criticism.

## 2. Benatar's argument

Benatar describes himself as identifying faults with a 'common assumption' to the effect that "one does no wrong by bringing into existence people whose lives will be good on balance" because (a further assumption) "being brought into existence (with decent life prospects) is a benefit (even though not being born is not a harm)" (1997:345).

He begins by noting some relatively uncontroversial empirical facts, including that "bad things happen to all of us" (1997:345) and that you need to exist in order to suffer: "Only existers suffer harm". The same, of course, goes for good things – "Pleasures, joys, and satisfactions can be had only by existers". Even at this stage, Benatar's priorities are discernible. The three vague plural nouns of "pleasures, joys, and satisfactions" are all he has to say about good things. For the bad we get "hardship", "poverty", "disability", "ill-health", frailty", "pain", "disappointment", "anxiety", "grief", and "death". "Suffering" comes up three times, and he finds it worth pointing out that suffering can be "excruciating" but wastes no adjectives on joys or satisfactions. Death is a harm he finds worth mentioning repeatedly, while life doesn't make the list of goods, not even as a means to enjoying other goods.

He then considers the "cheerful" who hold that a life should be assessed according to the balance of pleasure and pain, where a life that is on balance pleasurable is worth being born for. He rejects this "because there is a crucial difference between harms and benefits which makes the advantages of existence over non-existence hollow but the advantages real" (1997:345). Taking pains and pleasures as exemplars of harms and benefits, he asserts that the following four claims are 'uncontroversial':

1) the presence of pain is bad
2) The presence of pleasure is good
[...]
3) the absence of pain is good, even if that good is not enjoyed by anyone

---

2   All page references are to Bentar (1997).

3   And maybe more. Non-human animals suffering the harm of existence but whose parents are incapable of practical deliberation will continue to suffer unless energetic Benatarians embark on a global programme of (painless) sterilization for them. Committed members of the last generation should probably also organise the delayed destruction of all non-suffering life to make sure sentience doesn't evolve again. Better safe than sorry.

4) the absence of pleasure is not bad unless there is somebody for whom this absence is a deprivation. (1997:345-6).

The supposed asymmetry between (3) and (4) is the keystone of the 'anti-natalist' case. Benatar claims that this view is "widely shared", and cites a number of reasons in support of his claim. Among them it is supposedly the "best explanation for the commonly held view that while there is a duty to avoid bringing suffering people into existence, there is no duty to bring happy people into being" (1997:346). A further reason is that it "seems strange" to "give as a reason for having a child that the child one has will thereby be benefited" even though "sometimes we do avoid bringing a child into existence because of the potential child's interests" (1997:346). The last reason offered (in Benatar 1997) is the "related asymmetry [...] in our retrospective judgments", such that we can regret bringing someone into existence for their sake, but cannot regret not bringing someone into existence for their sake, or the sake of anyone not already existing. "Remorse about not having children is remorse for ourselves" (1997:346).

Someone contemplating procreating is, Benatar argues, chosing between two scenarios – in one a further person (or persons in the ghastly case of multiple births) is brought into existence, in another nobody is. Given the asymmetry the scenarios can be represented as follows:

|    | Scenario A (X exists)         |    | Scenario B (X never exists)      |
|----|-------------------------------|----|----------------------------------|
| 1) | Presence of Pain (Bad)        | 3) | Absence of Pain (Good)           |
| 2) | Presence of Pleasure (Good)   | 4) | Absence of Pleasure (Not Mad)    |

**Figure 1** *(Benatar 1997:347)*

The anti-natalist conclusion falls out fairly directly: An actual life can be assessed by its balance of pleasure and pain, which could well be negative. (Benatar thinks that the balance is far more often negative than the living themselves realize, which is to say that most people mistakenly think their lives are much better than they are, but that is another matter.) According to Benatar a possible life not made actual, though, *has* to be better than neutral – it's a combination of the good (lack of suffering) and the merely not bad (which is all that absent pleasure amounts to). I am not making this up. Here's Benatar: "Because there is nothing bad about never coming into existence, but there is something bad about coming into existence, *all things considered* non-existence is preferable" (349, emphasis added). And "so long as there are *some* negative aspects [...] life is not preferable to never having come into existence" (349, emphasis added).

The most common first response, in my experience talking about Benatar in the classroom and upon explaining anti-natalism to non-philosophers, is to object that in many lives (at least) while there is some pain, there are also goods (including pleasures) that can outweigh the suffering. This is, of course, not so much an objection to the argument, as an expression of hostility to the conclusion. From Benatar's perspec-

tive this move, while it may be useful in assessing the lives of those who actually exist, is not an effective defence of procreation precisely because of the asymmetry between (3) and (4) as compared to (1) and (2). In the case of people who do not yet exist, he maintains that the absence of pain is good even if that good is not enjoyed by
anyone, whereas absence of pleasure is not bad unless there is somebody for whom
that absence is a deprivation. For the potentially existing, he concludes, preventing the
pain of existence is justified (it does good), but not so facilitating enjoyment of its
pleasures. So going on about the supposed fact that some of the existing have good
lives is, even if true (which he also mostly denies), irrelevant.[4] How plausible this response is depends in large measure on how well the asymmetry represented by claims
(3) and (4) above can be defended.

## 3. Evaluating Benatar's defence of the asymmetry

*Reason 1*

Benatar's first reason is that the truth of the asymmetry is supposedly the "best explanation for the commonly held view that while there is a duty to avoid bringing suffering people into existence, there is no duty to bring happy people into being" (346).
The view apparently explains the asymmetry because failing to bring a happy person
into existence is merely not bad – there's nobody to enjoy the 'missing' pleasure,
whereas bringing a suffering person into the world is bad, because the absence of suffering is good even if nobody enjoys it.

Even if there was some threshold level of common holding that was epistemically
justifying, we'd need evidence that the threshold was met or exceeded, and Benatar
provides none. (He also makes the related claim – again with no evidence – that "only
a few" (346) of those who think that there are positive duties think that there is one to
bring happy people into being.) Even if he did, and the view turned out to be *very*
commonly held, it wouldn't help by itself because that a view might be commonly
held yet false, which is why appeals to popularity are generally regarded as fallacious.
The very opposite view is, furthermore, commonly held, which is to say that lots of
people think that there *is* a duty to bring people into being.

The claim that there is a duty to procreate is commonly found in religious settings.
The God of Genesis says "be fruitful and multiply" to Adam and Eve (Genesis 1:28),
Noah (Genesis 9:1) and Jacob (Genesis 35:11, as well as the fish and fowl, in Genesis
1:22). He also kills Onan for spilling his seed upon the ground, even though it was
only a first offence (Genesis 38:4-11). These considerations have been extensively
used – among other things – as grounds for opposing abortion, same-sex activity, formal same-sex unions, masturbation, and bestiality. They're invoked repeatedly in
sometimes elaborate theories which give central place to the ideas that there is indeed
a duty to procreate, that the proper purpose of sex is procreation (hence the
unacceptability of gay sex, solitary sex, etc.) and that the proper purpose of marriage is
to provide a suitable institution for (among other things) procreative sex and child
rearing (hence the unacceptability of adultery, fornication, same-sex marriage, etc.).

Aquinas gives a highly influential – within Christianity – account of sex and sexual
vices of various kinds. Rape and incest are wrong by his lights because there is some-

---

4    It isn't *entirely* irrelevant, because the supposed satisfaction of (most of) the living can be used as part
of an objection to Benatar. The idea is that the living can infer from their own lives that those brought
into existence will be likely enough to come to approve of that fact. This is part of why Benatar argues
in later work (Benatar 2006) that most people have mistakenly high opinions of their own lives. I'm not
going to get into this here.

thing wrong with how people engaged in them relate to each other. But "unnatural vice" (including sodomy, fellatio, cunnilingus and masturbation) is wrong, and *more* wrong, because such activities are not suited to the *purpose* of sex, which is procreation (*Summa Theologiae*, Questions 153 and 154). This reasoning informs recent Catholic policy, including Pius XI's 1930 encyclical on marriage, which referers to the "horrible crime" of Onan (Gallagher 1993:399). Movements within the Catholic Church favouring more tolerant policy on contraception have failed, and the 1968 encyclical of Paul VI (*Humanae vitae, 2,* in Carlen 1981) sticks to Thomistic guns: the purpose of sex (the 'marital act'!) is procreation, any sexual activity that is not potentially procreative, and any act which thwarts procreation is wrong. The force of the duty has been so strongly felt that the ban on barrier contraception has firmly been maintained almost to the present in the face of compelling evidence that condom use reduces the transmission of various pathogens, especially the human immunodeficiency virus.

These putative reasons may not be very good even by the flickering light of theological argument. The fact that God also tells the fish and birds to "go forth and multiply" is taken by some to mean that the utterance must be read as more as a blessing than a command (Daube 1977:3).[5] And aficionados will happily point out that Onan's real crime was effectively practicing *coitus interruptus* to avoid impregnating his dead brother's childless widow, because a child would have divided Onan's inheritance. On this view what angered God was Onan's failure to respect the duties he owed his dead brother, so the episode doesn't warrant a policy on birth control or masturbation. That experts can find some wiggle room doesn't change the fact that the crude interpretations have commanded wide support among many, for millennia.

I'm pressed for space here, and could not begin to survey the main expressions of the duty to procreate as they occur in other religions. For now I merely note that while most Protestant major denominations endorsed the view that contraception was permissible in the decades between the 1930s and 1960s (Stanford & Larimore 1998), this was almost invariably by way of statements that took care to recognize a duty to procreate in conventional marriages, but where contraception might allow other ends of (married) sexual activity to be pursued, and to allow the timing and spacing of child birth to be partly a matter of conscience for parents.

Outside religion, various nationalistic projects have recognised or asserted positive duties to procreate, and enacted policies of various kinds, including a tax on unmarried men under Mussolini (Albanese 2006:54), who also instituted formal maternity leave, a national holiday celebrating motherhood and infancy, and tax exemptions and prizes for fertility (Albanese 2006:55). Demographic nationalists are sometimes also hostile to homosexuality for similar reasons – it reneges on the duty to reproduce.

I'm not for a moment suggesting that we should think that there is a duty to procreate *because* either some band of misogynistic homophobes with imaginary friends or some gaggle of more modern nationalistic creeps claim there is one. Popularity carries no evidential weight here at all, except against the claim that the view that there is no duty to procreate is 'commonly held'. The view is very commonly *not* held, so the premise is false. Even if it was, being commonly held is not a generally decent

---

5    I note in passing that this reasoning is anachronistic. As late as the 19th century European courts were
     prepared to try (not always *in absentia*) and sentence non-human animals, including pigs, dogs, rats and
     various insects, for crimes including murder, indecency (!) and damage to property. There have also
     been trials of non-living objects, including sculptures, carts, swords, doorposts. For a recent discussion
     see Humphrey (2002, Chapter 18). A key historical treatment is Evans (1906).

epistemic reason, and we stand in need of a justification for thinking that it is in this case.

*Reason 2*

A further reason is that it "seems strange" to "give as a reason for having a child that the child one has will thereby be benefited" even though "sometimes we do avoid bringing a child into existence because of the potential child's interests" (346). It's hard to decide what to make of this. There are, after all, plenty of strange truths, and no shortage of non-strange falsehoods. But even if seeming strange was epistemically motivating (sub-atomic physics, general relativity, the germ theory of disease, etc., all being thereby damned), it's not clear that the claim really *is* strange, or strange enough, or strange to a large enough number of people.

We do indeed sometimes say that conditions are such that it would not be good to have a child, and this is sometimes because the prospects for a good life seem too tenuous, or of a desperately horrid life too high. Regarding this, Benatar is clearly correct. This, though, is entirely consistent with the fact that some of us also sometimes talk (without remarking on the strangeness of it) about the benefit of possible children *to the children themselves*. People just *do* say, sometimes, to those who are, or who they think would be, dedicated, generous, loving and effective parents things like "You should have a(nother) child. You would be good parents *for that child*." It's all very well to point at such views and call them names like "strange", but there's a burden of proof to be shouldered here. What is strange about them? Is it a truth-undermining kind of strangeness? What – if anything – is strange about saying that since you can't be kind to those who don't exist, you need to have children before you can be kind to them?

*Reason 3*

The last reason offered (in Benatar 1997) overlaps in some respects with the one just considered, and concerns the "related asymmetry [...] in our retrospective judgments", such that we can regret bringing someone into existence for their sake, but cannot regret not bringing someone into existence for their sake, or the sake of anyone not already existing. "Remorse about not having children is remorse for ourselves" (346).

This is a very strong claim. Elsewhere Benatar expresses a version of the claim without reference to regret: "Children *cannot* be brought into existence for their own sakes" (351, emphasis added). Is this true? One place to start approaching this question would be looking at Benatar's reasons, but they turn out to be statements of a claim weaker than the one being defended. The reason we 'cannot' regret the non-existence of the unborn is that *in fact* remorse about not-having children is self-directed. Well, even if it *was* true that remorse was like that, it doesn't follow that it *has* to be, any more than the fact that I'm not standing on one foot establishes that I *can't* do so. And we're surely within our rights to want to see a justification for thinking that it *is* like that at all. The premise effectively asserts an astonishing level of self-centrism in parental motivation. As with the supposedly 'strange' view discussed immediately above, why should we think that nobody *ever* regrets not having a child because of the benefits that child might have enjoyed?

Plenty of people clearly *think* they do things for their *actual* children – including paying massive opportunity costs in pursuit of highly convenient forms of adult entertainment, allocating substantial material resources, and taking sometimes remarkably extravagant steps to secure their welfare after the death of the parent. Perhaps all of this really is self-serving, not genuine kindness but the fool's kindness of those Benatar repeatedly derides as the 'cheerful'. Of course, if nobody ever really did anything for the sake of anyone else, then it would be more believable that nobody ever brought anyone into existence (partly) in order to do good for them. But we need to be given reasons for thinking so. And they need to be very good reasons for it not to turn out that losing the chance to be kind in these ways *for the sake of the recipients*, is either never regretted, or outright impossible to regret.

In very brief review, then, the three reasons we're given don't seem up the heavy lifting we'd want to motivate the end of humanity. Two of the key premises seem to be false – the putatively common isn't that common, and the putatively strange not very strange. In those cases even if the premises were true, being commonly held isn't generally truth conducive, and being strange isn't generally truth-defeating. Finally, it's not clear that people don't regret what Benatar says they don't, and even if it was true that they didn't, that wouldn't prove that they *couldn't*.

## 4. Against the asymmetry

Recall Benatar's table of consequences (in section 2 above). This is supposed to represent the costs and benefits of someone coming (or not coming) into existence. We can ask at least two questions about this table: Does it leave anything out? Is it correctly filled in?

On the question of completeness, we can unproblematically agree for present purposes that the two columns are mutually exclusive and collectively exhaustive – a person either exists or she does not. It is less clear that we can say the same about the rows, because it is far from obvious that the only relevant considerations concern pleasure and pain. Benatar considers pains and pleasures as 'exemplars of harms and benefits' (345). That much seems fair enough, but being exemplary is far from being exhaustive. If there were benefits and harms besides pleasures and pains, they ought to be factored in, in case they made a difference.

I propose that there could be least one missing row, and that relates to (human) life itself. It is by no means controversial or sensational to claim that an individual human life is a valuable thing. (Smilansky (1995) has in fact argued from this and other premises to a conclusion directly opposed to Benatar's, to the effect that there is a duty (an inclining and conditional one) upon those who can to have children). If we accept the premise that an individual life is valuable, along with the claims that the presence of value is good, and its absence bad, then we might revise Benatar's table as follows:

| | Scenario A<br>(X exists) | | Scenario B<br>(X never exists) |
|---|---|---|---|
| 1) | Presence of Pain<br>(Bad) | 3) | Absence of Pain<br>(Good) |
| 2) | Presence of Pleasure<br>(Good) | 4) | Absence of Pleasure<br>(Not Mad) |
| 5) | Presence of a valuable human life<br>(Good) | 6) | Absence of a valuable human life<br>(Bad) |

**Figure 2 (adapted from Benatar 1997:347).**

Now things are messier. Benatar's version has the advantage of very elegant simplicity – actual life might be some balance of good or bad that's not easy to figure out, but never having existed has *got* to be better than neutral. But with two goods and a bad in the 'existing' column, and one good, one bad and one not bad in the 'never existing' column, you need to assign quantities to the cells to work out any net advantage. Clearly you probably *shouldn't* have children during the siege of Stalingrad, but maybe you could (or even should?) in some other cases.

I've barely sketched this line of criticism of Benatar, and so need to be careful not to make too much of it. The point I take myself to have made is merely that *if* there are harms and benefits besides pleasures and pains which deserve to be factored in, this might change the outcome. Benatar might well respond that *any* absent benefit is merely 'not bad' (unless someone loses out), whereas any absent harm is 'good' (even if there is nobody to benefit), and so trying to populate the table with further rows of non-pleasure benefits and non-pain harms is a pointless distraction. But the reasons he's offered for that asymmetry aren't convincing, and so it's difficult to see that it should be allowed to hold trumps without additional defence. I hope to develop the argument for adding at least one row in future work.

What about how the table is populated? We are asked to agree that absent pains are good, even if there is nobody to enjoy their absence, but that absent pleasures are merely 'not bad' unless there is someone who is deprived.

Let's start with the latter claim. It seems very plausible. Why think that absent pleasures are merely 'not bad' unless someone exists to lose out on them? One reason is that pleasure is a state of an entity, rather than an entity itself. The notion of an independently existing, free-floating pleasure in the absence of someone to enjoy it, that is, feels slightly nonsensical. Nobody enjoys a party that nobody goes to partly *because* without anyone there, there's no party at all.

This doesn't only go for pleasures and people. Someone who doesn't own an Alfa Romeo, saying "I never have any Alfa Romeo reliability issues" is not making the same claim as an owner asserting the same words. The former one is likely making a joke. (The latter may well be lying.) The plausibility of Benatar's claim (4), that absent pleasures without possible enjoyers are merely 'not bad' arises, then, at least in part because our default serious understanding of 'absent pleasure' is something like "pleasure that isn't happening in a case where it is *possible* that it could".

It's not that we *can't* make sense of the idea of absence of a state because of the absence of whatever it can be a state of. We recognize that, in some sense, slaughtering the poor would lead to "poverty reduction", and that firing everybody would mean that there would be no "workplace accidents". But those are unusual interpretations – not what we're normally thinking or intending when we support poverty reduction or reduced workplace accidents. What we mean is more like 'less poverty without losing people', or 'fewer accidents without reduced employment'.

I've drifted into using illustrations that are about absent harms (poverty, accidents) while, I hope, making the same point. This is because it seems that the considerations supporting Benatar's premise (4) count against his premise (3). It's not *good* in our default, serious sense, for there to be free-floating pain that nobody suffers from, because when we approve of the absence of pain we mostly mean the absence of suffering without the absence of the sufferer. We want our anaesthetists to prevent the pain of surgery by means *other* than preventing us from existing. So absent pains are good when there's someone who gets to suffer less.

Benatar unsurprisingly disagrees. Having introduced his table, he considers some variations in how it is populated, and rejects the option of filling it in so that absent pain isn't positively good. He says that way of assessing absent pain in the right hand column is "too weak" and that avoiding "bringing a suffering child into existence is more than merely 'not bad'" (348). The formulation of his objection is striking, and also invites at least two interpretations which confer spurious plausibility to it. We can agree that bringing into existence a person whose life will on balance have more pain than pleasure is a bad thing. But if we agree with that, we are not agreeing with what Benatar should be allowing himself to say here. That's one kind of spurious plausibility, because the design of his argument precisely requires us not to confuse the case of the lives of the actual with merely possible lives. So he doesn't mean *that*.

We also *can't* interpret the sentence, despite the fact that its construction makes this tempting, as saying "taking an already suffering entity and bringing it into existence" because the non-existent have no properties and don't suffer. From a folk dualist point of view it's all too easy to imagine the immaterial minds of the not-yet born waiting around, and thus to interpret "bringing a suffering child into existence" as taking an already sad mind and making things worse by adding the burden of existence. Benatar sn'doet intend any such interpretation, of course. My point is merely that the tenses he uses invite it – the present continuous 'suffering' hints at suffering that's already going on when being brought into existence.

So Benatar's claim about "bringing a suffering child into existence" doesn't give an independent reason for regarding the absence of pain as good in the absence of sufferers, which is what we need here.

There's room for one remaining objection. We assuredly do sometimes speak approvingly of the absence of pain in cases where this absence is achieved by the non-existence of the sufferer. When contemplating the fate of an individual we know will suffer from terrible birth-defects, leading to a life of little more than suffering, many of us do approve of an outcome where birth is prevented *because* there is 'less pain'.[6] We also do the same thing in some end of life cases, where it is difficult or impossible to see, because of the nature and extent of someone's injuries or illness, that a continued life would be desirable. But when we say 'there's no more pain' in these cases, I submit that our approval depends on an evaluation of the left hand column of the table, precisely the sort of consideration that cannot independently motivate regarding absent pain as good in the right hand column. Suppose that a mostly health young person has a heart attack that is highly treatable, and where were it treated they would have decades of decent life afterwards, but they contingently don't receive treatment in time and die. In that case we precisely cannot comfort their loved ones by pointing out that there's 'no more pain' – the relevant contrast case is different when there's hope worth taking seriously.[7]

## 5. Conclusion

Although there's much more that could be said, I've argued for two main conclusions here. First the reasons Benatar (1997) offers for his crucial asymmetry are less convincing than they should be, especially for an argument calling for as drastic an outcome as human extinction. Second, there are independent reasons for suspecting that the inequality is implausible. Pains that are absent because there's nobody to benefit

6    I'm grateful to Elisa Galgut for making this point in the case of birth defects.
7    This response occurred to me in discussion with Thaddeus Metz.

from them are not good, and the cases where they seem to be good are ones where we're assessing the absence by the lights of the left hand column, which isn't what we need for a defence of the inequality. There may be better ways of looking after people than preventing them.

## References

Albanese, P. 2006. *Mothers of the Nation: Women, Families and Nationalism in Twentieth Century Europe*, Toronto: University of Toronto Press.

Aquinas, T. 1920. *The Summa Theologica of St. Thomas Aquinas*, (translated by Fathers of the English Dominican Province), New York: Benziger Brothers.

Benatar. D. 1997. Why it is better never to come into existence, *American Philosophical Quarterly*, 34(3), pp 345-55.

Benatar, D. 2006. *Better Never to Have Been: The Harm of Coming Into Existence*. Oxford: Oxford University Press.

Carlen, C. (ed.) 1981. *The Papal Encyclicals 1958-1981*, New York: McGrath.

Daube, D. 1977. *The Duty of Procreation*, Edinburgh, Edinburgh University Press.

Evans, E.P. 1906. *The Criminal Prosecution and Capital Punishment of Animals*, London: Heinemann.

Gallagher, J. 1993. Magisterial Teaching from 1918 to the Present, in C. Curran and R. McCormick (eds.), *Readings in Moral Theology No. 8: Dialogue about Catholic Sexual Teaching,* Paulist Press.

Horne, E. & Comeau, J. undated. *A Softer World*, number 494. ('Pretty and pointless' – http://www.asofterworld.com/index.php?id=494), accessed 11 December 2010.

Humphrey, N. 2002. *The Mind Made Flesh*, Oxford: Oxford University Press.

Smilansky, S. 1995. Is there a moral obligation to have children? *Journal of Applied Philosophy* 12(1), pp. 41-53.

Stanford, J.B. & Larimore, W.L. 1998. Birth Control, in Erwin Fahlbusch (ed.) *Encyclopedia of Christianity*, Grand Rapids: Wm. B. Eerdmans Publishing Co.

# Are Lives Worth Creating?

## Thaddeus Metz

Critical Notice of David Benatar, Better Never to Have Been (New York: Oxford University Press, 2006)

L'Chaim! (To life!)—Traditional Jewish toast

## 1. Introduction

The weaker one's premises, and the more surprising or even outlandish one's conclusion from them, the better one's philosophical argument, at least in one major respect. In his book Better Never to Have Been,[1] David Benatar presents an argument with this structure, concluding that it is generally all things considered wrong to procreate, such that if everyone acted in a morally ideal way, humanity would elect to extinguish the species. Virtually no commentators have given Benatar's reasoning a fair shake,[2] something that I aim to do. My goal is to pinpoint precisely where one would have good reason to step off the train of argument taking one to a place one does not want to end up.

I begin by clarifying Benatar's 'anti-natalist' conclusion with care, forestalling misinterpretations of it and also comparing and contrasting it and its major motivations with related positions in the literature (Section 2). Then, I critically explore the two major arguments Benatar gives for anti-natalism in his book. The most powerful and interesting argument, the one that has garnered the most attention (even if inadequate analysis), and the one that I devote the most space to discussing, is the notorious 'asymmetry argument' (Section 3). Here, Benatar argues that uncontroversial ideas about the differential valuation of benefits and harms entail that it is always a net harm to create a person. Benatar's other argument for anti-natalism is more familiar and less fiendish, but still quite worthy of reflection. It more or less argues in favour of a Schopenhauerian or Nagelian appraisal of the quality of human life from an extremely external point of view, the 'point of view of the universe', which entails that our lives are very badly off (Section 4). I conclude this critical notice by noting some ways to take discussion of Benatar's two anti-natalist arguments forward in other work and by adumbrating important topics in Better Never to Have Been that I have not addressed (Section 5).

---

1   Page citations in the text refer to this book.
2   Exceptions are Elizabeth Harman, 'Critical Study of David Benatar. Better Never to Have Been: The Harm of Coming into Existence', Nous 43 (2009): 776–785; and David DeGrazia, 'Is it Wrong to Impose the Harms of Human Life? A Reply to Benatar', Theoretical Medicine and Bioethics 31 (2010): 317–331.

## 2. Anti-Natalism and Benatar's Argumentative Strategy

By 'anti-natalism' Benatar means the view that it is generally wrong on balance to create new human persons. It is not merely the weak thesis that it is always wrong to some (pro tanto) degree to procreate, but it should not be construed so strongly as to imply that it is literally always wrong all things considered to do so. Benatar admits that there could be rare situations in which there is most moral reason on the whole to create a new person, when (and probably only when) it would substantially reduce the suffering of other, existent persons (182–193). It is still quite a robust thesis for Benatar to maintain that, apart from very unusual circumstances, there is no moral justification on the whole for procreating.

In an ecologically fragile world with seven billion people, more and more of whom are becoming consumers of meat, cars and sundry technological gadgets, anti-natalism is increasingly voiced and defended on the ground that the consequences of creating person X would be bad for other people Y (or even animals Z).[3] Such a rationale entails that it would be permissible to create people if there were fewer people or if many people lived in a way that were less destructive of the natural world. However, Benatar's anti-natalism is driven by different considerations and has radically different implications. For Benatar, 'a cumulative population numbering only one person would have been over-population' (166) for the reason that creating person X is always on balance bad for X.

Note Benatar's uncompromisingly strong claim about 'always' in the context of welfare, even if not morality. In the context of his asymmetry argument, Benatar aims to establish that it is invariably bad all things considered for a person to have been created, no matter how great the amount of goodness, and how little the amount of badness, that she undergoes afterward. As Benatar notes with characteristic frankness, his position entails that it would be wrong to create someone even if she were to experience 'a life of utter bliss adulterated only by the pain of a single pin-prick' (48); it would be wrong because such a life would still be on the whole bad for this person, or so Benatar maintains we are driven to believe by virtue of some uncontroversial claims.

Benatar's anti-natalism, the view that agents typically have the most moral reason not to create any more human persons, neither is nor implies the view that agents typically have the most moral reason to kill existing human persons, and, indeed, as I explain below, part of Benatar's rationale for anti-natalism implies a rejection of what he calls 'pro-mortalism'. He denies that it is morally permissible for one to kill other human persons for their sake, as they should have the autonomy to decide their own fate (196, 218), and the logic of his view commits him to thinking that it would often be imprudent for people to kill themselves.

To begin to grasp the plausibility of holding anti-natalism without pro-mortalism, consider the useful distinction that Benatar draws between two ways to understand the phrase 'a life worth living'. On the one hand, the phrase might connote the idea that a person's life is worth continuing, while, on the other, it might indicate the idea that person's life was worth starting. Benatar argues that the existing reasons in the literature for thinking that the two must stand and fall together are weak (20–28, 212–218). He

---

3   For an early proponent, see Paul Ehrlich, The Population Bomb (New York: Ballantine Books, 1968), and for a more recent case, see Thomas Young, 'Overconsumption and Procreation: Are They Morally Equivalent?', Journal of Applied Philosophy 18 (2001): 183–192.

points out that it is logically consistent to maintain both that that no one's life is worth starting and that people can, and often do, have lives worth continuing.

A crucial claim that makes sense of believing anti-natalism but not pro-mortalism is that death itself is something bad to be avoided. Interestingly, part of what makes a life on the whole bad and hence impermissible to create, for Benatar, is precisely the fact that it will end! Death is something undesirable on a par with pain, disappointment and grief (29, 89–91, 196, 212–217). 'Coming into existence is bad in part because it invariably leads to the harm of ceasing to exist' (213). Given that creating people is bad partially because their lives will end, Benatar should clearly not be construed as a pro-mortalist, someone who thinks people have most reason, whether moral or prudential, to end their lives sooner rather than later. In his view, once people have been (wrongfully) created, a moral agent ought, ceteris paribus, minimize the harm that he does to them, and since death is a harm, he usually ought not to kill them: 'Although it may be bad for anyone of us to die, it is still worse to die earlier than we need to' (196). Benatar's rejection of pro-mortalism can now be seen as sensibly combined with the view that creating people is always a net harm to them, so that it would have been better for them not to have been created in the first place.

Benatar's asymmetry argument for anti-natalism without promortalism is readily seen not to appeal to 'negative utilitarianism', the moral theory roughly according to which only the reduction of bad, and not the production of good, has ethical weight. More specifically, it is the basic principle that one's sole basic duty is to minimize the amount of pain, or more generally undesirable quality of life, wherever and however one can in the long run. Since that state of affairs would be achieved if no sentient being procreated, or even if all sentient beings were painlessly euthanized, negative utilitarianism entails that if an agent could do either one, he would be obligated to do it, regardless of the amount of pleasure or otherwise desirable quality of life these beings could have. However, Benatar is not a negative utilitarian. For one, as I have said above, he believes that people have a right to life and that death is itself a bad, and, for another, he counts the action of depriving an existing person of good to be pro tanto wrong.

Indeed, the logic of Benatar's asymmetry argument in some ways fits better with a standard deontological morality, one that accords negative duties not to harm stronger weight than positive duties to prevent harm or to benefit. Friends of non-consequentialism believe that it would be wrong to push a fat man in front of a trolley so as to prevent it from running over four persons, and that it would be wrong to forcibly harvest organs from one person so as to save the lives of four others who would die without them. In general, it is wrong to impose harm on some for the sake of helping others, let alone for the sake of oneself. Benatar argues in a similar way: since procreating is unavoidably a net harm for the one created, there is usually no moral justification in doing so for the sake of others, let alone oneself as a parent.

Benatar says little about the underlying moral theory that might underwrite the inference to anti-natalism. Logically speaking, the asymmetry argument has two major stages, the first one stopping at the welfarist conclusion that being created is a net harm for the individual, and the second inferring from that claim the anti-natalist, moral thesis that people ought not procreate. In between the welfarist, intermediate conclusion and the ultimate conclusion of anti-natalism there has to be a moral 'bridge' premise to the effect that one would be wrong to impose net harm on people under certain conditions.

However, Benatar does not carefully construct the bridge, resting content with vague mid-level principles such as these: serving one's own interests is usually not justified when doing so inflicts significant harm on others (98), and one ought not to treat people merely as a means (129–131).

When specifying and applying such mid-level principles with care, a lot turns on the precise nature and degree of harm being done to someone for the sake of oneself or others. And Benatar indeed acknowledges at certain points that if the harm on the one procreated were small enough, it could be morally justified to inflict it so as to prevent great harm to others or perhaps even to confer great benefits on others (98–99, 191–193, 207n6). After all, nearly everyone these days believes it is permissible to tax those who have acquired wealth without force or fraud in order to help others who are much worse off, where that is precisely to lower the quality of life of some (the rich) so as to raise that of others (the poor). In short, in order to derive the antinatalist conclusion, Benatar needs not merely the intermediate conclusion that procreation is always a net harm to the one created, but also the claim that it is a significant net harm to the one created— relevantly unlike taxing those who make over $100,000 a year.

Now, Benatar does argue that procreation is a significant net harm to the one created (60–92), but my present point is that he does not do so in the context of the asymmetry argument (18–59). Benatar's standard position is that the two arguments for anti-natalism work side by side and on their own, labelling the argument from the point of view of the universe as 'independent' (14, 61) support for the anti-natalist conclusion that the asymmetry argument is meant to support in its own right. However, reflection on the nature of the moral bridge principle that could plausibly lead one from the intermediate, welfarist conclusion that existence is always a net harm to the one created to the ultimate conclusion that it is immoral to procreate shows that the asymmetry argument cannot stand alone; it must be conjoined with an argument indicating that the net harm of procreation is great, which is the function of the point of view of the universe argument (and which Benatar presents in a separate chapter titled 'How Bad is Coming into Existence?').

In the following, therefore, I treat the asymmetry argument and the point of view of the universe argument as two parts of a single, overarching rationale for anti-natalism. With the former argument, Benatar purports to establish that being created is invariably a net harm (discussed in Section 3) and with the latter, he aims to show that it is usually a great harm (Section 4). From those two intermediate conclusions, he could then, by appealing to quasi-Kantian moral considerations, fairly draw the conclusion that it is almost always wrong on balance to procreate.

## 3. The Asymmetry Argument

At this point, readers are no doubt getting itchy, wanting to know how in the world someone could reasonably draw the conclusion that it is generally immoral to create a human person since it is always a net harm for her, even supposing that her life were well worth continuing for including substantial amounts of goodness and inconsequential amounts of badness. Having clarified Benatar's conclusion and his general argumentative strategy, I now proceed to the nitty-gritty, the way he executes it.

Benatar suggests, reasonably, that in order to know whether it is worth starting a person's life, we must compare the state in which the person exists with the state in which the person does not. He points out that most people judge whether a life is worth starting by looking solely at the good and bad within the life that would exist, but that fails to include all the relevant information: one must compare the tally of good and bad in the life of the existent person with the tally that would obtain were the person not to exist.

The rub is in the comparison of the tallies. Benatar begins by noting that the state in which the person exists is one in which there is (reasonably expected to be) badness, say, the experience of suffering pain, and in which there is (reasonably expected to be) goodness such as the feeling of pleasure. Where things get contested is Benatar's construal of the state in which the person has not been created: it is a condition in which no one will suffer pain, which he says is good, and in which no one will feel pleasure, which, for him, is not bad. Benatar suggests that, upon comparing these goods and bads, non-existence is better on the whole than existence. For one, existence includes states of both good and bad, whereas non-existence includes no states of bad, and only states of good (43–44). For another, with regard to pain, non-existence is clearly to be preferred, since the presence of pain is bad in existence and the absence of pain is good in non-existence, and with regard to pleasure, although the presence of pleasure is good in existence, that is 'not an advantage over non-existence, because the absence of pleasures is not bad' (41).

Where is the 'asymmetry' in this argument? It is between the valuation of pleasure (benefits) and pains (harms) in the state of nonexistence. There is symmetry between their valuation in the state of existence, as the former is good and the latter is bad. There is asymmetry in their valuation in the state of non-existence, as the absence of pain is good and the absence of pleasure is not bad. It is this latter claim that drives Benatar to infer that non-existence is preferable to existence.

### 3.1. Questioning the Arguments for Asymmetry

Why believe the asymmetry thesis? It is most carefully expressed as the combination of these claims: (A1) the absence of pain is good even if there is no one who exists and could have experienced the pain, and (A2) the absence of pleasure is not bad, unless there is someone who exists and would have been deprived of it. Why hold (A1) and (A2)? Benatar presents three basic arguments for believing them, which are a matter of contending that (A1) and (A2) best explain a variety of uncontroversial judgments, decisions and emotions. For each argument, I suggest that one can equally well explain the intuitions without appealing to the asymmetry thesis, after which I provide reason to doubt not only the asymmetry thesis itself, but also Benatar's contention that the asymmetry thesis is sufficient to entail that it is better never to have been.

First, Benatar points out that most of us (who are not positive, total utilitarians) believe that there is a duty not to bring suffering people into existence, but that there is no duty to bring happy people into existence. Our judgment that we must not create suffering people is best explained, in part, by (A1), the idea that the absence of pain is good even if there is no potential bearer of the pain. And our judgment that we do no wrong in failing to create happy people is best explained, in part, by (A2), the claim that an absence of pleasure is not bad unless someone already exists who could have experienced it. Or so Benatar argues.

Benatar is correct about our intuitions regarding the duties governing procreation, but they are not obviously best explained by the asymmetry thesis. First, the judgment that we have a duty not to create suffering people is at least equally well explained by the principle that it is permissible to start a life if and only if it would be worth continuing. And the judgment that we lack a duty to create happy people is well explained by the same principle; for it being permissible to start such a life does not imply a requirement to do so.

Consider how my explanation of the relevant judgments differs from Benatar's. I say that the duty not to create suffering people and the absence of a duty to create happy ones is best explained by the principle that it is permissible to start a life if and only if it would be worth continuing. A life is worth continuing, more or less, if: the good will (largely) outweigh the bad, and there will be no period of torturous badness. Working with this account of what it is for a life to be worth continuing, and adding in the substantive claims that suffering or unhappiness is bad and pleasure or happiness is good, I can straightforwardly account for the two judgments about the duty that obtains and the one that does not. Note that my explanation of these judgments appeals solely to facts about the nature of the lives that would exist upon their being created, whereas Benatar's appeals to those kinds of facts plus facts about non-existence. My explanation is simpler, for appealing to facts of fewer kinds, and, is also, I submit, more intuitive.

Benatar's second rationale for the asymmetry thesis starts with the allegedly uncontested data that people routinely and sensibly decide not to create a child because they expect the child will suffer, whereas people neither routinely nor sensibly decide to create a child because they expect the child to benefit. He maintains that the decision not to create a suffering child is best explained, in part, by (A1), the claim that the absence of pain is good even if there is no one who would have experienced it. And we could not account for the fact that we do not decide to 'have a child for that child's sake' (34n27) if absent pleasures were bad regardless of whether there exists a particular person who has been deprived of them. In other words, only on the supposition that (A2), the absence of pleasure is not bad unless there is already a potential bearer of it, can one account for the idea that it is unusual and odd 'to give as a reason for having a child that the child one has will thereby be benefited' (34).

Some will say that it is not 'strange' (34) to create a child at least in part for the reason that there would be another happy being on the planet. However, I am willing to grant Benatar the claim that it is strange. I rather contest the best explanation of why it is strange, supposing that it is. Benatar says that the reason it is strange is that the absence of pleasure is not bad if there is no potential bearer of it. However, an equally good explanation is that the absence of pleasure is not good unless there is already a potential bearer of it, which explanation is symmetrical with the alternative explanation I now suggest for why it is clearly not strange to decide not to create a child that one foresees will suffer. Benatar says that the reason people often and coherently decide not to procreate when they know the offspring will live a miserable life includes the idea that an absence of pain is good, even if there is no one who could have felt it (and that the experience of pain is bad). A no less reasonable alternative, however, is the idea that an absence of pain is not bad (and that the experience of pain is bad).

Here is Benatar's third major argument for the asymmetry thesis. He points out that it is common to exhibit emotions such as regret, sadness and feeling sorry about the fact that others are suffering, particularly those beings we have created, whereas it is uncommon to exhibit such emotions about the fact that no one was created and therefore missed out on pleasure or happiness. Again, Benatar suggests that these emotional reactions are best explained by the asymmetry thesis. In particular, we exhibit negative emotions toward unhappy lives because pain is bad and its absence is good, and we do not exhibit negative emotions toward nonexistent lives that lack happiness because the absence of happiness is not bad when there is no one to be deprived of it.

However, I submit that the objection I made to Benatar's second argument applies with equal force to his third. That is, an equally attractive explanation of why we exhibit negative emotions toward unhappy lives is that pain is bad and its absence is not bad, and an explanation that is no less plausible of why we do not exhibit negative emotions toward non-existent lives that lack happiness is that the absence of happiness is not good. A symmetrical account of the values of benefits and burdens under conditions of non-existence is a powerful alternative to Benatar's asymmetrical explanation.

### 3.2. Questioning Asymmetry Itself

Benatar is aware that a glaring alternative to asymmetry is the one I have advanced here (39–40), the idea that the absence of pain is not bad, supposing no potential bearer of it exists, and that the absence of pleasure is not good, supposing the same. He does not explore this alternative in the context of the arguments put forth in favour of asymmetry, but rather considers it as a rival to asymmetry itself. Now, there is probably no qualitative difference between claiming that the absence of pleasure upon the non-existence of a person is 'not bad', as per asymmetry, and saying that it is 'not good', supposing that the latter is not meant to imply that it is bad, as I have above. Benatar says that the former is 'more informative' (40) and hence to be preferred, but that is not a matter of substance. What this means is that the real linchpin of Benatar's argument appears to be not (A2), but rather (A1),[4] viz., whether one should construe the absence of pain upon the non-existence of a person as 'good', as per asymmetry, or as 'not bad', as per my suggested alternative.

On this score, Benatar at two points in the text defends his asymmetrical construal, claiming, first, that the judgment that the absence of pain is not bad 'is too weak. Avoiding the pains of existence is more than merely "not bad". It is good' (39). In reply, I submit that Benatar's reasoning here is fallacious, so that asymmetry does not follow. Note that the claim that the absence of pain, supposing no potential bearer of it exists, is good is an evaluative judgment about a state of affairs. In support of this claim, however, Benatar makes a normative judgment about an action. To say that 'avoiding' pain is 'good' is to say that one has reason to do something. It is not to say that the state of affairs in which there is not pain is desirable. The quoted statement is a non sequitur with regard to establishing asymmetry.

Benatar could respond that the best explanation of why there is good reason to avoid pain is that pain is bad and the absence of pain is good. However, an equally good explanation of why there is good reason to avoid pain is that pain is bad and its absence

---

4    However, see discussion below (3.3) about the pleasures of the existent not constituting a 'real advantage' over the absent pleasures of the non-existent.

is not bad. At this point, Benatar should be providing reason to favour the asymmetry explanation, which the quote above does not do.

The second time Benatar addresses this powerful rival to (A1), he says that claiming that absent pains are merely 'not bad' (as opposed to 'good')

> would commit us to saying that we have no moral reason, grounded in the interests of a possible future suffering person, to avoid creating that person. We could no longer regret, based on the interests of a suffering child, that we created that child. Nor could we regret, for the sake of miserable people suffering in some part of the world, that they were ever created (204).

However, these statements are mere assertion, in the face of what I have argued above. For example, we could easily regret, based on the interests of a suffering child, that we created that child, if we held the following: pain is bad and the absence of pain is not bad, even if there is no potential bearer of the pain. Knowing that one could have opted for a situation in which there was nothing bad, and instead opted for a situation in which there is something bad, is enough to ground negative emotional reactions such as regret. Similar remarks apply to the other cases Benatar mentions.

Furthermore, I submit that there are two major reasons to favour the symmetrical account of the valuation of happiness and unhappiness in conditions of non-existence, that is, to prefer the view that the lack of pain in non-existence would be not bad, and the lack of pleasure in nonexistence would be not good. One reason is the fact of symmetry itself. As many physicists, mathematicians and philosophers of science have pointed out, symmetrical principles and explanations are to be preferred, ceteris paribus, to asymmetrical ones. There is still substantial disagreement in the literature about precisely why symmetry provides pro tanto reason for belief, with considerations of elegance, simplicity and probability being invoked, any of which could presumably be extended from the realm of science to that of value, conceived objectively, or at least realistically.[5]

Second, the symmetrical account coheres better with uncontroversial judgments about the relationship between experiences such as pleasure and pain and their degree of dis/value. A natural story is this one: the amount of pleasure is well represented with a positive number, which number also tracks degree of goodness, and the amount of pain is well represented with a negative number, which number also tracks degree of badness. Roughly, the more pleasure, the better off one is, and the more pain, the worse off one is, such that one is neither well off nor badly off if one experiences none of either, viz., has a score of zero. Benatar's asymmetry principle is inconsistent with these straightforward principles, in that it deems the absence of pain to be good, i.e., well represented not with a zero, but with a positive number. There might well be reason to deviate from this schema in the final analysis, but my point is that it would take more argument than Benatar has provided in the book.

### 3.3. Questioning the Inference from Asymmetry to the Harm of Existence

So far, I have objected to Benatar's arguments for the asymmetry thesis, and have questioned the asymmetry thesis itself. Now I grant the asymmetry thesis, and consider

---

5   An extension that Robert Nozick has made in his Invariances: The Structure of the Objective World (Cambridge, MA: Harvard University Press, 2001), esp. pp. 81–83, 289–291.

whether it truly supports the conclusion that non-existence is preferable to existence. Return, now, to the two grounds on which Benatar bases this inference. First, recall his idea that existence includes states of both good and bad, whereas non-existence includes no states of bad, and only states of good. Benatar puts it this way:

> There are benefits both to existing and non-existing. It is good that existers enjoy their pleasures. It is also good that pains are avoided through nonexistence. However, that is only part of the picture. Because there is nothing bad about never coming into existence, but there is something bad about coming into existence, it seems that all things considered non-existence is preferable (43–44).

I believe this reasoning is too quick. If we grant asymmetry, then, yes, existers have good and bad, but non-existers have only good and nothing bad. But we lack enough information to judge whether nonexistence is preferable, or vice versa, because we have not been told anything about the magnitudes of the goodness and the badness. Intuitively, if the goodness of existing were much greater than the goodness of non-existence, and so great as to outweigh the badness of existing (which would not be torturous), then existence would be preferable to non-existence. Benatar is adamant that the asymmetry argument is designed to show merely that existence is always a harm, and that it does not indicate how great the harm is (48). However, in order to conclude that existence is a harm relative to non-existence, one seems to need to know something about the degree of badness and goodness involved.

Benatar does reply to this objection, but it basically involves him appealing to his second rationale for moving from asymmetry to the conclusion that it is better never to have been (45–47). Here, the idea turns on the concept of a 'real advantage' as opposed to a merely apparent one. With regard to pain, non-existence is clearly to be preferred, since the presence of pain is bad in existence and the absence of pain is good in non-existence. In addition, though, Benatar claims that with regard to pleasure, although the presence of pleasure is good in existence, it does not constitute a real advantage relative to nonexistence, since the absence of pleasures in that state are not deprivations.

> Just as absent pleasures that do deprive are 'bad' in the sense of 'worse', so absent pleasures that do not deprive are 'not bad' in the sense of 'not worse'. They are not worse than the presence of pleasures. It follows that the presence of pleasures is not better, and therefore that the presence of pleasures is not an advantage over absent pleasures that do not deprive (41–42).

Let me unpack the key, first sentence. The first clause says that if one exists, and if one is prevented from experiencing pleasure, then one is badly off in the sense of worse off than one could have been. The second clause says that if one has not been created yet, and so has not been deprived of pleasure, then one is not badly off (to complete the parallel) in the sense of worse off than one could have been. My question is: why believe the second clause? Why is one not badly off in the sense of worse off than one could have been had one existed?

Benatar provides an analogy intended both to illustrate and to motivate the crucial claim that experiencing the pleasures of existing is 'not a real advantage' relative to the absent pleasures in non-existence, or, equivalently, that the absent pleasures in non-existence are 'no worse' than the pleasures of existing (42). Consider two individuals, S (Sick) and H (Healthy), where S is prone to sickness but is able to recover quickly, and where H never gets sick but also lacks the ability to heal speedily. Of these two, Benatar makes the following point:

> The capacity for quick recovery, although a good for S, is not a real advantage over H. This, in turn, is because the absence of that capacity is not bad for H. H is not worse off than he would have been had he had the recuperative powers of S. S is not better off than H in any way …. (42).

This fascinating analogy is supposed to show that the pleasures of those who exist are not a real advantage over the absent pleasures of those who do not exist because the absence of those pleasures is not bad for those who do not exist. This reasoning is intended to finesse the above concern regarding the magnitudes of pleasures and pains, for no matter how great the pleasures of existing are, they simply do not count when compared with the absent pleasures of non-existence.[6]

Benatar's appraisal of the desirability of being H relative to S is surely correct, and so I focus on whether the analogy is strong. In the case of S and H, the capacity to heal is labelled a 'good' merely because it is needed to minimize the bad of ill-health. However, in the case of one who exists, feeling pleasure is a good not merely because it is needed to minimize the bad of pain. So, consider an explanation of why S's capacity to heal is not a real advantage relative to H that differs from Benatar's. Benatar says this is because 'it is not bad for H' to lack this capacity, but that is perhaps a broader principle than is warranted; a more narrow principle is that it is because H does not need this capacity to avoid a bad condition. And the narrower principle does not apply to the case of comparing an existing person with one not yet created.

Benatar's analogy has clarified the claim that the pleasures of those who exist are not real advantages relative to the absence of pleasures of those who do not exist, but it has not obviously justified it. That analogy, and the claim that pleasures of those who exist are no real advantage over absent ones in the case of non-existence, warrant more reflection than I give them here. In the rest of my discussion, for the sake of argument, I grant Benatar the asymmetry thesis and his claim that it entails that non-existence is preferable to existence in terms of the interests of the one who exists. Establishing that it would be better never to have been would be a major accomplishment in itself, but, of course, Benatar aims for more, trying next to infer anti-natalism, the claim that one morally should not procreate.

## 4. The Sub Specie Aeternitatis Argument

Suppose that with the asymmetry argument Benatar has shown that it is invariably a net harm for a person to have been created. If the amount of harm were small, then, as I pointed out above in Section 2, it could well be justifiable for others to create him nonetheless, say, for the sake of third parties. So, in order to draw an anti-natalist conclusion with confidence, Benatar needs to demonstrate that the harm of existence would be large.

---

6    For this point, see also David Benatar, 'Christopher Belshaw's Review: Better If It Had Never Been', available at: http://www.utilitarianism.com/benatar/betanar-reply.html.

Before considering Benatar's reasons for thinking that existing is dreadful, I note that there could be additional reasons, besides that of helping others, to create a person in spite of the fact that doing so would impose a (minor) harm on her. Benatar's reasoning focuses on the interests or well-being of an individual, with pleasure and pain being representative examples, but there are probably additional individual-centred values that would need to be weighed up against the former before coming to a conclusive judgment about whether one should procreate. For example, I have encountered the suggestion that if human life or personhood had a dignity, that might provide a moral reason to create a person, even if that person's well-being would not be fostered thereby.[7] In general, if a certain kind of entity has a superlative final value that demands respect, then there is some reason to ensure that it is instantiated (even if not maximally promoted), despite coming at some cost to less weighty goods such as happiness.

For another example, consider the value of meaning in life.[8] Elsewhere I have discussed cases in which meaning would plausibly accrue to an individual not merely in spite of the fact that she has been harmed, but precisely because of it. For a quick and dirty case, consider someone who volunteers to be bored, or otherwise have a lower quality of life, so that others will not.[9] Taking on harm can be a way to enhance meaning in one's life. If so, then the fact that existence is a net harm need not entail that it would be wrong to make someone exist, at least if the created person would still have an opportunity to make something meaningful of her woeful existence.

Again, the best way for Benatar to respond would be to demonstrate that the harm of existence is significant, so significant as to outweigh considerations of dignity, meaning or any other individual value, let alone the usefulness of one's existence as a way to help others. This is the function of the point of view of the universe argument, the conclusion of which is that 'even the best lives are very bad, and therefore that being brought into existence is always a considerable harm' (61).

To defend this conclusion, Benatar takes up all three of the major accounts of well-being in the literature, namely, hedonism, the desire satisfaction theory and the objective list view. With regard to the first two, appealing to facts about our lives that human beings have a tendency to downplay, Benatar plausibly contends that we undergo much more pain and frustration than we are initially willing to acknowledge.

I believe that the most vulnerable—and most interesting—part of Benatar's reasoning is in the context of the objective list view, according to which a person is better off for being and functioning in certain ways that are good not merely because they are pleasurable or desired. For instance, it is typical of objectivists to believe that one's life is going well insofar as one has made achievements, sustained friendly or loving relationships, acquired an education, maintained mental and physical health, and exhibited autonomy in decision-making. Against the objective list view, Benatar points out that the list is invariably constructed from a human point of view. Theorists and laypeople take the relevant mind-independent conditions to be good for human beings from a human

---

7   See David Spurrett, 'Hooray for Babies', South African Journal of Philosophy 30.2 (2011),197–206.
8   Benatar takes meaningfulness to be one aspect of well-being, something likely to appear on the 'objective list' version (82–84). I do not, instead deeming it to be a different value-theoretic category altogether.
9   See Thaddeus Metz, 'The Meaning of Life', in Edward Zalta (ed) Stanford Encyclopedia of Philosophy (2007), available at: http://plato.stanford.edu/entries/life-meaning.

perspective. When determining what is objectively good, virtually no one takes up the sub specie aeternitatis, the point of view of the universe. And Benatar finds a human-centred judgment poorly motivated.

Benatar presents several interesting arguments for questioning judgments of objective goods that are informed by a human perspective (82–84). First, he points out that they are likely to be informed by the limits of what human beings can expect or what is within our control, but he reasonably asks what reason there is to think that impossible standards should be excluded a priori when ascertaining the quality of human life. Second, Benatar notes that most of those writing on the meaning of life reject the subjectivist view that an individual's life is meaningful for obtaining the objects of her contingent propositional attitudes, e.g., desiring something and getting it, or adopting a goal and realizing it. Most maintain that the individual's viewpoint is too arbitrary to ground judgments of meaning, as it counterintuitively entails that, say, counting blades of grass could be a very meaningful project. By analogy, Benatar suggests, most should maintain that humanity's viewpoint is too arbitrary, and should rather opt for a more encompassing standpoint. Third, most of us believe that our lives are much better than those of non-human primates, let alone those of beings such as cats or mosquitoes. If so, Benatar asks, why should we not reasonably judge other possible lives to be much better than ours, so that our quality of life is seen to be poor on the whole?

These arguments merit careful and thoughtful responses, but rather than rebut Benatar's arguments,[10] I provide more food for thought by offering positive reason to doubt that the point of view of the universe is the relevant perspective to invoke when appraising the quality of human life. One of the arguments is dialectical, in the sense of appealing to premises that Benatar himself accepts, but that I do not work to show are true. The other is assertoric for appealing to claims that might be external to Benatar's worldview, but that I put forth as true.

The assertoric argument appeals to meta-ethical considerations about the likely source of our value judgments. I presume that readers will agree that human beings are a product of natural selection and, furthermore, that making value judgments was probably instrumental for us to flourish as much as we have. It is quite common for contemporary moral theorists to maintain that cooperating made it much more likely for us to succeed as a species and that cooperating was made much more likely by having acquired, biologically and socially, the disposition to make certain (emotionally coloured) judgments of what is good and bad, right and wrong, blameworthy and free from culpability. Now, if this naturalist story about the origin of our value judgments is broadly correct, then it is extraordinarily unlikely that they would be informed by the point of view of the

---

10   I have, in effect, responded to these arguments in some of my work on life's meaning. I have argued that intuitions about when a life is on the whole meaningful are best systematized so that, although judgments of when a life counts as 'meaningful on balance' are not a function of what a given human being or even the species on average can obtain, they probably are a function of what is maximally possible, given the laws of nature, for beings that were born human but that could morph into something non-human. Roughly, while I reject the view of those such as Martha Nussbaum and Leon Kass, that value judgments must be grounded in human nature, I accept the view, contra Benatar, that they must be grounded in what is available to human nature. See Thaddeus Metz, 'Imperfection as Sufficient for a Meaningful Life: How Much is Enough?', in Yujin Nagasawa and Erik Wielenberg (eds) New Waves in Philosophy of Religion (New York: Palgrave Macmillan, 2009), pp. 192–214.

universe. A resolutely human perspective would be what is most likely to have enabled us to evolve by virtue of judging the behaviour of oneself and others.

The remaining, dialectical argument against thinking that human life should be appraised from the point of view of the universe is a version of the familiar 'partners in guilt' strategy. For one, notice that Benatar makes plenty of judgments about what we ought to think, which views are more justified than others, and which theories are better than others. For instance, he maintains that we have sufficient reason to believe antinatalism, that it is more worthy of belief than is pro-natalism. Benatar is quite comfortable making judgments of shoulds and goods in the context of belief without appealing to the standpoint of the universe, making it incoherent for him to suggest that we must appeal to the standpoint of the universe when making judgments of shoulds and goods in the context of action.

For another, consider that Benatar routinely makes judgments of what is immoral and what is harmful, again, without appealing to the point of view of the universe. He claims to know that murder is immoral, that procreation is immoral, that it is wrong to treat people merely as a means, that pleasure is good, that pain is bad, etc. If he can know which conditions are good or bad without appealing to a non-human standpoint, then why can we not make judgments of how good or bad something is without appealing to such a standpoint? In short, to defend his own argument for anti-natalism, Benatar has often appealed to what appear to be human-centred evaluative and normative judgments, making it unfair for him to set a different, and extremely higher, standard at other points.

If we reject the point of view of the universe, and accept an objective list account of human well-being, at least where the non-experiential goods are more weighty than any hedonistic elements that might be on the list, then it is far from obvious that the best human lives are all that badly off. Many people are not utterly neurotic, are not entirely controlled from without, are not completely ignorant, are not systematically shunned by other human beings, are not devastatingly sick, and so on. Naturally, I would not like to have been plunked into the Congo in the 1990s and suffered from war, crimes against humanity, malnutrition, bugs and parasites, humidity and heat, and the lack of quality education, healthcare, infrastructure and transport. And I certainly do not look forward to old age and death. But I presume most readers are like me in deeming themselves to have acquired enough objective goods to judge their lives to be, if not good, then at least not very bad, from a human standpoint. And if Benatar has not convincingly argued that the harm of existence is great, then the door remains open to argue that non-welfarist considerations such as dignity, meaning in life and help to others could morally justify creating an individual, even if the asymmetry argument succeeds in showing that exist-ence would unavoidably be a net harm for her.

## 5. Conclusion

My critical notice has been critical, but that is to give Benatar's book the intense scru-tiny that it deserves and should be taken as a sign of respect; Benatar's defence of anti-natalism is extraordinarily thoughtful and worthy of reflection. I have sought to add to the literature by carefully questioning the premises and inferences that lead Benatar to draw the conclusion that it is almost always wrong to procreate, and I like to think that I have indicated several places where a reader could sensibly elect to disembark from the train of argument heading toward anti-natalism.

Of course, even if I have succeeded in reasonably questioning Benatar's justification of anti-natalism, it does not follow that I have provided conclusive reason to reject that view or even his justification for it. I have pointed out, for instance, that the field should reflect more on Benatar's intriguing claim that the pleasures of those who exist are not a 'real advantage' over the absent pleasures of non-existence, since no one is deprived of them in that context. It should also ask whether Benatar could find strong reason for thinking that the absence of pain is not merely not bad, as I have suggested, but also good, as per his asymmetry thesis. And the field needs to think more about why the point of view of the universe continues to be so compelling to value theorists such as Benatar, and how one might find a principled way to reject its relevance. Where, if at all, one can reasonably draw the line between a very subjective standpoint, say, a blip of the experience of a single individual, on the one hand, and the sub specie aeternitatis, on the other?

There are several other issues that Benatar takes up with erudition and insight that I have not addressed in this article. A key example is his discussion of precisely when a person is created and its implications for the morality of abortion, with Benatar maintaining that abortion in the early stages of pregnancy is usually morally required because no person has been created by that time. Also revealing are his discussions of the ethics of population and extinction as well as of when appealing to intuitions is informative or misleading. In all, Better Never to Have Been has made me think, and I submit to the reader that engaging with it would, at the very least, prevent one's life from being as bad as it would have been without doing so.[11]

---

11    I thank the editor, Ward Jones, for comments on an earlier draft of this article.

# Better to Be

## David Boonin

Suppose a couple knows that if they conceive a child, the child's life on the whole will contain a million units of pleasure and a hundred units of pain. Call this the Lucky Couple. If the Lucky Couple decides to conceive, will their act of conceiving harm the resulting child? Most people would say no. To harm a person is to make things worse for that person than they would otherwise be. If the Lucky Couple conceives a child, the child will experience a great balance of pleasure over pain. If the Lucky Couple does not conceive a child, the child will not exist at all, and thus will not experience any pleasure or any pain. It is not worse to experience a great balance of pleasure over pain than not to experience any pleasure or any pain. And so, most people will conclude, if the Lucky Couple decides to conceive, their act of conceiving will not harm the resulting child.

David Benatar is not like most people. In his provocative and elegantly argued 2006 book *Better Never to Have Been*, Benatar defends the claim that acts of conception that take place in circumstances like those in my case of the Lucky Couple harm the child who is created.[1] More generally, he argues that the creation of any sentient creature whose life contains at least some pain or suffering is bad for that creature overall and thus harms it. Since, in the world as it is, every sentient creature does experience at least some amount of pain or suffering during its existence, it follows that in the world as it is, each act of creating sentient life harms the creature created by the act. This is a highly counterintuitive thesis and it has implications about the wrongness of conception, the rightness of early abortion and the goodness of extinction that are, if anything, even more counterintuitive. But while Benatar's fundamental claim is difficult to believe, it arises from an admirably simple and ingenious argument whose premises are not only plausible, but difficult to deny. In Part I of this paper, I will explain Benatar's argument. In Part II, I will develop an objection to it. In Part III, I will defend the objection from two arguments that might be made in response to it. I will conclude that Benatar's argument, although surprisingly forceful, is ultimately unsuccessful.

I.

Benatar's argument is based on the claim that there is an important asymmetry between pleasure and pain. This claim, in turn, is grounded in the intuitive response he expects most people to have to four different kinds of cases. I will introduce the principle underlying Benatar's argument by locating it in the context of one kind of case in

---

1    David Benatar, *Better Never To Have Been: The Harm of Coming into Existence*. Oxford: Clarendon Press, 2006. All page references are to this book.

particular and will postpone treatment of the other three cases that Benatar appeals to until after I have raised an objection to his argument. So let us begin by considering what I will call the Blessed Couple and the Cursed Couple. The Blessed Couple knows that if they conceive a child, the child's life on the whole will contain a million units of pleasure and zero units of pain. The Cursed Couple knows that if they conceive a child, the child's life on the whole will contain zero units of pleasure and a million units of pain. What does morality say about the choice that each couple faces?

It is difficult to resist the thought that there is an important moral asymmetry between the two cases. This is because it is difficult to resist the thought that while it would be wrong for the Cursed Couple to conceive the Cursed Child that they could conceive, it would not be wrong for the Blessed Couple not to conceive the Blessed Child that they could conceive. That is certainly my own intuitive reaction to the two cases, and I expect that most people will respond to them in the same way. If your intuitive response to the two cases is instead to view them as morally on a par, or if you believe that a consequentialist moral theory that treats them as morally on a par trumps whatever asymmetric intuitions you might otherwise have to the contrary, then the problem posed by Benatar's argument will be unable to get a grip on you. But if, like most people, you are strongly inclined to say that it would be wrong for the Cursed Couple to conceive the Cursed Child but not wrong for the Blessed Couple not to conceive the Blessed Child, then boy does Benatar have an argument for you. I will assume for the purposes of this paper, then, that it would be wrong for the Cursed Couple to conceive but not wrong for the Blessed Couple not to conceive.

If there really is such an evaluative difference between the Blessed Couple and the Cursed Couple, there must be some general principle that accounts for it. Benatar's argumentative strategy is to identify the general principle that he thinks best accounts for the difference and then to show that this principle entails that we are mistaken about the case of the Lucky Couple. In order to preserve our beliefs about the Blessed Couple and the Cursed Couple, that is, we will have to concede that the Lucky Couple does, in fact, harm the child it conceives, even though the child's life on the whole will contain a million units of pleasure and only a hundred units of pain.

Benatar presents the general principle he appeals to as a set of four claims:[2]

(1)  the presence of pain is bad

(2)  the presence of pleasure is good

(3)  the absence of pain is good, even if that good is not enjoyed by anyone

(4)  the absence of pleasure is not bad unless there is somebody for whom this absence is a deprivation

A few clarifications are in order before we turn to the question of why we should accept this set of claims and what, if anything, it implies about the case of the Lucky Couple.

I take it that (1) and (2) are straightforward and uncontroversial. They assert that pain in itself is a bad thing and that pleasure in itself is a good thing. It should be clear, moreover, in what sense they are to be taken to be bad in itself and good in itself: they are bad or good *for* someone, namely the person who experiences them. But (3) and (4), and the asymmetry between them, require a bit more attention. Let me begin with (4). The claim that the absence of pleasure is not bad unless there is somebody for

---

2    Benatar (2006: 30).

whom this absence is a deprivation suggests (although it does not strictly entail)[3] that the absence of pleasure is, in fact, bad, when it is the deprivation of pleasure for a particular person. This may sound as if Benatar means to say that the absence of pleasure in such a case is bad in itself, in the way that the presence of pain is bad in itself, but several pages later he clarifies that "when I say that [the absent pleasure that is a deprivation of a particular person] is bad, I do not mean that it is bad in the same way that the presence of pain is bad. What is meant is that the absent pleasure is relatively (rather than intrinsically) bad. In other words, it is *worse* than the presence of pleasure."[4] This suggests that we can restate (4) as follows:

(4)    the absence of pleasure is *worse than* the presence of pleasure only if there is somebody for whom this absence is a deprivation.

which in turn suggests that we can restate (3) as follows[5]:

(3)    the absence of pain is *better than* the presence of pain even if there is nobody for whom the absence of pain is a benefit.

And this, in turn, raises a question about (3).

Unlike (1) and (2), which make claims about something's being good or bad *simpliciter*, (3) and (4) make relational claims about one thing's being better or worse than another. (4) makes a claim that one thing is worse than another only in the case where the same person exists in both scenarios that are being compared. It says, for example, that Larry existing without pleasure is worse than Larry existing with pleasure. This claim raises no particular difficulty about what is meant by one thing's being worse than another. The former scenario is presumably worse than the latter because it is worse *for Larry*. But (3) makes a claim about one thing's being better than another not just in the kind of case where the same person exists in both scenarios being compared, but also in the kind of case where the person exists in one scenario and doesn't exist in the other. It maintains not only that Larry existing without pain is better than Larry existing in pain, but also that there being no pain because there is no Larry is better than Larry existing in pain. The former claim again raises no particular difficulty about what is meant since in that case Larry existing without pain is presumably better than Larry existing in pain because it is better *for Larry*. But the latter claim does raise a problem: how can Larry's not existing at all be better *for Larry* than Larry's existing in pain? For one condition to be better than another for Larry seems to require that both conditions be conditions *of Larry*, and it is a familiar point that non-existence is not a condition that characterizes Larry when Larry doesn't exist. Saying that Larry is non-existent is just another way of saying that there is no Larry, and so no condition of Larry at all.

Benatar offers two responses to this problem,[6] but I will focus here only on one. Following Feinberg, Benatar points out that it seems perfectly intelligible to say of some existing person that he would be better off dead. This seems intelligible, on Benatar's account, not because it means that if he dies he will then be in a condition that is better for him than his current condition, but because it simply means that from the point of

---

3    The absence of pleasure as a deprivation might be good, for example, if the person deserves to be deprived of the pleasure. I will follow Benatar in ignoring such potential complications.
4    Benatar (2006: 41).
5    This is not to insist that Benatar would not also endorse the claim that that absence of pain is intrinsically good under such conditions, but for purposes of explicating and analyzing the argument, it will prove to be simpler to render (3) and (4) parallel in this respect.
6    See Benatar (2006: 21-2).

view of his own well-being, he should prefer not to exist at all rather than to exist in his current condition. When (3) maintains that the absence of pain is better than the presence of pain even if there is nobody for whom the absence of pain is a benefit, then, the relational claim can be understood in this sense. Just as it can make sense to say of a particular person that it is better for him that he no longer exist than that he continue to exist given that his existence involves a certain amount of pain, so it can make sense to say of a person who would otherwise have existed that it is better – and better *for him* — not to exist than to exist in a certain amount of pain.[7] Of course, we can identify the already existing person in whose interest it is to cease existing while we cannot identify the particular person who would have existed and who would have been worse off for having existed. But, at least on Benatar's account, "we can still say that whoever that person would have been, the avoidance of his or her pains is good when judged in terms of his or her potential interests. If there is any (obviously loose) sense in which the absent pain is good *for* the person who could have existed but does not exist, this is it."[8] With all of this in mind, then, we can restate Benatar's set of claims more precisely as follows:

(1)   the presence of pain is intrinsically bad

(2)   the presence of pleasure is intrinsically good

(3)   the absence of pain is better than the presence of pain if either (a) there is an actual person whose interests are better served by the absence of the pain or (b) the presence of the pain would require the existence of a person who would not otherwise exist and whose potential interests are better served by the absence of the pain

(4)   the absence of pleasure is worse than the presence of pleasure only if there is an actual person whose interests are better served by the presence of the pleasure.

Since the four claims together maintain that the presence of pleasure and pain are symmetric with respect to intrinsic goodness and badness but that there is an asymmetry between the absence of pleasure and pain with respect to the relational properties of being better than and worse than, I will refer to the conjunction of these four claims as Benatar's *Relational Asymmetry Principle* (RAP).

Why should we think that the Relational Asymmetry Principle is true? The answer, according to Benatar, is that accepting the principle provides the best way for us to make sense of our intuitions about cases like the Blessed Couple and the Cursed Couple. If the Cursed Couple conceives, there will be a child existing in pain rather than no child at all. According to RAP (3b), the absence of pain is better than the presence of pain if the presence of the pain would require the existence of a person who would not otherwise exist and whose potential interests are better served by the absence of the pain. And so RAP implies that by conceiving the Cursed Child, the Cursed Couple would make things worse for that child. If the Blessed Couple decides not to conceive, there will be no child at all rather than a child existing with pleasure. According to RAP (4), the absence of pleasure is worse than the presence of pleasure only if there is an actual person whose interests are better served by the presence of the pleasure. Since if the Blessed Couple does not conceive there will be no such actual person, this means that if the Blessed Couple does not conceive the Blessed Child, they will not make things worse for that child. RAP, in short, seems to entail that what the Cursed

7    Benatar (2006: 30-1).
8    Benatar (2006: 31).

Couple does by conceiving makes things worse for the Cursed Child while what the Blessed Couple does by refraining from conceiving does not make things worse for the Blessed Child. And this, in turn, seems to provide a natural explanation for why it is wrong for the Cursed Couple to conceive but not wrong for the Blessed Couple not to conceive.

So far, so good. There seems to be a morally relevant difference between the Blessed Couple and the Cursed Couple. There also seems to be a problem about how to account for the difference. And Benatar's Relational Asymmetry Principle provides a plausible solution to that problem. But things go from good to not so good once we apply RAP to the case of the Lucky Couple. If the Lucky Couple conceives a child, re-member, the child's life on the whole will contain a million units of pleasure and a hundred units of pain. Intuitively, it seems that the child will not be harmed by being conceived in this case. But RAP seems to show that we are mistaken about this.

Following Benatar, we can think about what RAP would entail about the case of the Lucky Couple by considering the relevance of the pain that the child would suffer and the relevance of the pleasure that the child would enjoy independently. With respect to the hundred units of pain that the child will suffer if the Lucky Couple conceives, RAP entails that the child's existing will be worse for the child than the child's not existing. RAP (3b) maintains that the absence of pain is better than the presence of pain even if there is no actual person who is benefited by the absence of pain. So, with respect to the choice between existing and not existing, the hundred units of pain count against bringing the child into existence. Even though it is true that if the child is not con-ceived there will be no actual person who is benefited by the absence of the hundred of units of pain, RAP (3b) maintains that the absence of pain still makes it better for the child that he not exist than that he exist.

With respect to the million units of pleasure that the child will enjoy if the Lucky Couple conceives, however, the implications of RAP are crucially different. In particu-lar, the principle entails that in this respect, the child's existing will not be better for him than the child's not existing. RAP (4) maintains that the absence of pleasure is worse than the presence of pleasure only if there is an actual person whose interests are better served by the presence of the pleasure. But in the case of the Lucky Couple, the absence of the million units of pleasure would be the result of the absence of any child to be deprived of it. So, with respect to the choice between existing and not ex-isting, the million units of pleasure do not make it better for the child that he exist than that he not exist.

The result of combining these two considerations seems difficult to avoid, but just as difficult to accept. With respect to the hundred units of pain, non-existence is better for the child than existence. With respect to the million units of pleasure, existence is not better for the child than non-existence. So non-existence has one advantage over existence – it avoids the badness of the child's suffering pain – but existence has no advantage over non-existence: the fact that the child would enjoy pleasure makes exis-tence no better for the child than non-existence because the absence of pleasure is not worse for the child than the presence of pleasure when there is no actual child to be deprived of the absent pleasure. If non-existence has an advantage over existence and existence has no advantage over non-existence, then non-existence is better than exis-tence. So non-existence is better for the child than existence in this case. If the Lucky Couple conceives, they will cause the worse thing to happen from the point of view of the interests of the child they would conceive. Relative to non-existence, he will not be better off as a result of the million units of pleasure. But relative to non-existence, he will be worse off as a result of the hundred units of pain. So the Lucky Couple will make things worse for the child by conceiving him. The act of conceiving him will harm him. And since your life and my life contain at least some pain as well, you and I were harmed by being conceived, too. We would all have been better off never having been.

## II.

Benatar's argument for this unwelcome conclusion depends on his claim that his Relational Asymmetry Principle provides the best explanation for the moral asymmetry between cases like that of the Blessed Couple and the Cursed Couple. One way to object to Benatar's argument, then, would be to identify an alternative principle that does an even better job of explaining the asymmetry and that produces a different result in the case of the Lucky Couple. And I want to argue that we can, in fact, identify such a principle if we start by appealing to a symmetric version of Benatar's principle, one in which (1)-(3) are the same as in RAP but in which the claim made about the absence of pleasure in (4) is symmetric to the claim made by RAP (3) about the absence of pain. What I will call the *Relational Symmetry Principle* (RSP), then, amounts to taking RAP (1)-(3) and conjoining them with:

(4) the absence of pleasure is worse than the presence of pleasure if either (a) there is an actual person whose interests are better served by the presence of

the pleasure or (b) the absence of the pleasure would require the absence of a person who would otherwise exist and whose potential interests are better served by the presence of the pleasure

If RAP (3) is logically coherent, then surely RSP (4) is logically coherent as well. If the absence of pain can be better than the presence of pain even when there is no actual person who enjoys the absence of pain, that is, then the absence of pleasure can be worse than the presence of pleasure even when there is no actual person who is deprived of the absent pleasure. Benatar himself concedes this much.[9] My claim in the rest of this paper will be not only that RSP is as coherent as RAP, but that RSP can be used to undermine Benatar's argument.

To see how this can be accomplished, let us begin by considering what my Relational Symmetry Principle would entail about the case of the Cursed Couple and the Blessed Couple. If the Cursed Couple conceives, the resulting child's life on the whole will contain zero units of pleasure and a million units of pain. RSP (3b) is identical to RAP (3b). It says that the absence of pain is better than the presence of pain if the presence of the pain would require the existence of a person who would not otherwise exist and whose potential interests are better served by the absence of the pain. And so RSP, just like RAP, makes it plausible to say that by conceiving, the Cursed Couple would make things worse for the Cursed Child. If the Blessed Couple conceives, on the other hand, the resulting child's life on the whole will contain a million units of pleasure and zero units of pain. RAP (4) entailed that by not conceiving, the Blessed Couple would not make things worse for the Blessed Child. But RSP (4b) maintains that the absence of pleasure is worse than the presence of pleasure even if the absence of the pleasure would require the absence of a person who would otherwise exist and whose potential interests are better served by the presence of the pleasure. So my RSP,

---

9   Benatar (2006: 31fn23).

unlike Benatar's RAP, entails that the Blessed Couple would make things worse for the Blessed Child by not conceiving.

Does this mean that the Relational Symmetry Principle is unable to account for the asymmetry between the Blessed Couple and the Cursed Couple? It does not. The asymmetry between the Blessed Couple and the Cursed Couple can be accounted for by appealing to an asymmetry between pleasure and pain that is different from the asymmetry that Benatar appeals to and that is fully consistent with affirming the Relational Symmetry Principle. The asymmetry is that with respect to pleasure, no actual person is made worse off by the decision about whether to conceive him regardless of whether the better or worse outcome is selected, but with respect to pain, whether an actual person is made worse off by the decision about whether to conceive him depends on whether the better or worse outcome is selected.

If the Blessed Couple decides to conceive the Blessed Child, for example, then things will be better from the point of view of the interests of the Blessed Child, and the Blessed Child will therefore not be made worse off by the decision. If the Blessed Couple decides not to conceive the Blessed Child, then things will be worse from the point of view of the interests of the Blessed Child, but the Blessed Child will not exist and so will not be an actual person who has been made worse off by the decision. Regardless of which choice the Blessed Couple makes, then, no actual person will be made worse off by their decision. But pain is different from pleasure in this respect. Whether an actual person will be made worse off by the Cursed Couple's decision about whether to conceive depends on the choice they make. If the Cursed Couple decides not to conceive the Cursed Child, then things will be better from the point of view of the interests of the Cursed Child. No actual person will be made worse off by their decision both because there will be no actual person to be affected by their decision and because their decision made things better rather than worse. But if the Cursed Couple decides to conceive the Cursed Child, then things will be worse from the point of view of the interests of the Cursed Child, and the Cursed Child will exist to be made worse off by this fact. There will therefore be an actual person who has been made worse off by their decision. While in the case of pleasure no actual person is made worse off regardless of whether the Blessed Couple choose the better or worse outcome, in the case of pain, whether or not an actual person will be made worse off depends on whether the Cursed Couple chooses the better or worse outcome.

Because of this asymmetry between pleasure and pain, the Relational Symmetry Principle that I am proposing as an alternative to Benatar's Relational Asymmetry Principle can account for the claim that it would be wrong for the Cursed Couple to conceive the Cursed Child but not wrong for the Blessed Couple not to conceive the Blessed Child. The Relational Symmetry Principle can do this by appealing to what I will call the *Actual Persons Principle* (APP), where by an "actual person" I mean a person who exists at some point in time:

> APP: When choosing between two options, it is prima facie wrong to make the choice the acting on which will result in its being the case that there is an actual person for whom your act made things worse.

RSP entails that if the Cursed Couple conceives the Cursed Child, this will make things worse for the Cursed Child. Since the Cursed Child will exist, the Actual Persons Principle entails that this will make the Cursed Couple's act prima face wrong. RSP also entails that if the Blessed Couple does not conceive the Blessed Child, this will make things worse for the Blessed Child. But since if the Blessed Couple does not conceive the Blessed Child, the Blessed Child will never exist, and since the Actual Persons Principle focuses only on the harmful effects on people who actually exist at some point in time, the principle will not entail that the Blessed Couple's act is prima facie wrong. Thus, while Benatar's Relational Asymmetry Principle can account for the asymmetry between the Blessed Couple and the Cursed Couple, my Relational Symmetry Principle can account for it as well, provided that it is conjoined with the Actual Persons Principle.

Benatar's RAP, as we saw in Part I, entails that the Lucky Couple harms the child that it conceives. What does my RSP entail about this case? If the Lucky Couple conceives, the resulting child's life on the whole will contain a million units of pleasure and a hundred units of pain. As in the case of RAP, we can follow Benatar and see how the case looks from the point of view of RSP by considering the relevance of the pain that the child would suffer and of the pleasure that the child would enjoy independently. With respect to the hundred units of pain that the child will suffer if the Lucky Couple conceives, RSP entails that existing will be worse for the child than not existing. RSP (3b), just like RAP (3b), maintains that the absence of pain is better than the presence of pain if the presence of the pain would require the existence of a person who would not otherwise exist and whose potential interests are better served by the absence of the pain. So, with respect to the choice between existing and not existing, my RSP, just like Benatar's RAP, treats the hundred units of pain as counting against bringing the child into existence.

With respect to the million units of pleasure that the child will enjoy if the Lucky Couple conceives, RAP (4) maintains that the absence of pleasure is worse than the presence of pleasure only if there is an actual person whose interests are better served by the presence of the pleasure. Since if the child is not conceived there will be no actual person who is deprived by the absence of the million of units of pleasure, RAP maintains that the absence of pleasure does not make it worse for the child not to exist than to exist. But my RSP is crucially different from Benatar's RAP in precisely this respect. RSP (3) is identical to RAP (3), but where RAP (4) maintains that the absence of pleasure is worse than the presence of pleasure only if there is an actual person who is harmed by the absence of pleasure, RSP (4b) maintains that the absence of pleasure is worse than the presence of pleasure even if there is no actual person who is harmed by the absence of the pleasure because the absence of the pleasure requires the absence of the person who would otherwise exist with the pleasure. So RSP maintains that the absence of pleasure does make it worse for the child not to exist than to exist. With respect to the choice between existing and not existing, the million units of pleasure count in favor of bringing the child into existence according to my RSP, while they do not count in favor of bringing the child into existence according to Benatar's RAP.

Regarding the hundred units of pain, then, RSP maintains that existence is worse than non-existence, and regarding the million units of pleasure, RSP maintains that existence is better than non-existence. Since the total amount of pleasure outweighs the total amount of pain in this case, the magnitude of the advantage that existence has over non-existence is greater than the magnitude of the advantage that non-existence has over existence. And so, in the end, RSP entails that in the case of the Lucky Couple, the advantages of existence outweigh the advantages of non-existence. Benatar's

Relational Asymmetry Principle entails that the Lucky Couple harms its child by conceiving it. But my Relational Symmetry Principle does not entail this.

We now have two principles that are capable of accounting for our asymmetric judgment in the case of the Blessed Couple and the Cursed Couple: Benatar's Relational Asymmetry Principle and my Relational Symmetry Principle. The question, then, is which principle provides the better account. There are three reasons to conclude that my Relational Symmetry Principle does.

The first reason to favor my RSP over Benatar's RAP is that RSP entails that the Lucky Couple does not harm its child by conceiving it while RAP entails that the Lucky Couple does harm its child by conceiving it. It may seem that I am begging the question here. It may seem that I am saying "we should believe that the Lucky Couple does not harm the child it conceives because RSP entails that it doesn't, and we should believe RSP because RSP entails that the Lucky Couple does not harm the child it conceives." That would, indeed, be circular. But that is not what I am saying. What I am saying is this: Benatar provides, as a reason for endorsing RAP, the claim that RAP accounts for the difference between the Blessed Couple and the Cursed Couple. Accepting the deeply counterintuitive claim that the Lucky Couple harms its child by conceiving it is simply the price we have to pay in order to preserve our judgments about the cases of the Blessed Couple and Cursed Couple. But RSP shows that we can account for the judgments in these two cases without paying that price. If, among two competing explanations for the judgments in the Blessed and Cursed Couple cases, one has fewer counterintuitive implications in additional cases than the other, then that is a legitimate, non-circular reason for preferring it. The case of the Lucky Couple therefore provides a legitimate, non-circular reason to prefer RSP over RAP. And once we have selected RSP over RAP for this legitimate, non-circular reason, there is no longer any reason to doubt the common sense judgment that the Lucky Couple does not harm its child by conceiving it.

A second reason to prefer my RSP over Benatar's RAP is independent of RSP's implications for the case of the Lucky Couple. Instead, it arises from the fact that while both RSP and RAP involve affirming the existence of an asymmetry between pleasure and pain, the asymmetry that RSP appeals to is perfectly straightforward while the asymmetry that RAP appeals to is quite counterintuitive. The asymmetry that my RSP appeals to arises directly from the fact that pleasure is good and pain is bad. Since pleasure is good, the worse outcome regarding pleasure is when it is absent. Since pain is bad, the worse outcome regarding pain is when it is present. There is nothing surprising or mysterious about this. In order for an actual person to be made worse off by something, he must actually exist at some point in time. There is nothing surprising or mysterious about this, either. But these two perfectly straightforward observations are enough to ground the asymmetry between pleasure and pain that my RSP appeals to in accounting for the asymmetry between the Blessed Couple and the Cursed Couple: since existing is the worse outcome in the case of Cursed Child, there is an actual person who is made worse off if the Cursed Couple makes the worse choice. Since not existing is the worse outcome in the case of the Blessed Child, there is no actual person who is made worse off if the Blessed Couple makes the worse choice.

But the asymmetric claim that Benatar's RAP appeals to should seem quite surprising. It seems odd to say that the absent pain of non-existence makes it better for the Cursed Child not to exist but that the absent pleasure of non-existence does not make it worse for the Blessed Child not to exist. How can the absence of something have an effect on the would-be child's welfare in one case but not in the other? Benatar, of course, provides a reason for accepting this asymmetry: the claim that accepting it is necessary in order to account for the asymmetry between our moral judgments in the case of the Blessed Couple and the Cursed Couple. But my RSP shows that Benatar's RAP is not necessary in order to account for this feature of our moral judgments. Once we see this, we lose our reason to endorse the asymmetry that Benatar appeals to. And once we lose our reason to endorse the asymmetry that is appealed to by RAP, the fact that the asymmetry itself is intuitively less plausible than the asymmetry appealed to by RSP provides a second independent reason to prefer my RSP over Benatar's RAP.

A final reason to prefer RSP over RAP is also independent of its implications for the case of the Lucky Couple. It arises from the fact that while both RSP and RAP can produce the intuitively correct answers in the case of the Blessed Couple and the Cursed Couple, there is an important difference between the two principles in terms of the additional assumptions that have to be accepted in order for them to be able to do so. Neither RSP nor RAP by themselves yield any conclusions about what it would be right or wrong to do. Neither principle makes any reference to right or wrong, obligatory or impermissible, should or should not. Instead, they make judgments about which states of affairs are good or bad, or better or worse. Without some sort of bridging principle, therefore, neither can justify any conclusions about what should or should not be done. And this is what generates the third reason to prefer my RSP over Benatar's RAP: the bridging principle needed in order for RSP to account for our judgments in the Blessed Couple and Cursed Couple cases is superior to the bridging principle needed in order for RAP to do so.

As I noted earlier, RSP can account for the asymmetry between the Blessed Couple and the Cursed Couple by appealing to what I called the Actual Persons Principle.

> APP: When choosing between two options, it is prima facie wrong to make the choice the acting on which will result in its being the case that there is an actual person for whom your act made things worse.

In order to account for the asymmetry between the Blessed Couple and the Cursed Couple by appealing to RAP, however, we must instead depend on what I will call the *Actual and Possible Persons Principle* (APPP), where by a "possible person" I mean a person who will never exist, but who would have existed had the other option been selected:

> APPP: When choosing between two options, it is prima facie wrong to make the choice the acting on which will result in its being the case that there is an actual or possible person for whom your act made things worse.

That Benatar's argument requires us to assume the Actual and Possible Persons Principle is clear from the following considerations. Benatar claims that we must say that the absent pleasures if the Blessed Child is not conceived do not make it worse for the child that he not be conceived. He claims that we must say that it is not worse for the Blessed Child that he not be conceived so that we can avoid having to say that it would be wrong for the Blessed Couple not to conceive the Blessed Child. But the claim "not conceiving the Blessed Child does not harm the child" is necessary to sustaining the claim "not conceiving the Blessed Child is not morally wrong" only if it would be morally wrong for the Blessed Couple to harm the Blessed Child by not conceiving him. The Actual Persons Principle does not entail that this would be wrong: even though not conceiving the Blessed Child would make things worse for the Blessed Child, not conceiving the Blessed Child would not be wrong because it would not result in an actual person for whom refraining from conceiving the Blessed Child had made things worse. Only if we include merely possible people in the scope of our considerations can Benatar's argument for RAP succeed. And so Benatar's argument requires us to accept the Actual and Possible Persons Principle.

But there are two reasons to prefer the bridging principle required by my RSP to the bridging principle required by Benatar's RAP. The first is that the RSP bridging principle is simpler. The Actual Persons Principle posits only one kind of entity whose interests we must consider: people who at some point actually exist. The Actual and Possible Persons Principle includes this kind of entity plus a second and very different kind of entity: those people who do not exist and who will never exist but who would have existed had a different choice been made. All else being equal, a simpler principle should be preferred to a more complex principle, and this provides one reason to prefer the bridging principle required by RSP to the bridging principle required by RAP.

The second reason to prefer the RSP bridging principle to the RAP bridging principle is that the RSP bridging principle appeals to a consideration whose moral salience is less controversial. The fact that an act would harm an actual person is generally recognized as relevant to the question of whether the act would be wrong. But the fact that an act would be worse for the interests of a merely possible person who will never exist if the act is performed is not already accepted to be relevant in the same way. Indeed, to say that we must consider the interests of people who will never exist is quite controversial. All else being equal, a principle whose salience is less controversial should be preferred to a principle whose salience is more controversial. And this provides a second reason to prefer the bridging principle required by my RSP to the bridging principle required by Benatar's RAP.

Benatar, of course, might maintain that all else is not equal, that RAP itself has a great amount of explanatory power because it can account for our asymmetric moral judgments in the case of the Blessed Couple and the Cursed Couple. But, as I have already argued, RSP can account for these cases as well. If the bridging principle required by RSP is simpler and less controversially salient than that required by RAP, and if RSP has at least as much explanatory power as RAP,[10] then we have a third and final reason to prefer RSP to RAP. Combined with the fact that RAP implausibly en-

---

10   It might be suggested that in two important respects, Benatar's RAP has more explanatory power than my RSP. This is because Benatar claims that the argument arising from his RAP solves Derek Parfit's non-identity problem and mere addition paradox (2006: 178) and because there is no obvious route from my RSP to a solution to either puzzle. Limitations of space do not permit a detailed response to this suggestion, but the outline of my response would run as follows. Both puzzles arise when we are confronted with a two-option choice: the choice between conceiving a blind child or a non-identical and otherwise comparable sighted child, for example, in the case of the non-identity problem, and the choice between what Parfit calls A and B in the case of the mere addition paradox. In the case of the former puzzle, it is difficult to account for the intuitive judgment that making the first choice rather than the second choice would be morally wrong and in the case of the latter puzzle, it is difficult to avoid the conclusion that B would be better than A, which in turn seems to entail what Parfit calls the Repugnant Conclusion: that what he calls Z would be even better still. Benatar's argument for the claim that coming into existence is always a harm can help us to sidestep these two problems, but it cannot really help us to solve them.

tails that the Lucky Couple harms their child by conceiving it while RSP more plausible entails that they do not, and with the fact that the asymmetry that RSP appeals to is more plausible than the asymmetry that RAP appeals to, we have three good reasons to prefer RSP over RAP. And by justifying the choice of RSP over RAP, we justify rejecting Benatar's argument for the claim that the Lucky Couple harms their child by conceiving it.

III.

I have argued that we can justify rejecting Benatar's argument by showing that RSP better accounts for our intuitions about the Blessed Couple and the Cursed Couple than does RAP and by showing that RSP entails that the Lucky Couple does not harm the child it conceives. I want now to consider two responses that might be offered on Benatar's behalf. The first response arises from the fact that Benatar's defense of RAP as a whole appeals to its ability to explain our asymmetric intuitions in four kinds of cases, not just the kind of case involved in the Blessed and Cursed Couples. Even if RSP proves superior to RAP in the context of the first kind of case, then, Benatar's RAP might still prove superior overall. The second response arises from the fact that Benatar briefly responds to an objection that is in some respects similar to the one that I have developed here. One might then ask whether his response would apply to my objection as well.

Let us begin with the supplemental cases that Benatar appeals to in supporting RAP. The first such case is this: "Whereas it is strange (if not incoherent) to give as a reason for having a child that the child one has will thereby be benefitted, it is not strange to cite a potential child's interests as a basis for avoiding bringing a child into exis-

---

The claim that it would be better to conceive no child at all than to conceive either a blind child or a different sighted child, for example, does not help to explain why it would be wrong to conceive the blind child rather than the sighted child if those were the only two options. The claim that the blind child would have less happiness to compensate for the harm of being brought into existence might be used to justify the claim that it would be wrong to conceive the blind child rather than the sighted child, but the claim that the blind child would have less happiness than the sighted child could just as easily be used to justify the claim that it would be wrong to conceive the blind child rather than the sighted child without appealing to the claim that either child would be harmed by being brought into existence. So while Benatar's argument could establish that the right thing to do would be to not conceive at all, and while not conceiving at all would enable us to avoid choice situations in which the non-identity problem arises, his argument does not offer a solution to the problem, in cases where it does arise, that depends on our accepting the Relational Asymmetry Principle in particular.

Similarly, the claim that a world with zero people would be better than either Parfit's world A or world B does not help us to resolve the paradox that is created by the fact that what Parfit calls A+ seems to be at least as good as A, that B seems to be better than A+, that this seems to show that B is better than A, and that this seems to show that Z is even better still. Indeed, the very same paradox can be generated without talking about worlds filled with people at all: A can represent the state of affairs in which you live for another 40 years at a very high level of welfare, B can represent the state of affairs in which you live for another 80 years at a level of welfare that is lower than in A but more than half as great, and Z can represent the state of affairs in which you live for an extremely long amount of time at a level of welfare that is just barely better than no welfare at all but such that the total amount of welfare your life as a whole will contain is greater than it will be in A or B. And so, again, Benatar's argument could establish that the best world to choose in terms of population size would be one in which the puzzle about the relationship between A, B and Z would not arise, but it does not really offer a solution to the problem in cases where it does arise.

tence."[11] RAP accounts for this asymmetry by maintaining that bringing a happy child into existence does not really make the child better off whereas bringing an unhappy child into existence really does make the child worse off. But RSP can account for this asymmetry just as easily. It can explain why it is not strange to cite a potential child's interests as a reason not to conceive, as in the case of the Cursed Couple. It can explain this because it maintains that creating an unhappy child causes harm to an actual person and because it is not strange to cite the negative impact on the interests of an actual person as a reason not to bring the child into existence. And it can also explain why it is strange to give as a reason for conceiving a happy child that the child will thereby be benefitted. The reason that this is strange is not that it is not true. According to RSP, it is true that a happy child benefits from being brought into existence. And so it is true that the Blessed Couple would benefit its child by conceiving it. The reason it would be strange for the Blessed Couple to give this as a reason for conceiving the Blessed Child is that, if they don't bring him into existence, there won't be any actual child whom they have failed to benefit. In cases where it clearly does make sense to cite as a reason for doing a particular action the fact that doing the action would benefit someone, it makes sense because there is an actual person who stands to benefit from the action being done and who will have to do without the benefit if the action is not done. But when the Blessed Couple is deciding whether or not to conceive, there is no actual person who stands to benefit from their deciding to conceive and no actual person who will have to do without a benefit if they decide not to conceive. And there is nothing about RSP that prevents us from appealing to this consideration in explaining our intuitions in the first supplemental case that Benatar appeals to.

Benatar's second supplemental case involves reasons for regret rather than reasons for action.[12] If we bring an unhappy person into existence, we can later regret this for the sake of the unhappy person himself. If we decline to bring a happy person into existence, on the other hand, we may regret this for our own sake, but we cannot really regret it for the sake of the person we could have conceived. RAP is again able to account for this asymmetry. We have harmed the unhappy person by creating him, and so regret for this for his sake is appropriate, but we have not harmed the potential but not actual happy person by not creating him, and so regret for his sake is not appropriate. As Benatar puts it, "The reason why we do not lament our failure to bring somebody [happy] into existence is because absent pleasures [unlike existing pains] are not bad."[13]

But RSP can account for this asymmetry just as well, too. If the Cursed Couple conceives the Cursed Child, then RSP entails that they have made things worse for this child, just as RAP does. Since their child will be an actual person, there will therefore be an actual person they have harmed and thus an actual person for whose sake they can appropriately regret their action. If the Blessed Couple does not conceive the Blessed Child, then RSP, unlike RAP, does entail that they have made things worse for the Blessed Child. But since in that case the Blessed Child does not exist, there exists no one for whose sake they can regret their decision. And so, as on the RAP account, they can regret their choice for their own sake, but not for the sake of any actual

---

11   Benatar (2006: 34).
12   Benatar (2006: 34-5).
13   Benatar (2006: 35).

person that they have harmed. The case of asymmetric sources of regret then, like the case of asymmetric reasons for action, provides no reason to prefer RAP over RSP.[14]

Finally, Benatar appeals to an asymmetry between our response to distant places where people are suffering and our response to distant places that are uninhabited.[15] When we learn of a distant place where people are suffering, we are sad for those people. But when we learn, say, of an uninhabited island, we are not sad for the people who, if they had existed, would have happily lived there. RAP is once more able to account for this asymmetry: the suffering people are worse off because of their suffering but the non-existent people are not worse off because of their not existing. And so we are right to feel bad about the existing pains and not feel bad about the absent pleasures. But RSP can once again account for the asymmetry, too. We feel bad for the suffering actual people not just because their suffering makes things worse for them but because their suffering is something bad that is actually happening to them. And while the non-existing happy people really would have benefitted from being brought into existence, according to RSP, it is nonetheless the case that nothing bad is happening to them by their not having been brought into existence – indeed, nothing at all is happening to them since they don't exist – and so their absent pleasures, while worse than existing pleasures, give us no reason to feel bad for them. There is simply no them for whom we can feel bad.

The result of considering all four cases that Benatar presents in defense of his argument, then, is that we have three reasons to favor RSP over RAP — the reason arising from the case of the Lucky Couple, the reason arising from the more plausible asymmetry that RSP appeals to, and the reason arising from the more parsimonious and more salient bridging principle that RSP depends on — and no reason to favor RAP over RSP, since all the cases that RAP can account for can also be accounted for by RSP. The first kind of response to my objection to Benatar's argument, then, should be rejected.

The second kind of response to my objection arises from something that Benatar says about the distinction between positive and negative duties. Immediately after arguing that RAP is supported by its ability to explain our intuitions in cases like the Blessed and Cursed Couples, Benatar notes that someone might propose an alternative explanation that does not involve the asymmetry between RAP (3) and RAP (4). Specifically, he anticipates someone suggesting that the difference can be accounted for by appealing to the distinction between a negative duty not to cause harm and a positive duty to actively "bring about happiness". If we have a duty of the former sort but not of the latter sort, then this might explain why the Cursed Couple has a duty not to conceive while the Blessed Couple does not have a duty to conceive. And it could explain this without appealing to the sort of asymmetry that Benatar's principle involves. Benatar responds to this possibility as follows: "I agree that for those who deny that we have any positive duties, this would indeed be an alternative explanation to the one

---

14   It may also be worth noting that if the example of regret really does pose a problem for my RSP, then a parallel example poses the same problem for Benatar's RAP. If the Cursed Couple does not conceive, then there is no one for whom they can feel pleased about their decision. If the fact that there is no one for whom the Blessed Couple can feel regret if they do not conceive means that conceiving the Blessed Child would not have made things better for him, then the fact that there is no one for whom the Cursed Couple can feel pleased if they do not conceive would mean that conceiving the Cursed Child would not have made things worse for him. But RAP and RSP both agree that conceiving the Cursed Child would make things worse for him.

15   Benatar (2006: 35).

I have provided. However, even of those who do think that we have positive duties only a few also think that amongst these is a duty to bring happy people into existence."[16] Since virtually everyone who believes in positive duties will still deny that it would be wrong for the Blessed Couple not to conceive, that is, a response to Benatar's argument that depends on denying the existence of such duties will prove unsatisfactory.

It may seem that this alternative account of why it is not wrong for the Blessed Couple not to conceive is the same as the alternative explanation that I have provided in this paper, and that the objection that I have raised in this paper is therefore one that Benatar has already satisfactorily answered. But this is not so. It is true that the RSP-based response that I have endorsed maintains that the Blessed Couple's child will be better off if they conceive it than if they don't. And it is also true that the RSP-based response maintains that the Blessed Couple nonetheless has no moral obligation to conceive the child. It is therefore true that the objection to Benatar that I have defended here maintains that the Blessed Couple has no moral obligation to do the act that would be better for the child they would conceive.

But it does not follow from this that the RSP-based objection to Benatar's argument depends on the claim that we have no positive moral duties. The RSP-based account is compatible with the claim that we have a great many positive duties, provided only that they are positive duties that we have to other actual people, people with actual lives that will go worse for them in various ways if we refrain benefitting them. If there is a child drowning in front of you, or an injured motorist lying by the side of the road, or a person starving in some distant country, for example, the RSP-based objection to Benatar's argument can allow that it would be morally wrong for you not to provide assistance. Indeed, even in cases where your assistance would simply make already happy people even happier, the RSP-based objection to Benatar's argument is consistent with the claim that it would be morally wrong for you not to provide it. If an already very happy child is about to enjoy a delicious ice cream sundae, for example, and if it would taste even better if you were to let him have one of your extra cherries to put on top of it, then the RSP-based account could allow that it would be morally wrong for you not to donate the extra cherry you happen to have to the child.

The RSP-based account can allow that you would have positive duties in any or all of these cases because in these cases there is an actual person whose life will go less well if you do not benefit them. If the Blessed Couple declines to conceive, by contrast, there will be no actual person whose life will go less well as a result. And so the claim made by the RSP-based account that I have offered here, the claim that it is not immoral for the Blessed Couple to refrain from conceiving since doing so does not result in there being an actual person who is made worse off as a result, is consistent with (but does not require us to accept) the claim that we have a prima facie positive duty to benefit actual people and not just a negative duty not to harm them. It is not the fact that the Blessed Couple would (merely) benefit the Blessed Child by conceiving it that renders it morally acceptable for them not to conceive the child on this account. It is the fact that if they don't conceive the child, there will be no actual person whose life will go less well as a result: no actual person that they have harmed and no actual person that they have failed to benefit.

---

16    Benatar (2006: 32).

Those who believe that we have positive duties to help others, then, can consistently embrace my objection to Benatar's argument, as, of course, can those who deny that we have such duties. And since my objection to Benatar's argument enables us to avoid the highly counterintuitive implications of his thesis, it isn't simply that they can accept my objection. They should.[17]

17  I would like to thank Eric Chwang and Elizabeth Harman for their comments on an earlier version of this paper, David Benatar for his comments on several earlier versions, and the participants at the November 23-24 anti-natalism workshop at the University of Johannesburg for feedback that was useful in making revisions on the final draft.

# Is Having Children Always Wrong?

## Rivka Weinberg

Life stinks. Mel Brooks knew it, David Benatar knows it,[1] and so do I. Even when life does not stink so badly, there's always the chance that it will begin to do so. Nonexistence, on the other hand, is odor free. Whereas being brought into existence can be harmful, or at least bad, nonexistence cannot be harmful or bad. Even if life is not clearly bad, it is at the very least extremely risky. David Benatar argues, somewhat notoriously, that since it is better never to exist, one is harmed by being brought into existence and, therefore, procreation is likely always wrong and certainly always morally problematic.[2]

Procreation is an activity widely engaged in and often considered virtuous, life affirming, and generous. It is important to know whether, contrary to most views, procreation is always morally problematic or even impermissible. Most people find it deeply counterintuitive to consider the fact that having children may always be wrong, yet many have found Benatar's arguments difficult to escape. I have the opposite problem: I am very sympathetic to the intuitions that inspire these arguments and I think the conclusion is probably right. But I have yet to find an argument to support it.

In this paper, I will explain Benatar's arguments and show how, though they are often relied upon, and widely cited, they do not succeed in showing that procreation is always wrong due to the harmfulness of existence.[3] I will be forced to conclude that, until such time as a more convincing argument is conceived of, procreation has not been shown to be always morally wrong or always morally problematic.

### I Are Pleasure and Pain Asymmetrical?

Benatar grounds his argument regarding the harm of coming into existence on the claim that there is an asymmetry between pleasure and pain. Benatar argues that al-

---

1    See David Benatar, *Better Never to Have Been: The Harm of Coming Into Existence*, Oxford University Press, 2006 and "Why It Is Better Never to Come into Existence," *American Philosophical Quarterly*, 34 (3), 345-355, July 1997.

2    Benatar, *op cit.*

3    Caspar Hare, "Voices from Another World: Must We Respect the Interests of People Who Do Not, and Will Never, Exist?" *Ethics* 117(3), 512-513, 2007; M. Häyry, "A Rational Cure for Prereproductive Stress Syndrome," *Journal of Medical Ethics*, 30, 377-378, 2004; David Wasserman, "The Non-Identity Problem, Disability, and the Role of Prospective Parents," *Ethics* 116(1), 132-152, October 2006; Elizabeth Harman, "Can We Harm and Benefit in Creating?" *Philosophical Perspectives*, 18, 2004; Frances Kamm, "Is There a Problem with Enhancement?" *The American Journal of Bioethics*, 5(3), 5-14, May 2005; and Stuart Rachels, "Is There a Right to Have Children, *The Philosophical Review*, 114(2), 288-290, 2005, among many others.

though, *a:* the absence of pain is good, even if that good is not enjoyed by anyone; *b:* the absence of pleasure is not bad unless there is somebody for whom this absence is a deprivation.[4] I will refer to Benatar's pain/pleasure asymmetry as "Benatar's Asymmetry". From *a* and *b*, Benatar concludes that it is always better never to come into existence since nonexistence is always 100% good by virtue of its being a state of absence of pain. Existence pales by comparison because no matter how good it is, it is never 100% good;[5] it is thus never more advantageous than nonexistence. Put another way, Benatar's asymmetry is intended to show that, since the absence of pain is good even if it's not enjoyed by anyone (*a*) and the absence of pleasure is not bad unless there is someone deprived by the absence (*b*), nonexistence is a win-win situation. It's all good. Existence, on the other hand, is sometimes bad. And, since all good is better than partially good, existence is worse than nonexistence. Since existence is worse than nonexistence, we harm, and hence wrong, people by bringing them into existence.

Benatar defends his asymmetry on the basis of its alleged explanatory power. He argues that his asymmetry best explains four other plausible beliefs:[6]

*1. Although there is a duty to avoid bringing unhappy people into existence, there is no corresponding duty to bring happy people into existence.*[7]

Benatar argues that the reason we think that there is a duty not to bring suffering people into existence is that the presence of this suffering would be bad (for the sufferers) and the absence of the suffering is good (even though there is nobody to enjoy the absence of suffering).

*2. It is strange to claim that one had a child for the reason that the child will be thereby benefited but it is not strange to say that one avoided having a child for the sake of the child's interests.*[8]

Benatar further argues that his asymmetry best explains belief *2*. If belief *2* were false, he argues, there would be a moral reason for many people to have many more children, but that is not the case (see belief 1).

*3. Whereas one can regret bringing a child into existence for the sake of that very child, one cannot regret not bringing a child into existence for the sake of that very child (that one would otherwise have brought into existence).*[9]

Here too, Benatar argues that although we regret bringing a miserable child into existence (for the sake of the child), "The reason we do not lament our failure to bring somebody into existence is because absent pleasures are not bad."[10]

*4. Although we are sad for miserable people who live far from us, we are not similarly sad for people who, had they existed, would have been happy.*[11]

---

4    Benatar, *"Why it is Better Never to Come into Existence,"* op. cit., p. 346; *Better Never to Have Been,* op. cit., p.30. For the remainder of my discussion of Benatar's argument, I will cite the later work.
5    *Better Never to Have Been,* op. cit., p.37.
6    Benatar, *op. cit.,* p.31.
7    Benatar, *op. cit.,* p.32.
8    Benatar, *op. cit.,* p.34.
9    Benatar, *op. cit.,* p.34.
10   Benatar, *op. cit.,* p.35.
11   Benatar, *op. cit.,* p.35.

Benatar accounts for this belief by reminding us that, "we regret suffering but not the absent pleasures of those who could have existed."[12] And, the argument goes, his asymmetry best explains this belief.

As explained above, Benatar argues that, given his asymmetry, coming into existence is always a harm (since existence, at best partially good, is worse than nonexistence, which is always all good).[13] Whether this follows from his asymmetry, I will leave open. It does not matter because Benatar's asymmetry ought not to be granted. Recall that Benatar's argument in favor of his asymmetry is based on its explanatory power. Setting aside the fact that many would dispute the plausibility of the four beliefs that Benatar's asymmetry supposedly explains (indeed, the implications of Benatar's view may be more counterintuitive than the four beliefs are intuitive), I will accept their plausibility and argue that there are two far simpler and more fitting explanations of the beliefs which Benatar argues are best explained by his asymmetry. The first explanation is a simple and obvious metaphysical fact, the second a (related) common moral principle. The common moral principle that explains the four beliefs is the view that our moral obligations are to persons who do or will exist, i.e. to persons with moral standing.[14] We are thus obligated to refrain from causing persons to suffer but we are not obligated to confer benefits upon hypothetical entities that will never exist since merely hypothetical entities have no moral standing and hence can make no moral demands upon us. Only persons who do or will exist are candidates for our duties. Those not convinced by this view can ignore this explanation in favor of the metaphysical fact that also explains the beliefs Benatar cites, namely: All interests are contingent upon existence. Unless an entity exists at some point, it cannot have any interests because, in the absence of an entity that exists at some point, there is no real subject for the interest. (In my view, the metaphysical fact grounds the moral principle but that is not critical to the ways in which they both better explain the four beliefs). I will now show how the above-mentioned metaphysical fact and moral principle explain the four beliefs that Benatar thinks are best explained by his asymmetry.

The important metaphysical fact is that all interests are contingent upon existence at some point since in the absence of an existent entity, we have no real subject for interests at all. Thus, there may be a duty to avoid bringing unhappy people into the world because those existent, interested people would be unhappy, presumably setting back their interests in happiness. But, there's no corresponding duty to bring would-be-happy people into existence because "failing" in that "duty" would not cause anyone's interests to be set back. Since interests are contingent upon existence, unhappy existent persons' unhappiness counts, morally, and makes sense, metaphysically. That's why we may have a duty to avoid bringing unhappy people into the world. In contrast, the hypothetical happiness of merely hypothetical entities, who never did exist and never will, does not count morally or make sense metaphysically, since there are no real subjects for said happiness. That's why we have no duty to bring people into existence who would be happy, were they to exist. There are no real subjects for that duty. That explains the first belief.

---

12  Benatar, *op. cit.*, p.35.
13  Benatar, *op. cit.*, pp. 37-49.
14  Caspar Hare has argued that we ought not to confine our concerns to those who do or will exist (see "Voices from Another World: Must We Respect the Interests of People Who Do Not, and Will Never, Exist?" *Ethics* 117(3), 2007, pp. 498-523). I believe his view fails but for reasons irrelevant to this paper. I argue against this unusual view here and elsewhere (see "Existence: Who Needs It? The Non-Identity Problem and Merely Possible People," *Bioethics*, forthcoming).

It may be strange to claim that one procreated in order to benefit one's child since the act of procreation is undertaken before there is any subject for whatever benefit one may have in mind. Having a child in order to benefit that very child may seem a conferral upon no one because interests are contingent upon existence. However, since the child, presumably, will eventually exist, many people actually think that it is not strange to claim that one procreates to benefit one's child. Still, if it is strange to make that sort of claim, it's because there seems no subject for the benefit. It may not, however, seem strange to say that one avoided having a child for the sake of that child's interests because that decision is made by imagining one's existent, suffering child and that existent, suffering person is someone with interests. Of course, once one decides not to have that child there again seems no one who has benefited from or been considered by that decision and that is why many think, contra Benatar's 2, above, that it actually does seem strange to say that one avoided having a child for the child's sake. Still, if it is not strange to refrain from procreating for the sake of the person that would exist, if procreated, it is because the person who would exist if you did procreate would be an existent suffering person, with interests that you have foreseeably (and unjustifiably) thwarted. We tend to think it wrong to deliberately create miserable people because we care about existent people and don't want them to have been deliberately created to suffer unduly. (We don't have similar views about the need to create people to benefit since there seems no one to suffer the cost of not having been created.) If we deliberately do procreate the miserable, we can foresee that our action will result in a real person's suffering and that gives us a reason to refrain from procreation in that case, for the sake of the foreseeable existent person. (We need not do an action in order for its foreseeable results to give us reason not to do that action.) When we foresee that procreation will result in an existent person's relentless suffering, it is the foreseeability of the existent person's suffering that gives us reason not to procreate, just as foreseeing that we would have to break a promise gives us reason not to make the promise for the sake of the person to whom we would have made, and broken, the promise.[15] One might decide against procreating the miserable to comply with the norm that constrains the way we act toward interested beings for the sake of interested beings. In this way, the fact that interests are contingent upon existence explains the second belief.

One may regret bringing a child into existence for the sake of that child since, presumably, something about that interested being's existence is so terrible as to make you regret bringing that child into existence (for the child's sake). However, it is more difficult to understand regret for not bringing a child into existence for sake of that child since there is no real subject for that sort of regret. Since interests are contingent upon existence, we can't regret not doing something for the sake of a nonexistent entity since there is no real subject for that regret, but we can regret doing something for the sake of an existent entity since there is a subject for that regret. The fact that interests are contingent upon existence thus explains the third belief.

We may be sad for miserable people who live far from us since interested existent persons can be the subject of our feelings. Of course we are not similarly sad for nonexistent people who would have been happy had they existed. There are no subjects for those sorts of feelings since, in the absence of existent entities, there is no one to

15   I thank David Boonin for this analogy.

feel sad for; there are no interested entities to care about.[16] The fourth belief is therefore also explained by the fact that all interests are contingent upon existence.

Thus, the fact that existence is required for interests explains all that Benatar's asymmetry is supposed to explain and, in my view, the explanation it provides is simpler and more consistent with our ordinary moral and metaphysical views: it does not require us to deem existence always harmful (counterintuitive to many) and it does not require us to think that the absence of a negative sensory state is good even if no sensory being exists to enjoy its absence or even to simply exist in its absence (complicated). Instead, the explanation provided by the fact that existence is required for all interests is simple and intuitive: of course a non-existent entity cannot have interests because there is no real subject for any interests. No subject, no interests. Simple and intuitive.

For those who prefer to keep metaphysics out of ethics, here is how a common sense moral principle can explain the beliefs that Benatar's asymmetry is supposed to explain (and can do so more simply and in a manner more consistent with common moral views). The moral duty to avoid bringing unhappy people into the world, if it is, in fact, a duty, can only be based on our duties to those who will exist and suffer unduly. If we violate this duty, we will cause real people to suffer. We have no corresponding duty to bring happy people into existence because our duties are confined to those who do or will exist, not to those who could exist but will not. Not bringing happy people into existence harms no one because there is no real person to suffer nonexistence but bringing a miserable person into existence harms that real person.

Similarly, if it is strange to say that one procreated to benefit one's child, the strangeness is due to the fact that our duties to benefit are confined to those who do or will exist, making it odd to think of existence itself as a benefit conferred. It may not be equally strange to say that one refrained from having a child for the sake of the child's interests since if one did have a child, it would be a person to whom one had duties of beneficence. If that child's life would be devoid of value, having that child might foreseeably violate duties of beneficence toward that child. The foreseeability of the violation of our duties of beneficence to those who will exist if we do procreate serves as a reason for us not to procreate. Just as I don't make an existing person suffer because that would foreseeably result in my violation of my duties toward that (real) person, I don't create a miserable person because that would foreseeably result in my violation of my duties toward that (real) person.[17] If the child's life would be fantastic, however, some may well think of themselves as having procreated in order to benefit that child with its fantastic life. This argues against the plausibility of the belief Benatar seeks to explain. If we accept the belief, however, we can explain it best, I think, by deeming it an intuition about conferring existence as a benefit, and our responsibility for the foreseeable results of our actions, that is explained by our views re-

16  Our views in these kinds of cases can be foreseen prospectively and experienced retrospectively. We can predict that we will be sad or regret causing (or having caused) or hearing about the suffering of real people but we won't be sad or have regrets about hypothetically possible entities that will never exist but would have been or would be happy had they existed.

17  See metaphysical explanation of this belief, above, for further clarification regarding how one can refrain from doing something for the sake of the person whose interests would be foreseeably set back by the act even though refraining from the act results in no one's interests being affected at all (with the exception of those already in existence whose interests may be affected by the decision to refrain from procreation).

garding the kind of entities toward whom we can have duties. That explains the first two beliefs.

Onto the third. We can regret bringing a child into existence for the sake of that child since that existing child is owed our beneficence and our bringing that child into existence may violate our duties of beneficence toward that child (see above). We cannot regret not bringing a child into existence for the sake of that very child since our duties are confined to those who do or will exist, leaving us with no reason to regret anything with respect to a non-existing merely hypothetical person.

Finally, we are sad for the distant miserable since we may have some duties of beneficence person who are far from us,[18] and we therefore regret and may be sad about their misery. We are not similarly sad for people who would have been happy had they existed because we have no duties toward non-existing hypothetical persons, regardless of how happy "they" might have been were "they" to have been persons.

Since Benatar's asymmetry relies on its unique explanatory power for its force, and that explanatory power has been met by what I take to be two more persuasive explanations of the beliefs the asymmetry allegedly explains, I see no reason to accept the asymmetry. Just as the absence of pleasure is not bad unless there is someone for whom it is a deprivation, the absence of pain is not good unless there is someone for whom it is a benefit.[19]

Whereas Benatar's *b* is true, his *a* is false; pleasure and pain are symmetrical: good or bad, respectively, only insofar as they affect interested entities.

Existence remains, then, what it has generally been thought to be: a mixed bag of benefits and burdens, generally deemed worthwhile so long as the burdens are outweighed, overridden, or relatively less important than the benefits. Thus, the denial of Benatar's asymmetry refutes his claim that procreation is always wrong because one is always harmed by being forced out of blissful nonexistence into the mixed bag of existence. The alternative explanations of the beliefs do not, by themselves, tell us whether procreation is usually or always permissible but they do tell us that procreation is not always wrong due to the fact that existence is always a harm by virtue of the asymmetry between pleasure and pain. Whether existence is harmful because life is bad is a separate issue that I will address in the next section of this paper.

Benatar might claim that his asymmetry is not about persons at all but is, instead, about states of affairs. On this view, a world with no pain is a state of affairs that is intrinsically good but a world without pleasure is not a state of affairs that is intrinsically bad. Indeed, Benatar's asymmetry is explicitly about states of affairs in the absence of interested parties. However, pleasure and pain are essentially interest-bound goods, good or bad only in virtue of the interested subjects that they affect.[20] In the absence of subjects, pleasure and pain are meaningless terms; there is no value in the uninhabited states of affairs that contain their "presence" or "absence." Even if some goods, e.g. beauty, may be seen as intrinsically good regardless of the existence of interested beings, the same cannot be said regarding pleasure and pain. Sentience is implied by the very meaning of the terms pleasure and pain; they are *feelings*, impossible and meaningless in

---

18  Distance *per se* does not do away with our duties of beneficence even if it can sometimes substantially weaken or eradicate said duty if the distance poses practical or epistemic barriers to our beneficence or, on some views, if we have stronger duties to those within our social or political community and only weak duties to distant persons.

19  Please see endnote no. 1 on pages 36-37 below.

20  See Nagel's argument to the effect that the very subjectivity of pleasure and pain is the source of their objective value. (Thomas Nagel, *The View From Nowhere*, Oxford University Press, 1986, pp. 158-162).

the absence of *feelers*. It is therefore no accident that Benatar's arguments in favor of his asymmetry speak of duties, interests, and regrets in reference to sentient beings (there being no other way to meaningfully talk about pleasure and pain). Even though Benatar's asymmetry seems to be about states of affairs, his arguments in favor of his asymmetry speak of pleasure and pain in reference to people and these arguments all fail once we note that all interests are contingent upon existence (at some point in time) and/or our duties are restricted to entities that exist at some point.

But, even if Benatar's asymmetry fails, we may still wonder about the general notion that it is more important to avoid pain than it is to acquire pleasure, or something along those lines. If this intuition, which is not all that uncommon, is correct, then it truly is always better not to come into existence since existence virtually always includes some suffering. But there seems no obvious reason for this asymmetrical intuition to be true, aside from the tendency of some toward risk aversion. Common life choices testify against the asymmetry between pain and pleasure: we cross busy streets, drive cars, ride bicycles, eat at restaurants, shake hands with strangers – sometimes even kiss them as a greeting. We accept risks in our pursuit of what we take to be of value and not just in order to avoid pain. The expression, "life is risk or nothing at all" implies that a bland, safe life is worse than the risk of misfortune, or at the very least no better. That's what many people seem to think, and, in the absence of evidence or argument to the contrary, seem entitled to continue to think.

## II Does Life Really Stink?

The facts of life remain to be addressed. Benatar argues that life is, overall, objectively bad and that procreation is, therefore, wrong.[21] Is life bad? Before we address that question, it is worth noting that in order for procreation to always be wrong due to life's badness, the badness must be bad enough to override the interests that existing people have in procreating.[22] But I leave that aside for now and turn back to the assessment of life and the human condition.

Most people, though certainly very far from all, think their lives are well worth living and that they are relatively happy and well off,[23] despite the fact that all life includes significant suffering.[24] Benatar is well aware of this and attributes the common, positive subjective assessment of one's life's quality to what he takes to be the human tendency to accentuate the positive and unrealistically overlook the negative.[25] Benatar cites psychological studies showing the human tendency to forget or ignore one's life's negatives and adopt a rose-colored glasses perspective on one's life. There is also research showing that depressed people tend to have a more realistic view of their own abilities and their future prospects. Note that this research does not show that depressed people have a

---

21 Benatar, *op. cit.*, pp. 69-93.
22 See Rivka Weinberg, "Procreative Justice: A Contractualist Account," *Public Affairs Quarterly*, 16(4), October 2002, 405-425.
23 See Diener, Ed., Carol Diener, "Most People Are Happy," *Psychological Science* 7(3) 1996, pp. 181-185; David G. Meyers and Diener, Ed., "The Pursuit of Happiness," *Scientific American* 274(5), 1996, pp. 70-72; Angus Campbell, Philip E. Converse, and Willard L. Rodgers, *The Quality of American Life*, The Russell Sage Foundation, New York, 1976, pp. 24-5; Margaret W. Matlin and David J. Stang, *The Pollyanna Principle: Selectivity in Language, Memory and Thought,* Schenkman Publishing Company, Cambridge, MA, 1978; pp. 146-7; among many others.
24 Some may dispute that but I think it would be very difficult to find someone who lived more than a few days or so yet experienced no significant suffering. In any case, for argument's sake, it is worth granting this point.
25 See Benatar, *op. cit.,* pp. 64-69.

more accurate view of reality, generally speaking, or of the human condition. Benatar argues that the tendency to focus on the good things in life (irrationally, in his view) is something of an adaptive preference, both psychologically and evolutionarily: we are alive, so we are highly motivated to put a good spin on it while we are stuck here; and a tendency towards accurate assessments of life would be naturally selected against since it would likely decrease reproduction and increase the likelihood of suicide.[26] He argues that life is, objectively, bad, which we would likely recognize were our perspectives not skewed by our Pollyanna tendencies and evolution's natural selection of unrealistic optimists.[27]

Of course Benatar is right to note that it helps us cope to think that our lives are worth living or even good. But being unrealistic Pollyanna optimists does not, by itself, entail that the bad parts of life would decisively outweigh the good if considered from a more objective perspective.[28] One cannot simply dismiss the argument that subjective, positive assessments of life can be taken as evidence for life's goodness. One must wonder whether the perspectives of individual people must suffice for our assessment of the value of human life, yet from which other perspective can this assessment matter to us? More importantly, which other perspective can we possibly access? These questions make it hard to be persuaded by the view that life seems good to people but, from the objective perspective of the universe, is actually bad for them.[29] If life is bad *for* us, it seems like it must be bad *to* us. This is not because all value is inherently subjective but is, instead, because the perspective of ourselves and other people are the only ones available to us from which we can, in any meaningful way, conduct the evaluation of the value of human life.

The common preference for life is not analogous to standard adaptive preference cases wherein, for example, an oppressed woman expresses a preference for her second class social status. That woman's perspective might be skewed by her lack of other, better, viable options and we, on the outside, may be better positioned to understand this. Life, however, is something we are all stuck in (so long as we deem suicide a less attractive option, as most do) so there seems no "outside" position from which to assess the preference for human life. We are not only stuck in life, we are even more stuck, so to speak, in the confines of the perspectives of ourselves and other people, from which, to most, life usually seems worth living despite its challenges. Sometimes even *because* of its challenges.

In his 1999 Academy Award acceptance speech, the director Roberto Begnini enthusiastically and sincerely thanked his parents, "for the greatest gift of all: *poverty!*" The actress Cate Blanchet, whose adored father died suddenly when she was ten, "has called bereavement 'a strange gift.' In many essential ways….her father's death was the shadow that informed her brightness. 'It's chiaroscuro,' she said."[30] This sort of outlook is not limited to the film industry (though, as in all other things, we hear from them most because they get the most air time). The psychologist Victor Frankl famously did not regret his excruciating experience in the Nazi death camps because he felt that the experience enriched his understanding and appreciation of the meaning of life.[31] One may argue that it is the benefits that are valued in these cases and not the pain that it took to acquire them but that is not how the value is described by the people in the examples above. They describe the pain itself not as an unfortunate yet necessary means to benefit but as itself a benefit. A very depressed and lonely friend of mine, to my great surprise, once said em-

26 Benatar, *op. cit.*, pp. 65-69.
27 Benatar, *op. cit.*, pp. 64-93.
28 I thank Paul Hurley for this point.
29 See Benatar, *op. cit.*, pp. 81-86.
30 John Lahr, "Disappearing Act," *The New Yorker*, February 2, 2007.
31 Victor Frankl, *Man's Search for Meaning*, Hogger and Stoughton, 1971.

phatically, "I *love* life." I laughed very hard at this and looked at him quizzically. He looked back at me, surprised at my obtuseness, and said, "Yes, of course I'm unhappy right now, but basically, I love life and have always loved life."

Of course, this life affirming view is not the only way to perceive life. H.L. Mencken said, "How little it takes to make life unbearable: a pebble in the shoe, a cockroach in the spaghetti, a women's laugh." Now this (minus the misogyny) comes much closer to my life outlook but I see no vantage point from which to argue that my outlook is, "objectively," or in some other authoritative sense, correct. Although life is treacherous, many people claim that suffering can be meaningful – even enjoyable, etc. From what vantage point can this claim be authoritatively denied? I don't see any vantage point accessible to us that can claim this sort of authority.

The fact that suffering can be meaningful or valuable does not mean that we are morally permitted to inflict suffering on others,[32] because we cannot rely on subjective interpretations to justify our (initially) pain-inducing action. If life was objectively bad for people or only pain-inducing then the fact that people may tend to retrospectively invest it with meaning and value might still not, by itself, make procreation morally permissible. But the fact remains that we have no perspective from which to judge that life is, objectively, bad. There are different ways of viewing and experiencing life, obviously. My point is not that most people find life worthwhile and therefore it likely is worthwhile. As we know, the ubiquity of a view is not conclusive evidence of its truth. Rather, my point is that among the different ways of experiencing or viewing life, no way is more authoritative or objective than another, nor has Benatar shown that one is. We therefore have no vantage point from which to conclude that the view that life is meaningful, worthwhile, or good is mistaken. We are forced to take people's views at face value and most people claim to experience and consider life meaningful, worthwhile, and good. (Remarkable but there it is.)

I conclude, perhaps too simply, that people are strangely constituted:

> But what a shining animal is man
> Who knows, when pain subsides, that is not that,
> For worse than that must follow – yet can write
> Music, can laugh, play tennis, even plan

*– Edna St. Vincent Millay, Sonnet CLXXI*[33]

People may be the sort of creatures born to enjoy their suffering. If that is the case, it is still not clear that it is wrong to procreate, especially given our interests in procreation. Alternatively, life may be enjoyable or meaningful to all but the most deprived or depressed. In either case, it seems unwarranted to conclude that procreation is always wrong due to the badness of life. Life does seem bad to me and my melancholic kind[34] but that may just be us. So long as we have no way to prove the optimists wrong, so long as we are in the extreme minority,[35] and so long as people have a very strong interest in procreation, it

---

32  Victor Frankl, *Man's Search for Meaning*, Hogger and Stoughton, 1971.
33  I thank David Benatar for raising this objection.
34  If the kind of melancholic outlook that I refer to here can be shown to be genetically transmitted, it may make procreation by the melancholic quite problematic indeed.
35  Although my point is that there is no authoritative or objective perspective from which to assess the value of human life, generally, if most people found life not worth living that would, in my view, count

seems unpromising to claim that procreation is always wrong due to life's inherent or "objective" badness.

## III Death

Does the fact that we will die, and live most of our lives with this knowledge, make life tragic? "All our stories have sad endings. We all die in the last act."[36] According to The World Health Organization, about 56.6 million people died in 2001.[37] The sheer number of deaths as well as the ubiquity of premature death due to disease, war, and natural disasters, is cited by Benatar in partial support of his view that we exist in a world of suffering.[38] (Benatar has much evidence grounded in everyday life to this effect, though, so even if he is wrong about death's contribution to life's badness, the effect of taking death off his list might not be all that significant.) Does life contain too much death to be good? On its face, this seems eminently plausible. Death is bad, life is full of it and always ends in it, ergo life is bad.

However, more needs to be said in order for us to assess how the badness of death affects quality of life and the nature of human existence. On some existentialist views, death robs life of its meaning and purpose since all that we devote ourselves to necessarily ends (often abruptly, unexpectedly, and inconveniently) and comes to nothing. Yet Benatar does not commit himself to this existentialist conception of death's badness. Instead, he seems to take death as straightforwardly and simply bad. It might be instructive to hear more about what Benatar thinks makes death bad. Nowadays, many view death as bad because it deprives the person who died of continued (good) life. But if death is bad because it deprives us of continued life, does that not imply that life is good? Claiming that life is bad because we die can seem like claiming that a gourmet dinner was bad because it didn't last forever, so Benatar cannot be referring to the deprivation account of the badness of death in his listing death as something that makes life so terrible. Perhaps he is thinking of the loss of loved ones that death causes those still alive to suffer, though this loss is sometimes a gain (depending on how the person who dies would affect others if she continued to live instead). Finally, it is worth noting that it is also common to think that death infuses life with precious meaning precisely because it renders life finite and precarious. In order to assess the impact death has on human well-being, we must arrive at a clearer understanding of the nature and value of death. Only then can we decide how death affects life. As things stand, Benatar has not demonstrated that the bare fact of death renders life not worth living.

## IV Suicide

If suicide is painless, it may offer us an easy way out of some of our procreative worries. We may think that if our children feel like existence is not a risk worth taking, or is plainly worse than nonexistence, then they can just kill themselves and be done with it. They can, in effect, undo what we have imposed upon them. But, as many have noted, suicide is difficult and not just because one tends to get used to living.[39] Suicide requires some skill, it can result in very unpleasant effects if it doesn't work out as planned (if you jump out the window and live, your life will likely be even worse than it

as an important reason against procreating (since we ought not, *ceteris paribus*, deliberately procreate the miserable).

36  Mary Pipher, *The Shelter of Each Other*, Ballantine Books, Random House, 1996, p. 119.
37  World Health Organization, *The World Health Report* 2002 (Geneva: WHO: 2002), p. 186.
38  Benatar, *op. cit.,* 88-92.
39  See Benatar, *op. cit.,* pp. 211-220.

was before your tried, and failed, to end it), it forces one to knowingly face death, and it usually causes great suffering to those who might miss us or feel guilty for not having made us happy enough to want to stick around. Lastly, it is not clear that death is the equivalent of nonexistence. It likely comes awfully close but many view existence as irreversible. Once in, you can never really opt out: you may die but you still, arguably, exist as a subject of reference, you almost certainly have had some effect on existent entities, and what's left of you after you die will continue to inhabit the world, albeit as fertilizer or ash, etc. Given these considerations, we ought not to be so easily comforted by the idea that suicide can undo procreative errors.

## V Conclusion

Given that most people not only do not regret being brought into existence but, to the contrary, are glad of it, I don't see how we can say that procreation is always wrong or always morally problematic due to life's badness *per* se or as compared with nonexistence. Life, while not quite the bowl of cherries the cheery seem to think, is (mysteriously) rather valued and enjoyed by most, even though, like all good things, it too comes to an end. So while I still think that life stinks, and is not worthwhile, I know of no argument to show that my view is somehow more "objectively" or "scientifically" correct. I am forced to conclude that procreation is not always morally wrong or problematic due to its objective or all-things-considered badness.[40]

*Endnote* 1

Benatar argues that since there is an asymmetry between the absence of pain and pleasure, it follows that it is always better never to come into existence, as his diagram illustrates.

| Scenario A: *x* exists | Scenario B: *x* never exists |
|---|---|
| 1. Presence of Pain (bad) | 3. Absence of pain (good) |
| 2. Presence of Pleasure (good) | 4. Absence of pleasure (not bad) |

In support of the above-diagramed asymmetry, Benatar rejects the alternative diagram that replaces 3 (good) and 4 (not bad) with 3 (good), 4 (bad), because if the absence of pleasure in scenario B is bad, then we would have to regret the nonexistence of x, something we do not actually deem regrettable. I accept that claim (though many don't). Benatar also rejects the alternative diagram that labels 3 (not bad) and 4 (not good) because he thinks that incorrectly implies that avoiding bringing a pure sufferer into existence is not a good thing, but just a "not bad" one. Yet the real reason we deem avoiding bringing a pure sufferer into existence a good thing is because it allows us to avoid option no. 1 (bad), under scenario *A*, not because it enables us to fulfill Benatar's option 3 (good) under Scenario B. Avoiding the conception of a pure sufferer is good because it allows us to avoid harming the interests of a (future) person, namely, the person who would exist under option 1, Scenario A. This has nothing to do with

40   I am very grateful and indebted to Jonathan Adler, Elizabeth Anderson, David Benatar, Jeanine Diller, Zev Gruman, Paul Hurley, Amy Kind, Thaddeus Metz, Suzanne Obdrzalek, Dion Scott-Kakures, Charles Young, the members of the Claremont Work-In-Progress Discussion Group, and the members of the Benatar Antinatalism Workshop for helpful comments and discussions.

Scenario B. We have no obligations to anyone in Scenario B because Scenario B does not include any interested entities.

The true Scenario B is different from any alternative that Benatar considers. The correct diagram replaces Benatar's 3 (good) and 4 (not bad), with 3 (neither good nor bad) and 4 (neither good nor bad):

| Scenario A: *x exists* | Scenario B: *x never exists* |
|---|---|
| 1. Presence of Pain (bad) | 3. Absence of pain (neither good nor bad) |
| 2. Presence of Pleasure (good) | 4. Absence of pleasure (neither good nor bad) |

According to my diagram, if $x$ never exists, then the absence of pain and pleasure are neither good nor bad because the nonexistent $x$ has no interests; pleasure and pain are neither good nor bad in the absence of any interested parties. It is only when $x$ does exist, under Scenario A, that $x$ has interests and, therefore, in Scenario A the presence of pain is bad and the presence of pleasure is good. As for the absence of pleasure and pain, symmetry reigns.

# Sick and Healthy: Benatar on the Logic of Value[1]

## Skott Brill

**Abstract**

David Benatar, in *Better Never to Have Been*, sets out two arguments in support of the view that coming into existence is always a net harm. Remarkably, the first argument seems to imply that coming into existence would be a net harm even if the only bad we experienced in our lives were a 'single pin-prick'. This argument hinges on a purported asymmetry: that whereas the absence of pains in non-existence is *good*, the absence of pleasures in non-existence is *not bad* (rather than *bad*). It also hinges on the non-badness at issue here being *relative* (no worse than the presence of pleasures in existence) rather than *intrinsic* (value neutral). To establish the crucial claim that the non-badness of absent pleasures in non-existence is relative rather than intrinsic, Benatar constructs an analogy involving two people, Sick and Healthy. In this paper, I show the inaptness of the analogy and also provide positive reason to doubt the soundness of the argument as it stands. What emerges from this critical analysis of the analogy is a plausible theory of value at odds with Benatar's argument as a whole.

One of the most widely and deeply held convictions over the centuries has been that coming into existence is, at least in most cases, a good thing for an individual. But that is not to say this conviction has gone unchallenged. From Siddhartha Gautama (the Buddha) over 2,500 years ago to Arthur Schopenhauer in the nineteenth century, pessimists about human existence have inferred from an alleged disproportionate amount of pain and suffering in our lives that we all would have been better off never having been born. In his recent book *Better Never to Have Been*, David Benatar revives this standard argument for pessimism (Benatar 2006: 60–92); however, he seems to regard his version of it as a fall-back argument, one he will go to if a separate argument for pessimism he sets out earlier in the book falls on deaf ears (Benatar 2006: 14). This

1     I am grateful to Thomas A. Mappes and to the journal's guest editor, Thaddeus Metz, for their helpful comments on earlier drafts of this paper. Also, I thank David Benatar for commenting on parts of the paper I delivered at the workshop on anti-natalism held at the University of Johannesburg in November 2011.

other argument does not rely on establishing a disproportionate amount of pain and suffering in our lives. In fact, it seems to imply that if the amount of pain and suffering in the world were drastically reduced—to as much as each of us experiencing no more than a 'single pin-prick'—coming into existence would still be worse than never existing (Benatar 2006: 48).[2] Benatar's bold, new argument, which has come to be called the 'asymmetry argument', is my focus here. Specifically, I focus on one of its two key lines of defense that heretofore has not received sustained attention: the Sick and Healthy analogy.[3] I show why this crucial analogy does not do the job Benatar needs it to do and consequently why the asymmetry argument as it stands is unsound. What emerges from this critical analysis of the analogy is a plausible theory of value that is damning to the asymmetry argument as a whole.

## 1. The Asymmetry Argument

Benatar asks us to consider X, either an actual person who might never have existed or a possible person who never exists but might have.[4] The question is: Would X be better off existing or never existing? If X never exists, X does not experience what X would as an existing sentient being, most notably pleasure and pain. Regarding pain, since pain is *bad* and the absence of pain is *good*, never existing is better than existing. Regarding pleasure, since pleasure is *good* and the absence of pleasure is *not bad* when there is nobody for whom this absence is a deprivation, never existing is no worse than existing. Therefore, if X never exists, X is both (1) better off for not experiencing pain and (2) no worse off for not experiencing pleasure, which makes X better off overall never existing. As Benatar sums up the matter:

> It is good that existers enjoy their pleasures. It is also good that pains are avoided through non-existence. However, that is only part of the picture. Because there is nothing bad about never coming into existence, but there is something bad about coming into existence, it seems that all things considered non-existence is preferable. (Benatar 2006: 44)

The matrix below is similar to one Benatar includes in his book to help make perspicuous the logic of the asymmetry argument (Benatar 2006: 38).

2   In this hypothetical case, coming into existence would only be *a bit* worse for each of us than never coming into existence. In our actual world, coming into existence is not a mere harm but, instead, a *serious* one. Benatar uses chapter 3, 'How Bad Is Coming into Existence?' to support this claim. He also views the argument in chapter 3 as a fresh version of the standard pessimist argument that hinges on showing that human existence includes a disproportionate amount of pain and suffering.

3   Thaddeus Metz, the only commentator so far who has given the analogy any attention, concludes his insightful, though brief, analysis of it with this remark: 'That analogy, and the claim that pleasures of those who exist are no real advantage over absent ones in the case of non-existence, warrant more reflection than I give them here' (Metz 2011: 248).

4   According to Benatar, the 'obviously loose' sense in which we can speak of the interests of a non-existent person who never exists (i.e., a merely possible person) is 'in terms of the interests of the person who would otherwise have existed' (Benatar 2006: 31). David DeGrazia (2010: 321) questions the intelligibility of this view. For my purposes, I assume that it is both intelligible and plausible.

| Scenario A<br>(X exists) | Scenario B<br>(X never exists) |
|---|---|
| (1)<br>Presence of pain<br>(Bad) | (3)<br>Absence of pain<br>(Good) |
| (2)<br>Presence of pleasure<br>(Good) | (4)<br>Absence of pleasure<br>(Not Bad) |

Figure 1.

Benatar insists that even if X in Scenario A has very little pain in life and a great amount of pleasure, non-existence would still be preferable to existence. Why that is so is not obvious, and some commentators have questioned it,[5] but here is one way to grasp the basic idea using the matrix and a calculation of value assignments (Figure 2).[6] Say that X in existence experiences a total of one unit of pain and one million units of pleasure, represented by -1 in quadrant (1) and +1,000,000 in quadrant (2). Since X would not have experienced that pain had X not existed, which would have been as good as that pain is bad, non-existence gets the counterpart in value to the one unit of pain: +1 in quadrant (3). And since the absence of pleasures in non-existence is not bad in the sense that it is no worse than the presence of pleasures in existence, this absence of pleasures in non-existence gets '+1,000,000'.

Scare quotes around this value are important and indicate that it is not intrinsic value. On Benatar's view, the absence of pleasures in non-existence is not good in itself; indeed, it lacks intrinsic value status altogether—good, bad, or neutral (Benatar 2006: 40, 41). However, since the absence of pleasures in non-existence is no worse than the presence of pleasures in existence—and correspondingly the presence of pleasures in existence is no better than its absence in non-existence—the absence of pleasures in non-existence assumes a sort of relative or virtual value equivalent to the presence of pleasures in existence. (It does so, anyway, if we insist on viewing the matter in terms of quantities of positive and negative values.) Now add up the values. Existence comes out at +999,999 and non-existence, +1,000,001. Non-existence wins.

---

5   DeGrazia (2010: 321) and Metz (2011: 246) have done so fairly and ably; Belshaw (2007) not so.
6   Benatar himself (2006: 48) resists any such calculation. Perhaps the main reason for this resistance is that, on his view, the relative non-badness of absent pleasures in non-existence has no intrinsic value status whatsoever (good, bad, or neutral) and so cannot be part of a straightforward utility calculation. Nevertheless, the example here, mindful as it is of his view, may be helpful, especially (or at least) for those who are strongly inclined to view the matter in terms of a calculation of quantities of value. For a nice alternative formulation, without a calculation of value assignments, see Harman (2009: 778–80).

| Scenario A<br>(X exists) | Scenario B<br>(X never exists) |
|---|---|
| (1)<br>Presence of pain<br>(Bad)<br>-1 | (3)<br>Absence of pain<br>(Good)<br>+1 |
| (2)<br>Presence of pleasure<br>(Good)<br>+1,000,000 | (4)<br>Absence of pleasure<br>(Not Bad)<br>'+1,000,000' |
| = +999,999 | = +1,000,001 |

Figure 2.

The asymmetry argument, of course, contains some controversial claims, the most glaring of which are the ones that constitute the asymmetry for which the argument is named (represented by the quadrants on the right): (3) 'the absence of pain is good even if that good is not enjoyed by anyone' and (4) 'the absence of pleasure is not bad unless there is somebody for whom this absence is a deprivation' (Benatar 2006: 30). Consequently, Benatar spends much of his time defending this asymmetry (hereafter the Asymmetry, with a capital 'A'). He does so by showing how four other asymmetries, which he alleges are 'quite plausible' and 'widely endorsed' (Benatar 2006: 31, 36), are each best explained by the deeper Asymmetry. If they are, then we have excellent reason to believe the deeper Asymmetry is true.

However, Benatar does not simply need to establish that the absence of pains in non-existence is good whereas the absence of pleasures in non-existence is not bad. He must also show that the non-badness at issue here is *relative* in the sense that it is no worse than the presence of pleasures in existence. It is imperative that Benatar establish that this non-badness is relative in this way because if it were *intrinsic* non-badness (value neutrality), then the absence of pleasures in non-existence would be worse than the presence of pleasures in existence, not to the same degree as something bad, but still worse. And if the absence of pleasures in non-existence were to some degree worse than the presence of pleasures in existence, then coming into existence could be a good thing. It would be a good thing whenever someone's life contained more than twice the good in it than bad.[7] To see this, assign the presence of pains in existence the arbitrary value -5 and the absence of pains in non-existence its counterpart +5. Now if the absence of pleasures in non-existence is 0, for neutral value, and the value of the presence of pleasures in existence is more than twice the disvalue of the presence of pains in existence, say +12, then the net value of existence

7   Benatar (2006: 45–46) insists that it is not only the proportion of pleasure and pain that determines the quality of a life. However, even if the proper assessment of the quality of a life is more complicated, the basic point stands.

is +7 whereas the net value of non-existence is +5. In this case, existence wins (Figure 3).

| Scenario A (X exists) | Scenario B (X never exists) |
|---|---|
| (1) Presence of pain (Bad) -5 | (3) Absence of pain (Good) +5 |
| (2) Presence of pleasure (Good) +12 | (4) Absence of pleasure (Not Bad) 0 |
| = +7 | = +5 |

Figure 3.

Note that the absence of pleasures in non-existence being intrinsically not bad in the sense of value neutral is consistent with there being an asymmetry between (3) and (4). So if Benatar succeeds in establishing an asymmetry by way of the four topical asymmetries, but one that is consistent with both intrinsic non-badness and relative non-badness, the asymmetry argument is unsound unless he goes on and establishes that the absence of pleasures in non-existence is specifically *relatively* not bad.[8]

## 2. The Analogy and Its Deficiency

Benatar employs what appears to be a compelling analogy to support his crucial claim that the non-badness of the absence of pleasures in non-existence is relative non-badness (Benatar 2006: 42–49). This analogy concerns two existers, S (Sick) and H (Healthy). S is sick regularly but has the capacity to heal quickly; H is healthy continuously but lacks the capacity to heal. Now Benatar believes it is clear that S's capacity to heal is no advantage over H's lacking that capacity. In other words, H's lacking the capacity to heal is not bad in the sense that it is no worse than S's capacity to recover quickly. The reason is that H is not deprived of the capacity to heal given H's state of being: continuous health (Figure 4). Similarly, X's experience of pleasures in existence is no advantage over X's absence of pleasures in non-existence; X's absence of pleasures in non-existence is not bad in the sense that it is no worse than X's experience of pleasures in existence. The reason is that X in non-existence is not deprived of the presence of pleasures given X's state of being: nonbeing.

---

8  In section 5, I address the issue of whether any of the four asymmetries support specifically relative non-badness.

| S | H |
|---|---|
| (1)<br>Presence of sickness<br>(Bad) | (3)<br>Absence of sickness<br>(Good) |
| (2)<br>Presence of capacity<br>for quick recovery<br>(Good) | (4)<br>Absence of capacity<br>for quick recovery<br>(Not Bad) |

Figure 4.

Since H will never get sick, it does seem as though H's lacking the capacity for quick recovery is no worse than S's having it. Notwithstanding, the analogy, I submit, fails to show that experiencing pleasures in existence is no better than not experiencing pleasures in non-existence. The key to understanding why is to understand a particular contrast closely associated with the fundamental difference between intrinsic value and instrumental value. So as not to beg any questions, the below explication of this fundamental difference and the important associated contrast concerns only things in existence: real razors, real pleasures, real hospice patients, real ants, and real dental patients.

First, the fundamental difference is that whereas the value of a thing that has only instrumental value is entirely dependent on its usefulness to other things, the value of a thing that has intrinsic value is independent of its utility (i.e., it has value *in itself*). A sharp disposable razor is instrumentally good. It has value, but only to the extent that it is useful to us. When the blade of this non-recyclable razor dulls, the razor loses all of its value and may be disposed of. A state of pleasure, on the other hand, has intrinsic value. Although it may not always be useful, it is nevertheless always good to have. Even when a person would have been better off, all things considered, without being in a state of pleasure, it is still true that being in that state of pleasure was good in itself to some degree. We say something similar about persons. Persons arguably have intrinsic value. Even a terminally ill hospice patient has it. Although she may no longer be useful to society, she still has value and is not disposable like a razor.

Now an important contrast closely associated with this difference is that unlike the goodness of a thing that has intrinsic value, the goodness of a thing that has only instrumental value is relative to the nature, condition, and circumstances of other things. Relative to many human beings, a sharp razor has value, but relative to an ant, it is valueless. Given the kind of thing an ant is, a razor is of no use to it and so is valueless. An intrinsic good like pleasure, on the other hand, is good for any creature to possess no matter its nature or condition or the circumstances in which it finds itself. If an ant were in fact to experience pleasure, that would be a good thing for it. Even if ants are as a matter of fact non-sentient, it is both intelligible and true to say that if an ant *were* to experience pleasure, it would be good. Moreover, even if acquiring an intrinsic good would hinder an ant to such an extent that the ant would be better off without it, all things considered (say, an ant's acquiring the mental state of pleasure would make the ant complacent and hence forego adequate food and shelter), it is nonetheless true to say that acquiring the good would, as far as it goes, be good for the ant. We say something similar about pain, something intrinsically bad. Even though a healthy tooth brought about by a dentist drilling and filling a cavity may justify the pain involved in drilling and filling it (and so the patient may be better off going to the dentist than not), it is unfortunate this pain has to be experienced, for the pain itself—that is, divorced from any associated good consequences—is a bad thing.[9]

Return now to Benatar's analogy. The capacity for quick recovery is an instrumental good. As such, its value depends on the nature, condition, and circumstances of the individuals for whom it has (or might have had) instrumental value. It is no wonder, then, that S, who possesses the capacity for quick recovery, is no better off than H, who does not. H's nature or condition is, or his circumstances are, such that H has absolutely no use for the capacity (like an ant that has no use for a razor). If, however, the capacity that S has and H lacks were an intrinsic good, matters would change; S would be better off than H, at the very least to the extent that S has it and H does not and ignoring all good and bad consequences of either possessing it or not. If the capacity for pleasure (or, say, friendship or creativity or aesthetic appreciation, provided these, too, are intrinsically good) were what S has and H lacks, then even if for some reason having it would not be in H's long-term best interest, S to some extent would be better off than H. S would have experiences that have value in themselves. H would not.

This analysis helps us to see why Benatar's analogy is deficient. The important contrast in the asymmetry argument is the presence and absence of an intrinsic good (pleasure); the one in his analogy is the presence and absence of an instrumental good (capacity for quick recovery). Since for *at least* existing things the value of an instrumental good depends on the nature, condition, and circumstances of those who may possess it, whereas this is not the case with an intrinsic good, H's being no worse off than S is no good reason to believe that X in non-existence is no worse off than X in existence. Indeed, if there is reason to believe anything at this point, it is that X in non-existence is worse off—that is, 'in terms of the interests of the person who would otherwise have existed' (Benatar 2006: 31)—because X in non-existence (unlike H) lacks an *intrinsic* good. Just as a *non-sentient* ant would be better off if it could experience pleasure, so too would a *non-existing* ant be better off if it could experience pleasure (again, 'in terms of the interests of the [ant] who would otherwise have existed'). This view reasonably assumes that, *in the absence of any countervailing consideration, there is more reason to believe that the logic of intrinsic value that applies to existing*

---

9    This theory of value may have the appearance of being more stringent than I intend it to be. For the purpose at hand, I am only committed to the view that there are some intrinsically valuable things whose value is independent of their utility or, more generally, the nature, condition, and circumstances of other things. There may be other intrinsically valuable things (intrinsically valuable only in the sense that they happen to be valued by us as ends) whose value is in part, or even in whole, dependent on their usefulness or, more generally, the nature, condition, or circumstances of other things. An example in the literature is the pen that Abraham Lincoln used to sign the Emancipation Proclamation. It is valued by many Americans as an end (and so in this sense may be called intrinsically valuable), and its intrinsic value is tied up in the instrumental role it played in U.S. history. See Kagan (1998) for this example, as well as other ones. See also Korsgaard (1983) and Rabinowicz and Rønnow-Rasmussen (2000). I am grateful to the editor for bringing this issue to my attention.

*things also applies to non-existing things than to believe (as Benatar does) that the logic of instrumental value that applies to existing things becomes part of the logic of intrinsic value when applied to non-existing things.* (I hereafter refer to this claim as the 'reasonable assumption'.) However, I do not want to get ahead of myself. All I am claiming at this point is that in view of the differing logics of intrinsic and instrumental value concerning existing things, H's being no worse off than S (a matter that involves an instrumental good) does not give us any good reason to believe that X in non-existence is no worse off than X in existence (a matter that involves an intrinsic good).

### 3. Benatar's Defense of the Analogy and the Deficiency of This Defense

Benatar is aware that the good at issue in the Sick and Healthy analogy is instrumental whereas the good in Scenarios A and B is intrinsic. He is also aware that this axiological discrepancy 'might be thought to be relevant' (Benatar 2006: 43). However, he contends that it is, in fact, irrelevant and concludes that the analogy is apt. In this effort, he begins by pointing to another discrepancy between S and H and A and B, an ontological one: S and H involve two existers whereas A and B involve one exister and one non-exister. Benatar asserts that any analogy involving an actual person and a possible person would be too much like A and B to shed any light on the issue of whether X in non-existence is any worse off than X in existence; thus the nature of the case in effect forces an analogy involving two existers.[10] But now, he continues, a problem arises in using an analogy with two existers in conjunction with an *intrinsic* good: the exister who lacks the good *is* deprived of it and so disadvantaged relative to the other exister. (Remember, unlike non-existers, all existers who lack an intrinsic good *are* deprived of it and are accordingly worse off, according to Benatar.) Consequently, on his view, using an analogy involving two existers in conjunction with an intrinsic good will beg the question against the asymmetry argument. The solution, he suggests, is to use two existers in conjunction with an *instrumental* good, which will make the analogy fair to the asymmetry argument.[11] Ultimately, then, only a case involving two existers in conjunction with an instrumental good (S and H) will properly simulate the tandem scenarios of one exister and one non-exister in conjunction with an intrinsic good (A and B).

This defense of the analogy, I submit, is unpersuasive. It is based on two *non sequiturs*, one built on top of the other. These *non sequiturs* are perhaps best identified as instances of the fallacy of Correct by Default:

1. Using an analogy involving an exister and a non-exister is inappropriate. (For it is too close to the matter at hand.)

2. Therefore, (by default) an analogy involving two existers is appropriate.

3. An analogy involving two existers in conjunction with an intrinsic good is inappropriate. (For, since all existers who lack an intrinsic good *are* deprived, such an analogy would beg the question against the asymmetry argument.)

4. Therefore, (by default) an analogy involving two existers in conjunction with an instrumental good is appropriate.

---

10  He makes this point in a footnote (Benatar 2006: 43).

11  'In analogies that compare two existing people the only way to simulate the absence of deprivation is by considering instrumental goods' (Benatar 2006: 43).

Both of these inferences are fallacious. In both cases, a good reason for not using one kind of analogy does not by itself establish the legitimacy of using another. It is possible that a third kind of analogy is the only appropriate one or, perhaps more likely for the matter at hand, that there simply is no appropriate non-question-begging analogy of any type to help determine whether the absence of pleasures in non-existence is worse, or no worse, than the presence of pleasures in existence. If I am an improper judge of my character, that does not justify concluding that, say, a complete stranger is a good judge of my character. A third or fourth type of person may be, or maybe no one is. Even if in relation to me there were no other type of person in the world than complete strangers, that would not thereby make them good judges of my character. Reasons that go beyond the one that I am a poor judge of my character (or the additional one that no other kind of person exists in the world than complete strangers) need to be given to support the claim that a complete stranger is a good judge of my character. Likewise, Benatar needs to give reasons for the legitimacy of using in his analogy two existers in conjunction with an instrumental good that go beyond his premises (1) and (3) above. Unless he does so, H's being no worse off than S does not give us any good reason to believe that X in non-existence is no worse off than X in existence. This takes us back to the aforementioned reasonable assumption: in the absence of any countervailing consideration, there is more reason to believe that the logic of intrinsic value that applies to existing things also applies to non-existing things than to believe (as Benatar does) that the logic of instrumental value that applies to existing things becomes part of the logic of intrinsic value when applied to non-existing things. (Applied to the matter at hand: in the absence of any countervailing consideration, there is more reason to believe X in non-existence is deprived of an intrinsic good—just like X in existence when lacking an intrinsic good—than to believe that X in non-existence, lacking an intrinsic good, is like H in existence, lacking an instrumental good.)

## 4.   Another Possible Countervailing Consideration

If Benatar, by way of the analogy, fails to show *directly* that relative non-badness is the kind of non-badness associated with the absence of pleasures in non-existence, perhaps he could establish it *indirectly* by showing that intrinsic non-badness is implausible.[12] Showing this would in effect constitute the kind of countervailing consideration that would render the main clause of the reasonable assumption null and void. Benatar, in fact, attempts such an argument. He contends that if non-badness were intrinsic (Figure 5):

> It would be better to be S than H if the value of (2) were more than twice the value of (1). (This presumably would be the case where the amount of suffering that (2) saves S is more than twice the amount S actually suffers.) But this cannot be right, for surely it is *always* better to be H (a person who never gets sick and is thus not disadvantaged by lacking the capacity for quick recovery). The whole point is that (2) is *good for S* but does not constitute an advantage over H. By assigning a positive charge to (2) and a '0' to (4), [the figure] suggests that (2) is an advantage over (4), but it quite clearly is not. The assignment of values in [this figure], and hence also [the corresponding assignment of values

---

12   Such an argument would be a sort of correct-by-default argument, but a non-fallacious one. While it is false that there must be an appropriate analogy, it seems true that if the absence of pleasures in non-existence is, in fact, not bad, then the non-badness must be either relative or intrinsic.

in a figure representing Scenarios A and B], must be mistaken. (Benatar 2006: 47)

| S | H |
|---|---|
| (1)<br>Presence of sickness<br>(Bad)<br>-5 | (3)<br>Absence of sickness<br>(Good)<br>+5 |
| (2)<br>Presence of capacity<br>for quick recovery<br>(Good)<br>+12 | (4)<br>Absence of capacity<br>for quick recovery<br>(Not Bad)<br>0 |
| = +7 | = +5 |

Figure 5.

There are, however, problems with this way of producing the needed countervailing consideration to upset the main clause of the reasonable assumption. First, if Benatar is unjustified in claiming that the case of H and S properly simulates Scenarios A and B (which the preceding analysis has shown), then this *reductio ad absurdum* objection to interpreting the case of H and S a certain way is groundless when applied to Scenarios A and B. That is, if we have no good reason to believe that the case of S and H is a good simulation of Scenarios A and B, then we have no good reason to believe that the absurdity in interpreting non-badness as value neutrality in the case of H and S carries over to Scenarios A and B.

Moreover, what if we did not know and did not concern ourselves with whether or not H has the capacity for quick recovery? What if all we knew and focused on is that H never gets sick? In this case, with the fourth quadrant ignored altogether, we would *still* get the counter-intuitive conclusion that it is better to be S than to be H (Figure 6).

| S | H |
|---|---|
| (1)<br>Presence of sickness<br>(Bad)<br>-5 | (3)<br>Absence of sickness<br>(Good)<br>+5 |
| (2)<br>Presence of capacity<br>for quick recovery<br>(Good)<br>+12 | |
| = +7 | = +5 |

Figure 6.

If so, then it seems the value neutrality of quadrant (4) in Figure 5 is not fundamentally responsible for yielding the counter-intuitive conclusion. Something else is. One possibility is Benatar's incorrectly leaving something out of his matrix. Where in the matrix, we might ask, is *H's capacity to never get sick* and all of its positive value in the sickness it prevents? While S's capacity to recover quickly is recognized and given its due in positive value for all the bad it prevents, H's corresponding—and, indeed, more impressive—capacity to never get sick is not even acknowledged. While this capacity is behind the absence of sickness in quadrant (3)—it is what accounts for H's not getting sick in the way S does—this remarkable capacity of H is not given any credit for the other preventative work it does. It is not, for example, given credit for preventing the extent of sickness that S's capacity to recover quickly is given credit for preventing. Once H's capacity to never get sick is afforded the value that S's capacity to recover quickly is afforded (in addition to the +5 units for preventing the extent of sickness S actually suffers), the numbers easily add up in favor of H over S and consequently no counter-intuitive sums in value result in interpreting the non-badness of H's absence of the capacity to recover quickly as being value neutral (Figure 7).

| S | H |
|---|---|
| (1)<br>Presence of sickness<br>(Bad)<br>-5 | (3)<br>Presence of capacity<br>to never get sick<br>(Good)<br>+17<br><br>(the prevention of sickness, which includes the equivalent of both S's actual sickness, -5, and possible sickness, -12) |
| (2)<br>Presence of capacity<br>for quick recovery<br>(Good)<br>+12<br><br>(the prevention of sickness, which would have been -12) | (4)<br>Absence of capacity<br>for quick recovery<br>(Not Bad)<br>0 |
| = +7 | = +17 |

Figure 7.

Now I suppose Benatar might suggest that it is incorrect to attribute to H the capacity to never get sick, if what is meant by that is having a certain genetic constitution, such as one resulting in stupendous antibodies. He might claim that something else, dumb luck, is responsible for H's never getting sick.[13] So in this case there is nothing special about H; he just always is at the right place at the right time—coincidentally away from bad germs. Be that as it may, it seems that dumb luck, though more ab-

13   In his book, Benatar simply states that H never gets sick; he does not tell us why.

stract, is something that can be predicated of H as much as stupendous antibodies. And it is something that has high value. If dumb luck is responsible for H's never getting sick, then H has something of high value that needs to be part of the calculation in the case of S and H.

There is also a second possible candidate for yielding the counter-intuitive conclusion that S is better off than H that differs from Benatar's own suggestion that it is the value neutrality in quadrant (4). This one, however, does not refer to something Benatar implausibly excludes from his matrix; it concerns something he implausibly includes: that S's capacity to recover quickly can be attributed a positive charge that is more than twice the disvalue of S's presence of sickness.[14] This claim implies that as the effects S's sicknesses would have on him worsen—were these effects not prevented by his capacity to recovery quickly—the greater overall value S has in his life, all else being equal. But S is not better off than he would have been had, say, some illnesses not lasted as long and consequently his capacity to recover quickly prevented only 6 units of pain instead of 12. The presence of 12 units of pleasure, instead of the presence of 6, can make S's life go better; the absence of 12 units of pain, instead of the absence of 6, cannot. The same is true across lives. Consider Vikki and Betsy, two women who live in different parts of the world, whose lives up till now have gone equally well, and who both have the capacity to recover quickly from illness. Both Vikki and Betsy get the flu, although different strains, and both recover quickly from their illnesses after having suffered the same amount. Now if it is true that Vikki would have suffered longer than Betsy had both not had the capacity to recover quickly—and so it is true that Vikki's capacity to recover quickly does more preventative work than Betsy's—that does not make Vikki's life at this point *better* than Betsy's. The amount of bad that 'preventative goods' prevent does not determine the quality of our lives, does not make them go better or worse. If our environments were more germ-filled, and consequently our antibodies were utilized more than they actually are, then, all else being equal, our lives would not have been any better. If this line of reasoning is correct, then the problematic quadrant in Figure 5 above is (2), not (4).[15]

In this section, I have set out Benatar's *reductio ad absurdum* objection to the view that the non-badness of absent pleasures in non-existence may be intrinsic non-badness (value neutrality). If sound, this *reductio* would constitute a forceful countervailing consideration to the main clause of the reasonable assumption. I have shown, however, that Benatar's objection is not sound. First, it hinges on the Sick and Healthy analogy whose aptness to Scenarios A and B was earlier shown to be problematic.

14  Insofar as the previous alternative candidate for yielding the counter-intuitive result presupposes that this major claim of Benatar's is true, the previous alternative candidate and this second one are incompatible. Since I believe this major claim is false, I view my previous alternative as a fall-back candidate, one which is more plausible than Benatar's own if his major claim, against what I believe, is actually true.

15  This line of reasoning may also make us begin to wonder whether, on the one hand, the whole business of attributing an inverse positive charge to the absence of something bad (absent due to a preventative capacity or something else, such as non-existence) is flawed. Of course, if it is flawed, the asymmetry argument, by virtue of the assignment of an inverse positive charge to the absence of pains in non-existence, in quadrant (3), is unsound. If, on the other hand, attributing an inverse positive charge to the absence of something bad is warranted, then it seems Benatar in the next chapter of his book drastically underestimates the good in our lives since he is silent about all the preventative work our good preventative capacities do on a daily, if not moment-by-moment, basis.

Second, it inexplicably excludes much of the value of H's capacity to never get sick while includes and attributes much positive value to S's capacity to recover quickly. And third, it turns on the questionable claim that the more bad a capacity of ours prevents, the better our lives go (so that we would have lived better lives had our world been worse and consequently our preventative capacities been employed more often).

## 5. Final Possible Countervailing Consideration

Recall my noting at the end of section 1 that Benatar maintains that four 'quite plausible' and 'widely endorsed' asymmetries are best explained by the deeper Asymmetry in his argument and that, if they are, we have excellent reason to believe the Asymmetry is true. Recall also my suggesting that it is one thing for these topical asymmetries to establish *an* Asymmetry, another thing for them to establish the particular Asymmetry the asymmetry argument requires. If the asymmetries show only that while the absence of pains in non-existence is good the absence of pleasures in non-existence is *intrinsically* not bad (i.e., value neutral), then Benatar may have strong support for *an* Asymmetry, but he would not have strong support for the right one.

Now Benatar could respond to this point, as well as to my above criticisms of the Sick and Healthy analogy, by claiming that the topical asymmetries do, in fact, straightaway support the right Asymmetry: that while the absence of pains in non-existence is good, the absence of pleasures in non-existence is *relatively* not bad (i.e., no worse than the presence of pleasures in existence). And if they do, then the asymmetry argument does not depend on the Sick and Healthy analogy establishing, either directly or indirectly, that the non-badness of absent pleasures in non-existence is *relative* non-badness. Each of the topical asymmetries in this case would amount to a successful countervailing consideration rendering null and void the main clause of the reasonable assumption: there is more reason to believe that the logic of intrinsic value that applies to existing things also applies to non-existing things than to believe (as Benatar does) that the logic of instrumental value that applies to existing things becomes part of the logic of intrinsic value when applied to non-existing things.[16]

Let us see, then, whether the topical analogies do, in fact, support the claim that the absence of pleasures in non-existence is specifically relatively not bad and thereby collectively constitute a successful countervailing consideration to the main clause of the

---

16  Since this kind of move might appear to be viable, I address it. However, the following passage indicates that Benatar himself (at least when he wrote the book) is not motivated to make it, that he believes the topical asymmetries establish a general asymmetry and the Sick and Healthy analogy establishes more specifically that the non-badness of absent pleasures in non-existence is *relative* non-badness (no worse than the presence of pleasures in existence): 'The analogy need not be read as proving that quadrant (2) [the presence of pleasures in existence] is good and that quadrant (4) [the absence of pleasures in non-existence] is not bad. That asymmetry was established in the previous section [by the four topical asymmetries]. Instead, the analogy could be interpreted as showing how, given the asymmetry, (2) is not an advantage over (4), whereas (1) is a disadvantage relative to (3). It would thereby show that Scenario B is preferable to Scenario A'. (Benatar 2006: 43) Moreover, all the effort Benatar makes to defend the aptness of the Sick and Healthy analogy is further evidence that he thinks the topical asymmetries themselves do not establish that the non-badness of absent pleasures in non-existence is specifically relative non-badness and that the analogy, therefore, is needed to do this extra work. If all he wanted the analogy to be is an example of how the absence of something good can be no worse than the good thing itself, then the objections to the analogy in the book that he addresses are patently inappropriate and his responses to them unnecessary.

reasonable assumption. In what follows, I italicize the clauses that would directly constitute the countervailing consideration.[17]

Here is the first asymmetry: 'While there is a duty to avoid bringing suffering people into existence, *there is no duty to bring happy people into being*' (Benatar 2006: 32). But, in short, the fact that there is no duty to bring happy people into existence may be explained as much by the absence of pleasures in non-existence being value neutral as by its being no worse than the presence of pleasures in existence. If the absence of pleasures in non-existence is value neutral (not bad, not good), instead of bad, then while we may have a moral reason to procreate, we certainly do not have a *duty* to do so, especially in view of all the countervailing reasons not to procreate (e.g., the substantial burdens children place on parents). In contrast, why avoiding bringing suffering people into existence rises to the level of duty is that it involves *causing bad*, and much of it, to befall someone.

Here is a second asymmetry: 'Whereas, at least when we think of them, we rightly are sad for inhabitants of a foreign land whose lives are characterized by suffering, *when we hear that some island is unpopulated, we are not similarly sad for the happy people who, had they existed, would have populated this island*' (Benatar 2006: 35). But that we are not similarly sad about the island case may be explained as much by the absence of pleasures in non-existence being value neutral (instead of its being bad, as actual people suffering is) as by its being no worse than the presence of pleasures in existence. And if by 'not similarly sad' Benatar means 'not sad *at all*,' then that seems false, as Saul Smilansky has argued.[18]

Unlike the first two, the final two asymmetries might more strongly appear inconsistent with the view that the non-badness of the absence of pleasures in non-existence is intrinsic non-badness (value neutrality). One of these asymmetries is this: 'Whereas *it is strange (if not incoherent) to give as a reason for having a child that the child one has will thereby be benefited*, it is not strange to cite a potential child's interests as a basis for avoiding bringing a child into existence' (Benatar 2006: 34). First, Benatar's language here (in particular the term 'incoherent') suggests that he believes there is some deep logical problem with citing a not-yet-conceived child's interests as a reason for procreating and, of course, the non-identity problem comes to mind as that deep logical problem. But that cannot be, for the non-identity problem would be as much a problem for citing a potential child's interests as a basis for avoiding bringing a child

---

17  I believe, in part for reasons that Smilansky (2008), DeGrazia (2010), and Metz (2011) give, that Benatar has not shown that these four alleged asymmetries establish *any kind* of deeper Asymmetry. However, since the focus of this paper is the Sick and Healthy analogy and not the four asymmetries, I include below only what I think is required to call into question Benatar's possible claim that the asymmetries themselves establish that the non-badness of absent pleasures in non-existence is specifically *relative* non-badness. All that is required for this purpose is to show that the topical asymmetries equally support the other kind of Asymmetry (the one involving *intrinsic* non-badness).

18  'When experiencing a happy and moving occasion (such as visiting a beautiful area) I often regret that people close to me have died, and so cannot enjoy the pleasure which I experience. If the region is nearly empty, it would be natural for me to think that it is a pity that more people do not live among all this beauty. The presence of more people would be good, and it would be equally good whether this presence came through immigration or because more people had been born there. So (I feel) the existence of currently non-existent people would in itself be good. Moreover, just as I am glad to be alive, I think that people who could exist but do not (because they have died or because they were not born) are missing something' (Smilansky 2008: 570).

into existence, and Benatar earlier in the book explains how he can successfully deal with that problem (Benatar 2006: 31).[19]

Perhaps, then, the problem with citing the potential child's interests in the one case is this consideration, which Benatar states a few lines later: 'If having children were done for the purpose of thereby benefiting those children, then there would be greater moral reason for at least many people to have more children' (Benatar 2006: 34). Now, again, if the absence of pleasures in non-existence were downright *bad*, then we may well expect there to be greater moral reason to have more children than we believe there is. However, if the absence of pleasures in non-existence is only value neutral (intrinsically not bad), then, in view of all the burdens and sacrifices having children place on parents, it is not at all surprising that we do not feel more moral pressure (or believe we have greater moral reason) than we do to have more children. As for a possible world in which children impose no burdens or sacrifices on parents at all[20]—a world so way out there that it is quite difficult to mentally inhabit—who knows, perhaps we would feel more moral pressure or believe ourselves to have greater moral reason to have more children. Remember, the greater degree of moral pressure or of moral reason in this possible world (compared to our own) would not be all that much. It certainly would be much less than the greater degree of moral pressure or moral reason in the case in which the absence of pleasures in non-existence were downright bad. A modest degree of additional moral pressure or moral reason in that possible world seems plausible to me.

Finally, there is this fourth asymmetry: 'We can regret, for the sake of an indeterminate but existent person that a benefit was not bestowed on him or her, but *we cannot regret, for the sake of somebody who never exists . . . a good that this never existent person never experiences*' (Benatar 2006: 34). Again, Benatar's language ('can regret', 'cannot regret') suggests that he thinks there is a deep logical problem when the object of inquiry is a *merely* possible person (i.e., someone who, as a matter of fact, never exists). But, once more, it seems that problem cannot be the issue for Benatar because the same problem would apply to something that it cannot for him, in this case the act of welcoming (or feeling good about) the absence of pain when the object of welcoming is a merely possible person. So perhaps Benatar's point is that, as a matter of fact, we just do not regret that a possible person does not experience pleasure. If so, then, as far as the issue of providing evidence that the non-badness at issue is relative (not intrinsic) is concerned, this asymmetry amounts to the second one involving our alleged lack of sadness about an unpopulated island, and my critical remarks about that second asymmetry apply equally to this asymmetry.

## 6. The Logic of Intrinsic Value and the Logic of Instrumental Value
So far, on the basis of my analysis, I have made three main claims: (1) that Benatar's Sick and Healthy analogy fails to show that the non-badness of the absence of pleasures in non-existence is relative in the sense that this non-badness is no worse than the presence of pleasures in existence; (2) that his *reductio* of the position that the

---

19  Benatar had to solve the non-identity problem in order to go forward with his important claim that the absence of pains in non-existence is good for X, a merely possible person who never exists. The point is that he cannot now turn around and *rely* on the same non-identity problem and claim that since X is a merely possible person, we cannot speak of X's interests.

20  Benatar (2006: 32–34) uses such a possible world in defending the first topical asymmetry (the one involving no duty to bring happy people into existence) against a similar objection that emphasizes burdens that children place on parents.

non-badness of the absence of pleasures in non-existence is intrinsic (value neutral) is untenable; and (3) that the four topical asymmetries that Benatar uses to support the deeper Asymmetry do not support the view that the non-badness of pleasures in non-existence is relative rather than intrinsic. If I am correct in believing that I have sufficiently supported these three claims, I am now warranted in going further in claiming that the main clause of the reasonable assumption has been shown to be justified: there *is* more reason to believe that the logic of intrinsic value that applies to existing things also applies to non-existing things than to believe that the logic of instrumental value that applies to existing things becomes part of the logic of intrinsic value when applied to non-existing things. Unpacked, this claim yields the following theory of the differing logics of intrinsic and instrumental value, which is damning to the asymmetry argument as a whole.

The logic of intrinsic goodness is such that, unlike the case of an instrumental good, the presence of an intrinsic good is *always* good. Ignoring possible bad side-effects of its presence, this feature of intrinsic goodness makes its presence always better than its absence, which in turn makes its absence *relatively bad* and *intrinsically value neutral*. Insofar as the presence of pleasures characterizes existence and the absence of pleasures characterizes non-existence, existence is better than non-existence. In other words, it is (impersonally) better that the universe contains sentient beings who experience pleasure than that it does not, all else being equal. And so X is (personally) better off existing than not as far as the presence and absence of pleasures are concerned and all else being equal. Parallel remarks can be made about the logic of intrinsic badness, such as pain. The logic of intrinsic badness is such that the presence of an intrinsic bad is always bad. This (again, ignoring extraneous consequences) makes its presence always worse than its absence, which in turn makes its absence *relatively good* and *intrinsically value neutral*.[21] Insofar as the presence of pains characterizes existence and the absence of pains characterizes non-existence, non-existence is (impersonally) better than existence. In other words, it is worse that the universe contains sentient beings who experience pain than that it does not, *ceteris paribus*. And so X is (personally) better off not existing than existing as far as the presence and absence of pains are concerned and all else being equal. Now whether X is better off existing or not *overall* has to do with whether the good in X's life outweighs the bad. *Good*, *bad*, and *neutral* and, when comparing instances of these three, *better* and *worse*—are part of the logic of intrinsic value, and they apply over both existence and non-existence. *Not bad*, in the sense of *no worse than good*, does not belong to the logic of intrinsic value. It belongs solely to the logic of instrumental value.

In turn, the logic of instrumental value is such that, unlike the case of an intrinsic good, the presence of an instrumental good is *not* always good. This makes its absence in some instances (think H) not bad in the sense of no worse than its presence in other instances (think S). If you possess and I lack what is instrumentally good for you but never for me, I am no worse off than you. Again, the logic of relative non-badness is

---

21  This view dovetails with Harman's comment (2009: 781): 'When we fail to bring someone into existence who would have suffered horribly, then we have failed to do *something we should not have done*. We have acted rightly, and we have avoided causing a bad state of affairs. None of this implies that there is anything [intrinsically] *good* about the current situation; but it might be mistakenly thought to imply that'. The reason for the mistake, I believe, is the failure to distinguish intrinsic and relative goodness. The absence of pains in non-existence, though not intrinsically good, is relatively so, that is, better than something that is intrinsically bad, such as the presence of pain.

solely a part of the logic of instrumental value. Benatar's principal mistake is pasting it to the logic of intrinsic value in cases in which existence and non-existence are compared.

## 7. Conclusion

For readers who understandably scratch their heads and wonder how in the world something merely *not bad* can be no worse than something *good*, there is no better teaching tool than the Sick and Healthy analogy. Since H never gets sick, lacking the capacity for quick recovery—something undoubtedly good for S who gets sick often—certainly makes H no worse off than S. But if the preceding analysis is correct, the analogy does nothing more for Benatar. Contrary to what he maintains, it does not give us any good reason to believe that the non-badness of the absence of pleasures in non-existence is relative non-badness in the sense that this non-badness is no worse than the presence of pleasures in existence. Ironically, if the analogy does anything more, it evokes reflection on the distinguishing features of intrinsic and instrumental value and gives us reason to believe the opposite: that the non-badness of the absence of pleasures in non-existence is intrinsic non-badness in the sense of value neutrality. If so, then the asymmetry argument is unsound, and it seems that what is left for Benatar to do, *qua* pessimist, is to revive the old standard argument that relies on establishing a disproportionate amount of pain and suffering in the world. Of course, that is exactly what he does in the next chapter of his ingenious, challenging, and provocative book.

## References

Belshaw, Christopher 2007. 'Better Never to Have Been: The Harm of Coming into Existence'. *Notre Dame Philosophical Reviews*. http://ndpr.nd.edu/review.cfm?id=9983.

Benatar, David 2006. *Better Never to Have Been: The Harm of Coming into Existence*. New York: Oxford.

DeGrazia, David 2010. 'Is It Wrong to Impose the Harms of Human Life? A Reply to Benatar'. *Theoretical Medicine and Bioethics* 31: 317–331.

Harman, Elizabeth 2009. 'Critical Study of David Benatar. *Better Never to Have Been: The Harm of Coming into Existence*'. *Nous* 43: 776–785.

Kagan, Shelly 1998. 'Rethinking Intrinsic Value'. *The Journal of Ethics* 2: 277–297.

Korsgaard, Christine M. 1983. 'Two Distinctions in Goodness'. *The Philosophical Review* 2: 169–195.

Metz, Thaddeus 2011. 'Are Lives Worth Creating?' *Philosophical Papers* 40, no. 2: 233–255.

Rabinowicz, Wlodek and Rønnow-Rasmussen, Toni 2000. 'A Distinction in Value: Intrinsic and for Its Own Sake'. *Proceedings of the Aristotelian Society*, New Series, 100: 33–51.

Smilansky, Saul 2008. 'Better Never to Have Been: The Harm of Coming into Existence'. *Philosophical Quarterly* 58, no. 232: 569–571.

# Better No Longer to Be[1]

## Rafe McGregor

## Ema Sullivan-Bissett

**Abstract**

David Benatar argues that coming into existence is always a harm, and that – for all of us unfortunate enough to have come into existence – it would be better had we never come to be. We contend that if one accepts Benatar's arguments for the asymmetry between the presence and absence of pleasure and pain, and the poor quality of life,[2] one must also accept that suicide is preferable to continued existence, and that his view therefore implies *both* anti-natalism *and* pro-mortalism[3]. This conclusion has been argued for before by Elizabeth Harman – she takes it that because Benatar claims that our lives are 'awful', it follows that 'we would be better off to kill ourselves' (Harman 2009: 784). Though we agree with Harman's conclusion, we think that her argument is too quick, and that Benatar's arguments for non-pro-mortalism[4] deserve more serious consideration than she gives them. We make our case

1    We would like to thank the AHRC for Ema Sullivan-Bissett's doctoral studentship which was held whilst this work was completed. We would like to thank the Mind and Reason research group at York; Keith Allen, Paul Noordhof, Christian Piller and Rachael Wiseman for their useful feedback, and Thom Brooks for his helpful commentary and encouragement, on an earlier version of this paper. We would also like to thank Thaddeus Metz for his comments and suggestions, as a result of which this paper was greatly improved.
2    We will not discuss whether Benatar's arguments for his anti-natalism work; for the purposes of this paper, we assume that they do. This is a point upon which the authors disagree.
3    Where pro-mortalism is understood as the claim that suicide is always preferable to continued existence. Though we think that this strong claim really does follow from Benatar's anti-natalism, towards the end of the paper we take a more charitable line and give back a bit of ground in allowing that perhaps only a weaker version of pro-mortalism follows from Benatar's position, namely, that suicide is (*almost*) always preferable. Even if only the weaker claim follows, we take it that this is significant.
4    We use the term 'non-pro-mortalism' to refer to Benatar's claim that his position does not entail pro-mortalism.

using a tripartite structure. We start by examining the prima facie case for the claim that pro-mortalism follows from Benatar's position, presenting his response to the contrary, and furthering the dialectic by showing that Benatar's position is not just that *coming into* existence is a harm, but that existence itself is a harm. We then look to Benatar's treatment of the Epicurean line, which is important for him as it undermines his anti-death argument for non-pro-mortalism. We demonstrate that he fails to address the concern that the Epicurean line raises, and that he cannot therefore use the harm of death as an argument for non-pro-mortalism. Finally, we turn to Benatar's pro-life argument for non-pro-mortalism, built upon his notion of interests, and argue that while the interest in continued existence may indeed have moral relevance, it is almost always irrational. Given that neither Benatar's anti-death nor pro-life arguments for non-pro-mortalism work, we conclude that pro-mortalism follows from his anti-natalism, As such, *if* it is better never to have been, *then* it is better no longer to be.

## 1. Anti-Natalism and Pro-Mortalism

### 1a: The Dialectic

Benatar's argument for anti-natalism is multi-faceted; first he argues that there is an asymmetry between the presence and absence of pleasure and pain, and second that the quality of lives of sentient beings is very poor. The prima facie case for Benatar's anti-natalism entailing pro-mortalism can be seen to be derived from the asymmetry, which briefly[5], is as follows: the presence of pleasure and pain are good and bad respectively; and the absence of pain is good while, significantly, the absence of pleasure is not bad[6] (Benatar 2006: 30). We take it that the most objectionable claims here are the ones Benatar makes about the absence of pleasure and pain, but our concern in this paper is with what follows from his position if it works, so we will not spend any time discussing the plausibility of the asymmetry. If we accept the asymmetry, we see that not existing is better than existing: in World A where DB exists, DB experiences pleasure – that is good – and he experiences pain – that is bad; in World B where DB does not exist, DB[7] does not experience pain – that is good – and he does not experience pleasure – importantly, that is not bad. This is because the absence of pleasure is only bad if there is somebody who is deprived by that absence, and given that 'one could not have been deprived by their absence if one had not existed', we do not have a case of deprivation for those who never exist (Benatar 2006: 1). As such, the absence of pleasure in these cases is not bad. The thought is then that World B is the better world, and any instance of procreation is an example of a World A situation. One is therefore morally obliged to abstain from procreation. Very roughly, this is Benatar's asymmetry argument for anti-natalism.

If one accepts Benatar's asymmetry between pleasure and pain, then prima facie one ought to accept that suicide is always preferable to continued existence. The reason for this is straightforward: if Benatar is right that it is better never to have existed, then non-existence must still be preferable to existing even when the agent in question has been unfortunate enough to be brought into existence. When the agent ceases to exist the result is: an absence of pain, which is good, and an absence of pleasure, which is

---

5    We assume familiarity with Benatar's position and will make only the briefest of introductory remarks.
6    See Benatar (2006: 39-40) for reasons why 'not bad' is used rather than 'not good' or 'neutral' to describe the absence of pleasure.
7    There is of course no DB in World B; we write in this way only for ease of exposition.

not bad. This is the basic case for the claim that Benatar's anti-natalism entails pro-mortalism.

Benatar, however, maintains that his anti-natalism does not entail pro-mortalism; he puts forward an explicit argument for this, which we will call the 'pro-life argument' and discuss in section three. The pro-life argument is a response to his observation that '[i]f our lives are quite as bad as I shall still suggest they are, and if people were prone to see this true quality of their lives for what it is, they might be much more inclined to kill themselves' (Benatar 2006: 69). Benatar rejects the claim that his position entails pro-mortalism on the following basis: 'the existent can have interests in continuing to exist, and thus harms that make life not worth continuing must be sufficiently severe to defeat those interests' (Benatar 2006: 213). The moral agent who accepts Benatar's asymmetry and also desires to minimise harm is therefore not required to commit suicide, as the frustration of her interests is a harm in itself. As such it is also legitimate to claim that there is a difference between a life worth starting and a life worth continuing – the threshold is higher in the former case. This is because the non-existent do not and cannot have any interests in coming into existence. The avoidance of harm achieved by not bringing them into existence is therefore decisive (Benatar 2006: 213).

There is also an implicit argument for non-pro-mortalism, which has been suggested by Thaddeus Metz. He claims that there is a further reason for the incompatibility of Benatar's anti-natalism with pro-mortalism: part of the harm of existence is that its end – death – is itself a harm (Metz 2011: 236). Benatar claims that '[a]lthough it may be bad for anyone of us to die, it is still worse to die earlier than we need to' (Benatar 2006: 196), and that '[c]oming into existence is bad in part because it invariably leads to the harm of ceasing to exist' (Benatar 2006: 213). It might seem that the claims that those who exist have an interest in continuing to do so and that death is a harm are equivalent. This would be the case if the harm posed by death is instrumental, i.e. if death is a harm because it frustrates the agent's interest in continued existence. However, Benatar does not qualify his claim about premature death by stating that it is usually worse to die earlier than later; he states simply: 'I assume that death is bad for the one who dies' (Benatar 2006: 196). We think this justifies us in taking death to be intrinsically – not merely instrumentally – bad for Benatar. Benatar never makes the explicit claim that the harm of death is a reason for continued existence, but if death is intrinsically bad, then an 'anti-death argument' could be employed in a case for non-pro-mortalism. Given that the agent already exists, the agent's death is – in this conception – a further harm. We shall discuss the anti-death argument in section two. Before this, though, we will show that Benatar's position is not just that coming into existence is a harm, but that existence itself is a harm.

*1b: Furthering the Dialectic*

The discerning reader may have noticed that the way we put the prima facie case for the claim that Benatar's view entailed pro-mortalism, left it open to an obvious objection. We suggested that if it is better never to have existed, then similarly non-existence must still be preferable even when the agent in question has come into existence. But if Benatar can claim that only coming into existence – and not existence itself – is a harm, then pro-mortalism will not follow from his position[8].

---

8    This is not to say that Benatar can reject the claim that his anti-natalism entails pro-mortalism *only* by arguing that *coming into existence* is a harm, rather we just want to say that if he can argue this, the prima facie case for his position entailing pro-mortalism fails.

Benatar's argument does not obviously require the claim that existence is a harm, only that coming into existence is a harm. Nonetheless, he goes to great lengths to show why the quality of life cannot be calculated by working out the difference between good and bad (Benatar 2006: 61-4), and why self-assessments of the quality of life are invariably over-optimistic (Benatar 2006: 64-9). Importantly for our purposes, he makes the following claims:

(1)   'I deny that *any* lives are worth starting' (Benatar 2006: 121, Benatar's italics).

(2)   '[I]t would be better if humans (and other species) became extinct' (Benatar 2006: 194).

(3)   'All things being equal, the longer sentient life continues, the more suffering there will be' (Benatar 2006: 209).

(4)   'I have argued that our lives are very bad. There is no reason why we should not try to make them less so, on condition that we do not spread the suffering (including the *harm of existence*)' (Benatar 2006: 210, our italics).

We take it that these four claims are sufficient to show that existence itself is a harm: if it should not be begun under any circumstances, and its continuation increases suffering such that extinction is preferable, then it is reasonable to hold that existence and not just *coming into* existence, is harmful.

We propose an analogy with smoking cigarettes. Consider the situation of someone who:

(1*)  denied that anyone should start smoking,

(2*)  advocated the global cessation of smoking,

(3*)  claimed that smoking was directly proportional to harm, and

(4*)  held that it was one's duty[9] to prevent others from smoking.

The primary reason for holding this view is that *smoking* is harmful, not just that *starting smoking* is harmful. Starting smoking is harmful because smoking itself is harmful. In the same way, the primary reason for holding Benatar's anti-natalist view is that *existence* is harmful, not merely that *coming into existence* is harmful. We shall therefore state Benatar's proposal as follows: (*coming into*) existence is always a harm.

It might be that Benatar could reject this analogy in the following way: even if one accepts the correlation between the two sets of statements above, if death itself is a harm, then it is not the case that ceasing to exist is analogous to stopping smoking. If it is true that death is harmful, but stopping smoking reduces harm, we have a disanalogy. We shall, however, show in part two that Benatar fails to prove that death is a harm, and that this is therefore not a premise upon which he can rely to sustain his non-pro-mortalism. So, we take it that coming into existence and existing are both harmful. Given this, anti-natalism and pro-mortalism follow: I can prevent harm by stopping someone coming into existence if I am an anti-natalist; I can reduce harm by terminating my own existence if I am a pro-mortalist.

## 2. The Anti-Death Argument
As outlined in the previous section, Benatar's case for non-pro-mortalism relies on his pro-life argument from interests and a more implicit anti-death argument based on the

---

9    Benatar does not use the word 'duty' in the corresponding quote (4). However, given that he is putting forward a normative anti-natalism, we take it that our use of it in the analogy is not contentious.

harm of death. This part will look to the Epicurean line as a way of undermining the anti-death argument. It is important for Benatar that the Epicurean line is mistaken, for if one accepts it then Benatar's anti-death argument for anti-natalism *not* entailing pro-mortalism is not going to hold. The burden of showing the error of the Epicurean line really is therefore one Benatar bears. Indeed, he recognises this problem and spends some time addressing it. As we have seen, the anti-death argument for non-pro-mortalism is that part of the harm of existence comes from the fact that that existence will end. Coming into existence is a harm in part because it 'invariably leads to the harm of ceasing to exist' (Benatar 2006: 213). So it might look like if one accepts that death is a harm, then one cannot get pro-mortalism from Benatar's anti-natalism.

Of course, the Epicurean would not accept the anti-death argument. Epicurus argued that death is not a harm, as it is not something which can be experienced. As he put it:

[W]hen we are, death is not come, and, when death is come, we are not. It is nothing, then, either to the living or to the dead, for with the living it is not and the dead exist no longer (Epicurus 2009: 406).

If one accepts the Epicurean line, we learn that – contra Benatar – death is not a harm. If death does not harm the one who dies, but does bring about an absence of pain, then one should adopt pro-mortalism (if Benatar's asymmetry holds[10]).

Clearly Benatar cannot accept this and he makes three points against the Epicurean line.

We should note though that at one point Benatar seems less worried by the Epicurean position than he ought to be. He says '[t]hose who think that death does not harm the person who dies may simply leave death off my list of harms' (Benatar 2006: 29, fn. 20). But of course if one does leave death off the list, Benatar becomes entirely reliant on his pro-life argument for non-pro-mortalism – his argument from interests – making his position more vulnerable. So it really is important for Benatar to argue for the claim that death is a harm; in what follows we suggest that he is unsuccessful in this.

The first point Benatar makes against the Epicurean line is that there are a number of ingrained views which – if we accept the Epicurean line – would have to be given up. These include the view that a murder victim is harmed by being murdered, that we ought to respect the wishes of the dead, and that a longer life is better than a shorter one *ceteris paribus* (Benatar 2006: 214). If one thinks that death is not a harm, one should reject these three views, which is counterintuitive.

At this point we should note what Benatar says about the counter-intuitiveness of his position. In response to any potential objectors who claim that Benatar's conclusions are too counter-intuitive to accept or even take seriously, Benatar has this to say:

[I]t is noteworthy that a view's counter-intuitiveness cannot by itself constitute a decisive consideration against it. This is because intuitions are often profoundly unreliable – a product of mere prejudice (Benatar 2006: 203).

Returning to the point at hand: Benatar quite rightly notes that an appeal to the counter-intuitiveness of the Epicurean line is not going to be sufficient to 'dismiss [it] out

---

10   Further, if the claims Benatar makes about the poor quality of our lives are also right, we have a stronger case for pro-mortalism: if our lives are terrible *and* non-existence is better than existence *and* death is not a harm, suicide looks preferable to continued existence. It is the last of these three claims which Benatar resists which we seek to support in this section.

of hand' (Benatar 2006: 215); it is particularly important to Benatar that the counter-intuitiveness of an argument is of no serious consequence to that argument's soundness given the conclusions he wants his readers to swallow. However, Benatar maintains that the counter-intuitiveness of his anti-natalism and the counter-intuitiveness of the Epicurean line differ in that the latter is 'far more radically counter-intuitive' than the former (Benatar 2006: 214). He suspects that there are more people who balk at the claim that murder does not harm the victim than the claim that coming into existence is a harm; and that many people accept the latter whilst there are very few who accept the former.

We think that Benatar is probably correct in his suspicions, but this is nonetheless a strange argument. We already know that pointing to the counter-intuitiveness of an argument is not on its own decisive; we have learnt this from Benatar's discussion in 'Countering the Counter-Intuitiveness Objection' (2006: 202-208). It is odd then that he goes on to claim that the Epicurean conclusion is *more* counter-intuitive than his own. It is worth quoting Benatar from this section:

> [W]hen one has a powerful argument, based on highly plausible premises, for a conclusion that if acted upon would reduce suffering without depriving the suffering person of anything, but which is rejected merely because of psychological features that compromise our judgement, then the counter-intuitiveness of that conclusion should not count against it (Benatar 2006: 207).

It strikes us that the Epicurean line fits the above bill[11]. Its premises are plausible, acting on it neither necessarily reduces nor increases suffering[12], and it looks as though Benatar rejects it 'because of psychological features that compromise our judgement' (Benatar 2006: 207). These psychological features are also displayed by the judgements we make which conflict with the Epicurean position. Indeed, as Benatar points out, '[t]he view that death is a harm to the one who dies is not an unreasonable view [...] It is the common sense view and underlies many important judgements we make' (Benatar 2006: 196). An example of one such judgement is that murder is a harm, but the Epicurean is of course committed to denying this. Further, we take it that if we can explain *why* it is that people hold views inconsistent with the Epicurean line, then all the better for the latter. With regard to the view that death is a harm, David Suits has done just that:

> Our common experience is of course our usual guide, and our common experience tells us that injuries may be mild or severe; they can be graded according to how much damage or pain they cause the victim, and how long it takes to recover. The more severe the injury, the greater the pain, and the longer it will take to recover. Some injuries, such as the loss of an eye or a limb, are so severe that part of the organism cannot recover, and one will remain forevermore in a damaged condition, which sometimes includes unending pain. It is easy to

---

11   One might make a case for its not doing so. Perhaps if we acted on Epicurean conclusions it would not be the case that we would 'reduce suffering without depriving the suffering person of anything', particularly if one thinks that the person who dies suffers a deprivation of some sort. However, this concern would not move the Epicurean because he denies that one is harmed or deprived by death.

12   One might think that acting on the Epicurean position by killing oneself would reduce suffering (that of the person who dies). However, as Benatar points out, if we follow the Epicurean reasoning, we derive the claim that death is not able to spare anybody from – or deprive anybody of – anything (Benatar 2006: 217). There might be room for claiming that acting on the Epicurean position reduces suffering *in the world* if not for the person who kills himself, but we leave this aside.

extend such observations to include death, which is then thought of as the most severe injury because the entire organism permanently fails and no recovery at all is possible. On this psychological slippery slope, if mild damage is a mild harm, then death must be the greatest of harms. *Our strong pre-theoretic conviction that death is a harm is a product of our usual way of thinking of things* (Suits 2001: 81-2, our italics).

This observation can also be used to explain why many people think that murder harms the victim: if death harms the victim, then murder – which brings that state about – does so too. To sum up our discussion of Benatar's first point about the Epicurean line: Benatar claimed in a previous section that a view's being counter-intuitive cannot, on its own, count against it (Benatar 2006: 207). In his discussion of the Epicurean position he claims that it is *more* counter-intuitive than his own and is at odds with a number of other views that many people have (Benatar 2006: 214). We suggested that this was an odd move to make given his preceding discussion and further offered a reason, drawing on Suits, for why people are affected by psychological factors that arguably compromise their judgment with regard to whether murder harms the victim – one of the views Benatar offered as in tension with the Epicurean line. Given this, although we read Benatar charitably enough to not construe him as using the counter-intuitiveness of the Epicurean position as a decisive argument against it, we take it that it does not help whatsoever in countering the Epicurean line.

The second point that Benatar makes in his discussion of the Epicurean line is that there is another distinction which can be drawn between it and his own view: 'a precautionary principle applies asymmetrically to the two views' (Benatar 2006: 214). This is to say that *if* the two positions are wrong, the consequences of acting on them differ significantly. If the Epicurean line is wrong in its claim that death is not a harm and people act on that claim by killing themselves or others, those who were killed would be seriously harmed. If Benatar is wrong in his claim that coming into existence is a harm and people act on it by not procreating, however, nobody is harmed because the non-existent do not suffer.

We have two things to say about Benatar's discussion here. Firstly, Benatar goes from assuming for sake of argument that his view is mistaken and draws conclusions from this by implicitly appealing to a major tenet of it. He asks us to assume that his position is wrong; that the claim that coming into existence is a harm is mistaken. However, Benatar establishes that claim from his four premises which make up his asymmetry. As such, he cannot conclude in his discussion on precaution that *if* his view is mistaken *then* nobody is harmed, because this assumes premise four of his asymmetry: 'the absence of pleasure is not bad unless there is somebody for whom this absence is a deprivation' (Benatar 2006: 30). Now it would not be too controversial to take this premise to be false – a utilitarian of a particular stripe may, for example, claim that abstaining from procreation really is a bad thing because the absence of the unborn child's pleasure is a bad thing, even though of course, that child has not been deprived[13]. So if premise four is incorrect – and it is conceivable that it might be – then it would not be true that refraining from procreating is not bad, something bad

13 Even if one accepted premise four, one might still claim that acting on Benatar's position does cause harm because somebody is in fact deprived by not being born. Saul Smilansky takes this line; he claims that he would feel regret for the unborn child and takes it that this potential child has lost out on a good life, and it thus might be that he really has been deprived (Smilansky, personal correspondence). If the absence of pleasure is bad when there is somebody for whom that absence is a deprivation, not procre-

(not 'not bad') has been done by acting on Benatar's position. And if we are to assume that his position is mistaken, we are presumably entitled to take any one of his premises to be mistaken too. It is thus inappropriate for Benatar to make an implicit appeal to the truth of one of his premises in his discussion of the consequences of acting on his position if it is mistaken[14].

Our second point is simply that, just as with the discussion on counter-intuitiveness, we fail to see the relevance. Benatar's point here against the Epicurean line addresses the consequences of acting on the view. Given that considerations of this sort are not epistemic in kind – they are not considerations regarding the truth of the view in question – we take it they are not relevant to Benatar's purposes; a philosophical enquiry which concerns itself with a view's truth. If Benatar is not offering these discussions as arguments against the *truth of* the Epicurean line (and he surely cannot be), then one might think that his inclusion of them just unfairly stacks the deck against the Epicurean, but does not do so with any substance.

The third point Benatar makes about the Epicurean line is that one cannot derive pro-mortalism from his asymmetry by supplementing it with the Epicurean line. This is because if death does not harm the one who dies, it cannot be good for them either. If we follow the Epicurean reasoning through from the claim that death is not a harm, we also derive the claims that death is not a benefit, and further that death is not able to spare anybody from – or deprive anybody of – anything (Benatar 2006: 217). Now it is not clear what work Benatar takes these claims to be doing, but it is worth trying to work this out as charitably as possible. We will not take issue with Benatar's suggestion that the above claims follow from the Epicurean position; it might be that there is some discussion to be had on whether or not they do, but it is not a discussion in which we will partake. Rather, for our purposes, we need to identify why Benatar thinks that it matters that these claims follow from the Epicurean line. Presumably – and we have to presume, because Benatar does not explain – the thought is this: one cannot get pro-mortalism from Benatar's anti-natalism coupled with an Epicurean view of death, because, on the basis of the latter we are to believe that death does not benefit or spare the one who dies. To motivate this point consider John: John is about to be tortured in the most awful of ways. One might think that John's death (before the torture) would prevent this awful fate from befalling him. But of course, the Epicurean (at least on Benatar's reading) is committed to saying of this case that given that death does not deprive us of good things, it does not prevent us from suffering awful things either. This might strike some people as odd. So if one is convinced by Benatar's anti-natalism and thinks that it would have been better never to have been *and* they

---

ating does – contra Benatar – look like a harmful act, and thus the precautionary principle does not apply. Of course, taking Smilansky's line may well be metaphysically costly, we only mention it to show that Benatar's claims about the precautionary principle are on shaky ground even if we allow him that 'the absence of pain is not bad unless there is somebody for whom that absence is a deprivation' (Benatar 2006: 30).

14   One might think that we have been uncharitable to Benatar here; could Benatar not assume that it is only his *conclusion*, namely that pro-creation is wrong, is mistaken? Need he be willing to drop all of the premises in his asymmetry? We take it that this is good point to raise and certainly the way that Benatar *should* go in response to this worry. However, it should be noted that in discussing this point Benatar uses the word 'view', not *conclusion*, which presumably is used as an umbrella term for the asymmetry and his views on the quality of human life. As such we take it that it is legitimate to expect him to be willing to drop the tenets of his view when he appeals to the possibility that his '*view* is mistaken' (Benatar 2006: 215, our italics). We thank Thaddeus Metz for bringing our attention to this.

take it that death is not a harm, it does not follow that they should commit suicide because – staying with the Epicurean reasoning – they will not be benefited or spared of anything by doing so.

If this is what Benatar is alluding to here, we – once again – think that he has failed to undermine the Epicurean line. In fact, this is another very odd position to take given that, as Benatarian anti-natalists, we are motivated by the asymmetry, the third premise of which is: 'the absence of pain is good, even if that good is not enjoyed by anyone' (Benatar 2006: 30). And because we take this to be the case it is not benefit with which we are concerned, but the reduction of pain. Our point (and indeed Benatar's point for his anti-natalism) is that *nobody needs to be spared* for suicide to be preferable. As Benatar points out, there is nobody 'suspended in the metaphysical void' (Benatar 2006: 129) who is spared by not being brought into existence, but that is not to say that we should not refrain from procreation. Equally, even if one is not spared by committing suicide, that is not to say that one should not do so; once again: 'the absence of pain is good, even if that good is not enjoyed by anyone' (Benatar 2006: 30).

We have shown that Benatar has not been successful in his brief attempt at countering the Epicurean position. He needs to do so because his anti-death argument for non-pro-mortalism – which relies on the claim that death is a harm – will not work against an Epicurean. If one takes an Epicurean line, coupled with Benatar's anti-natalism, one might take oneself to have arrived at pro-mortalism. However, the Epicurean line only undermines the anti-death argument for non-pro-mortalism[15], and although Benatar hints at this argument, he does not fully articulate it. We turn now to his explicit argument against the claim that his anti-natalism entails pro-mortalism.

### 3. The Pro-Life Argument

Benatar maintains that judgements concerning future-life cases (judgements about starting lives) are made at a different level from judgements we make about present life cases (judgements about continuing lives). He not only takes it that we *do* make judgements in this way, but also thinks that we *should* (Benatar 2006: 121). This is because there is a difference in the quality threshold between those lives worth starting and those worth continuing; the former is (and should be) set higher than the latter. The reason for this is interests: those in existence can (and usually do) have interests in their continued existence and those interests must be defeated for us to claim that the life is not worth continuing (Benatar 2006: 213).

We should note that Benatar is not opposed to suicide; in fact he states that his view does not preclude 'the possibility that suicide may more often be rational and may even be more rational than continuing to exist' (Benatar 2006: 219). This claim comes from the fact that what can keep people alive is an 'an irrational love for life', even

---

15  One might think the Epicurean could also say something with regard to the pro-life argument. Benatar claims that his argument for anti-natalism does not commit him to pro-mortalism because the existent have interests in continuing to exist, and life need be sufficiently severe to defeat those interests for suicide to become the preferable option. It looks like there is an implicit appeal here to the fourth premise of his asymmetry, 'the absence of pleasure is not bad unless there is somebody for whom this absence is a deprivation' (Benatar 2006: 30). If one has interests in continuing to exist, one's death would be a bad thing in that it would deprive one of future pleasures and satisfaction of interests. However, if one accepts the Epicurean line, then it seems that one's interests do not come into play precisely because the motivation behind premise four is rejected (i.e. an Epicurean would deny that a dead person can be deprived). We take it though that a stronger case can be made against Benatar's pro-life argument, and we will do so in the third section.

when that life has become sufficiently bad such that 'ceasing to exist would be better' (Benatar 2006: 219).

We believe that Benatar's notion of interests is questionable, juxtaposed as it is against his categorical claim that (coming into) existence is not only always a harm, but a *serious* harm (Benatar 2006: 93). He uses the example of someone who is severely disabled. Many people who agree that aborting a severely impaired foetus (for example, one with no legs) would be right, would not themselves commit suicide were they to lose their own legs in an accident at the age of thirty (Benatar 2006: 25). Once someone exists in the morally relevant sense, which Benatar believes occurs with the development of consciousness in foetuses at around twenty-eight to thirty weeks of age, then that person begins to have morally relevant interests (Benatar 2006: 148). Benatar holds that existence in the morally relevant sense is (usually) accompanied by a very strong interest in continued existence (Benatar 2006: 25). This interest in continued existence is sufficient such that even the moral agent who wishes to reduce harm is not required to commit suicide.

There are at least two problems with interests and the work required of them in Benatar's theory, one minor and one serious. First, Benatar does not provide much detail. Interests become morally relevant with the development of consciousness: at about twenty-eight weeks; from here conscious interests 'emerge gradually' (Benatar 2006: 148). Benatar does spend some time looking at 'non-negligible' (Benatar 2006: 147) empirical evidence for his claims, but such evidence does not look sufficient for them. However, we take it that this is a minor issue, which Benatar is no doubt aware of, and one which can be resolved with further empirical work.

The main problem with interests is revealed in the discussion on the rationality of suicide, it often being 'an irrational love for life' that keeps many people alive (Benatar 2006: 219). Benatar provides a detailed analysis showing why our self-assessments of our quality of life are invariably optimistic, a phenomenon he refers to as Pollyannaism.[16] Pollyannaism causes most people – no matter what their circumstances – to over-value their quality of life, and the quality of life of the children they may choose to bring into existence. If Pollyannaism is indeed rife amongst human beings, then it seems that many interests in continued existence over suicide lack a rational basis.

We'll adapt our smoking analogy, comparing our reading of Benatar's book with someone of an earlier generation discovering that smoking is harmful. We were already in existence when we read Benatar's book (our births being prior to publication), but having read it we are now convinced that the rest of our lives are going to be harmful. We are convinced by his argument – in particular the premise that 'the absence of pain is good even if that good is not enjoyed by anyone' (Benatar 2006: 30) – but desire to continue existing. Benatar's position is that because we are morally relevant beings with interests, our desire is not immoral, only (at least sometimes) irrational. Our position finds an exact parallel in the smoker of thirty years who discovers that her habit is harmful. An adult's decision to start or stop smoking is not usually considered a moral one. Most people do not find smoking a morally repugnant habit; the basis for disapproval is rationality: we disapprove of smoking because science has shown that the harms of smoking far outweigh the benefits. Even though we are operating in the sphere of the rational rather than the moral, however, we still maintain that our smoker *should* stop. We accept that she is unlikely to stop, and that this decision is

---

16    Benatar (2006: 64) employs the term coined by Margaret Matlin and David Stang (1978).

not a moral decision (unless she has dependents, in which case we might think otherwise), but the rationality of stopping smoking nonetheless carries normative valence. While it is not immoral to continue smoking, it is irrational, and we censure the decision on that basis. As in the case of continued existence, our censure comes from our concern for the individual: we do not want the smoker to continue to smoke because of the harm she is doing to herself.

Benatar's anti-natalism is normative; he is stating that it is wrong for all human beings to procreate, as (coming into) existence is always a serious harm. He is prepared to make the claim with respect to anti-natalism but not pro-mortalism, because my own moral relevance means that my interest in increasing harm by continuing to exist is not immoral. It is still *irrational*, however. If (coming into) existence is always a serious harm, then continued existence is also always a serious harm[17]. Benatar may have demonstrated that choosing to continue to harm oneself in this fashion is not immoral, but he is – given his views on Pollyannaism – bound to the view that the choice to continue to exist is always irrational[18]. In consequence, therefore: *it is always rational to commit suicide*.[19]

Benatar's commitment to the view that despite the moral relevance of interests, (coming into) existence is always a harm is firm:

> On the assumption that this interest [in continued existence] is not always defeated by the poor quality of life, death is not always a benefit. But is this assumption really reasonable, given how serious a harm I have said it is to come into existence? I think that it is, but saying that it is a reasonable assumption is not to make a very strong claim. It is to say only that the quality of life is not always so poor that ceasing to exist is a benefit. It leaves wide open the question of how often it is not so poor (Benatar 2006: 218).

Even if we allow that Benatar agrees to exceptions, his position at the very least entails that it is usually rational to commit suicide. His reluctance to admit of counterexamples to the harm of existence is obvious, however, and the final sentence above implies that such exceptions are rare indeed. Continued existence is thus for the most part – if not always – a serious harm. We shall therefore summarise Benatar's position as: *it is (mostly) rational to commit suicide*. The corollary of his reasonable assumption that death is not always a benefit is the reasonable assumption that death is mostly a benefit. This, *pace* Benatar, *is* a very strong claim. If one accepts his position, then suicide is rational for most of the 6.94 billion human beings currently in existence. Whatever numerical value one assigns to 'most', the consequence is that billions of people are better off dead, and that it would be rational for them to commit suicide. We are convinced Benatar is well aware of this. That he does not want to advocate the rationality of mass suicide is perhaps admirable, but it is a consequence of his anti-natalism which cannot be denied.

---

17   It might be the case that a weaker version of pro-mortalism follows from Benatar's position, one which has it that it is only when life becomes sufficiently awful that suicide is preferable to continued existence. We discuss this possibility in the postscript to the paper.

18   It might even be that Benatar is aware of this, at one point he claims that 'the desire to continue living may or may not be irrational, but even if it is, this is the kind of irrationality, unlike a preference for having come into existence, that should be decisive' (Benatar 2006: 219).

19   As we are not disputing the claim that the choice to continue existing is not immoral, we have omitted a discussion of the harm one's own suicide may cause others. Benatar rightly notes that the effect on family and friends is 'an important obstacle in the way of suicide' (Benatar 2006: 220).

Our view is that even in our charitable interpretation, Benatar's anti-natalism *does* commit him to pro-mortalism, and that his pro-life argument for pro-mortalism thus fails. In the smoking analogy, the recommendation that the smoker stop smoking is normative despite the appeal to rationality rather than morality. There is a simple reason for this, the historical coupling of morality and reason. The first attempt to prise them apart was not until the eighteenth century, when the Third Earl of Shaftesbury advanced his sentimentalist view of virtue as a feeling[20]. Shaftesbury's idea was developed by Hume, who not only separated morality and rationality, but argued for a reversal of the accepted principle that desire should serve reason. All three branches of normative ethics are based on reason, from Aristotle's virtues to Kant's categorical imperative, and Mill's maximisation of utility. Emotivists may challenge the connection, but every cognitivist theory has sought vindication in the rational basis of morality. As rational beings, people usually believe that they *ought* to act in a rational manner, even if their desires lead them astray. The normativity associated with the rational may have a lower cogency than that associated with the moral[21], but it nonetheless bears authority. We can grant that Benatar is right to state that continued existence is not immoral, but he offers a weaker version of pro-mortalism in its stead. There are two consequences of Benatar's asymmetry, therefore, and both should have been clearly stated:

(1)   Anti-natalism: *it is (always) wrong to procreate.*

(2)   Pro-mortalism: *it is (mostly) rational to commit suicide.*

## 4. Conclusion

To conclude: we first showed that Benatar's views on *coming into* existence entail that *existence* itself is harmful. We then discussed the Epicurean line, which threatens to undermine Benatar's anti-death argument for non-pro-mortalism: if existence is a harm and death is not, then pro-mortalism seems to follow. We discussed Benatar's three points against the Epicurean line and argued that none of them was successful, and that Benatar could not therefore base an argument for non-pro-mortalism on the claim that death is a harm. We then moved on to Benatar's pro-life argument for non-pro-mortalism, showing that while interests are sufficient to show that continued existence is not immoral, they are insufficient to show that it is not irrational, and that Benatar cannot therefore maintain that continued existence is rational as this is in tension with his claim that (coming into) existence is harmful. Our conclusion is therefore that Benatar's position entails pro-mortalism, where pro-mortalism is understood as the view that it is (mostly) rational to commit suicide. Thus: *if it is better never to have been, then it is better no longer to be.*

## Post Script

After a presentation[22] of this paper, a distinction was raised between two kinds of pro-mortalism; one which would recommend committing suicide *now* and another that would recommend doing so *later* (when one's life became sufficiently bad). We wanted to claim that Benatar's anti-natalism commits him to the first of these versions

---

20   Shaftesbury's influential work on ethics is notoriously unsystematic. His philosophy was published in a single volume, entitled *Charactersticks of Men, Manners, Opinions, Times* in 1711 (two years before his death).

21   The historical attempts to base ethics on rationality suggest otherwise, however.

22   Workshop on Contemporary Anti-Natalism. University of Johannesburg, 23rd-24th November 2011.

of pro-mortalism, but one might think that his position only commits him to the second. Of course, this is still a very bold claim and something that does not appear in Benatar's writings; so even if Benatar concedes only the second version of pro-mortalism, this is significant. However, we close by explaining why we remain convinced that Benatar's anti-natalism entails the first, stronger version of pro-mortalism, and that – as sections two and three sought to show – his anti-death and pro-life arguments to the contrary do not work.

There is some evidence in Benatar's writings that he might be willing to concede that his anti-natalism entails the second version of pro-mortalism. When discussing the Epicurean position, Benatar looks at the deprivation account of why death is bad for the one who dies. According to this account, death is bad for the one who dies because it 'deprives that person of future life and the positive features thereof'. However, as Benatar notes, this account is not committed to the claim that death is *always* bad. Rather, 'where the further life of which somebody is deprived is of a sufficiently poor quality, death is not bad for that person. Instead, it is good' (Benatar 2006: 216). Benatar's view on death is that it is 'sometimes a harm and sometimes a benefit' (Benatar 2006: 219), which supports his claim that '[l]ife can be so bad that it is better to die' (Benatar 2006: 218). As we have seen, Benatar thinks that it is often 'an irrational love for life' which can keep people alive, even when life has become sufficiently bad such that 'ceasing to exist would be better' (Benatar 2006: 219). All of this can be read as supporting a commitment to the weaker version of pro-mortalism outlined above.

However, to us, this looks like a weighing procedure, which Benatar explicitly warns against. He considers an opponent who might claim that a life's quality can be assessed 'by subtracting the disvalue of life's negative features from the value of its positive features' (Benatar 2006: 61). In response, Benatar claims that the quality of life *cannot* be calculated by working out the difference between good and bad (Benatar 2006: 61-4).

We learn from the asymmetry that any presence of pain is a bad thing and any absence of pain is a good thing. Benatar accepts the counterintuitive result one gets if they take this to its logical conclusion: even if a life had a tiny amount of pain – a pin prick at birth – it would still be better for that life not to have begun (Benatar 2006: 49). Now if this is the case, the first version of pro-mortalism according to which it is preferable to kill oneself *now* looks to follow. It may well be the case that our lives are not too bad now (relative to the lives of others, or our own lives in the future), and so perhaps we should wait until our quality of life becomes sufficiently terrible before we commit suicide. But, as Benatar points out, our daily lives are characterised by unpleasant states; 'hunger, thirst, bowel and bladder distension (as these organs become filled), tiredness, stress, thermal discomfort and itch' (Benatar 2006: 71). And we learn from Benatar's asymmetry that the absence of even these minor discomforts is a good thing, whereas the absence of the pleasures we will thus not experience is a not bad thing[23]. Also, Benatar claims that '[a]ll things being equal, the longer sentient life continues, the more suffering there will be' (Benatar 2006: 209). We take Benatar's claim here to be about sentient life on a larger scale, rather than as applied to any particular life, but it looks like it applies here too. It is quite clear that the longer a person

---

23   Unless you thought that the person who dies is deprived by the pleasures that they would have experienced had they continued to live. However, this is a claim that would not be accepted by the Epicurean position and thus shows further why Benatar needs to say something in response to it.

lives, the more suffering there will be. One can remove that suffering (the absence of which is good) by killing oneself. Not at some unspecified later date when such suffering becomes more intense, but now. Thus we have the first stronger version of pro-mortalism.

## References

Benatar, David 2006: *Better Never To Have Been: The Harm of Coming Into Existence*. New York: Oxford University Press.

Epicurus 2009: 'Death is Nothing to Us', in Zagzebski, L and Miller, T.D. (eds.), *Readings in Philosophy of Religion: Ancient to Contemporary*. United Kingdom: Blackwell Publishing Ltd, pp. 405-6.

Harman, Elizabeth 2009: 'Critical Study: David Benatar. Better Never to Have Been: The Harm of Coming into Existence'. *Nous,* Vol. 43, No. 4, pp. 776-785.

Matlin, Margaret W. And Stang, David J 1978: *The Pollyanna Principle: Selectivity in Language, Memory and Thought*. Cambirdge MA: Schenkamn.

Metz, Thaddeus 2011: 'Are Lives Worth Creating?'. *Philosophical Papers,* Vol. 40, No. 2, pp. 233-255.

Suits, David B 2001: 'Why Death Is Not Bad For The One Who Died'. *American Philosophical Quarterly.* Vol. 38, No. 1, pp. 69-84.

# Life Is Good

## Saul Smilansky

David Benatar has made a number of distinct claims leading to the conclusion that giving birth to people harms them, that it is overall impermissible to do so from a moral point of view, and that hence, giving birth needs to be strongly discouraged (Benatar 2006). In the response to his work, his exciting direct antinatalist arguments, primarily those concerning the asymmetries (such as his claim that being born is always a harm but not being born is never a harm), have taken center stage. The issue whether life is all that bad or is in fact good has been relatively neglected. I will take up this matter, and argue that there is a strong case to be made for the goodness of life, in a way that significantly affects the plausibility of Benatar's views.

Benatar himself sees the "goodness of life" issue as a central component of his position. Even if one grants the asymmetry arguments, *how* bad bringing people into existence would be depends on how bad life would be. Even more importantly, the badness of actual lives carries significant independent argumentative weight. According to Benatar, "If people realized just how bad their lives were, they might grant that their coming into existence was a harm even if they deny that coming into existence would have been a harm had their lives contained but the smallest amount of harm" (Benatar 2006: 60). Moreover, since the asymmetry arguments are controversial, and confront strong pronatalist arguments and intuitions, it matters a great deal for the way we will evaluate Benatar's position whether indeed "the best lives are very bad, and therefore that being brought into existence is always a considerable harm" (Benatar 2006: 61).

I will assume here familiarity with Benatar's position, and not take care to note the places where I agree with him. I will also not go in detail into the implications of my claims for Benatar's arguments, except for his claims against the view that life is good. Finally, I will consider the badness and goodness of life as composing one topic, as I think Benatar views this as well.

The goodness (or badness) of life is a matter of degree. I do not think that there is any one conclusive or decisive argument to be made either way on this topic of how good life is, yet I do think that there is a strong case for rejecting Benatar's overwhelmingly negative view, a case which can be constructed cumulatively, based upon a number of diverse considerations. Sketching some of these will be my aim here.

## 1. Happiness:

One way in which we can try to understand whether life is good is to ask the living: this is frequently done, and there is a large research literature that reports and compares people's replies on these issues, primarily couched in terms of happiness (for a general survey of the subjective well-being literature, see Diener 1999). In modern Western societies, consistently large numbers of people (over 80%) report fairly high to very high levels of happiness. One set of studies found that a full ninety-three per-cent of Americans report feeling very happy, pretty happy, or moderately happy (see Liszka 2005: 326). This means that all those people would be more or less perplexed by Benatar's views, not quite knowing what to make of them. For them, at least, life *is* happy, well-being prevalent, satisfaction wide-spread; in short, life is experienced as good, or at least quite good.

This is supported by the fact that nearly everyone views the premature termination of lives, both their own and others', as a huge loss. Would this not imply, then, that they view the continuation of life as something at least quite good? That the great ma-jority of people would view the painless cessation of their life as a terrible disaster and loss seems to me to show that people almost universally view living as being good for-tune.

It is not easy to claim that nevertheless people are not really happy; indeed it may not be clear what this means. Happiness seems akin to pain here: genuine first-per-sonal reports of pain have strong evidential weight, which are very difficult to dismiss, and analogous considerations seem to apply to happiness. Benatar does not deny that people report that their lives are good, and this makes it very difficult to claim that they experience their lives as being bad. At least insofar as we focus on happiness or well-being, it is not quite clear what Benatar means by saying that life is not good. If we think of this in the usual, experiential way, then life *does* seem quite good for most people. This generates a doubt whether Benatar is in fact relating to what most people mean when they think of the goodness of life (in terms of happiness or well-being), but then this threatens to considerably weaken the significance of his claim that life is not good, suggesting that perhaps he sees the "good life" eccentrically.

The fairly robust research results are significant in another way: divergences in hap-piness tend to make good sense. Societies that report higher levels of happiness are by and large the societies where we would expect this to be so, namely, advanced West-ern societies where economic existence is relatively secure, and where there is more personal security and freedom. These are the same societies into which many people want to immigrate, in order to improve their lives, for themselves and their children. Thus, "respondents in very poor nations such as India and Nigeria reported much lower SWB [subjective well-being] than people in wealthier nations even though pov-erty there has been endured for centuries" (Diener 1999: 286). Indeed, "the relation between wealth of a nation and average SWB is positive and strong. Gross National Product (GNP) per capita correlates approximately .50 with life satisfaction across 39 nations... wealthy nations appear *much happier* than poor ones" (Diener 1999: 288). It is important that on the social level things are broadly reasonable here (I will consider later some issues of individual personal divergence in levels of happiness). Human be-ings are often fickle on such matters, happiness is notoriously tied to expectations, and there is an important distinction between what people actually experience and the way they will later perceive those events, just to point out three complications, and yet one sees that happiness is very often higher when we would expect it to be, and lower where there are good reasons for this. This not only supports the significance of the re-sults of this research, but *explains* much of the prevailing unhappiness, on the broad social level. If we see that people find life bad when they are destitute or persecuted, this does not show that life as such is bad, or even that it is very likely to be bad but, on the contrary, it suggests that life is found good *unless there are good reasons to be unhappy about one's state, reasons such as great poverty or persecution.*

Since people consistently report levels of well-being that contrast with Benatar's claims about the badness of living, he needs to discredit these results. I will consider this matter below, but already one can see that discrediting common sentiments will not be easy.

The fact that the happiness results significantly track happiness-making features strengthens the qualitative credentials of the "pro-goodness" claim. On the broad social level people tend to be happy unless desperate or harmed, and this seems to indicate that possessing the baseline of a satisfactory life is quite common, and will typically result in a *reasonable* sense that life is by and large happy and well worth living, together with rational backing for those instances where people do not feel in this way. People's sense of well-being seems to be reasons-responsive in a way that lends credence to their reports.

## 2. Taking suicide seriously:

Suicide is a great embarrassment for Benatar's claims: people simply kill themselves in very low numbers. Indeed, they typically cling to life even when life objectively seems to be very hard and even hopeless. This prima facie supports the "pro-goodness" of life case, suggesting that there is, for most people, a great deal of good in their lives, which therefore seem worthwhile to preserve, even in the face of pain and loss of hope. Benatar has responded by providing an "error theory": roughly, people do not kill themselves because they are biologically built this way, the biased "psychological phenomena are unsurprising from an evolutionary perspective. They militate against suicide and in favor of reproduction" (Benatar 2006: 69). And it makes sense why human beings would develop in this way, for those biological creatures that would more easily commit suicide would procreate less, hence gradually ceding evolutionary control to those disposed to hang on, irrespective of the goodness of life. This is a powerful move. Yet I think that there are fairly decisive points that can be made against it, points which at least considerably weaken Benatar's counter-move.

It is important to look at the populations in which suicide is more prevalent. One category is that of the young, where suicide is the fourth-ranked cause of death for young males, and the third for young females, worldwide (Wasserman 2005). Much suicide seems to follow from the temporary instability of hormonal-affected youth, coupled with a less developed ability to take things in their stride and put them in perspective (as well as irrationality – in a surprising number of cases, the irreversibility of suicide does not seem to be grasped). Even with youth much suicide is explicable as an (over)reaction to specific harms or disappointments (abusive or over-demanding parents, bad grades, being left by one's boy-or-girlfriend), factors which in themselves do little to speak about the badness of life as such, rather than the badness of abusive parents and the like; and more broadly, these facts attest to the dangers latent in over sensitivity at a young, immature and vulnerable age to difficulties and disappointments.

That these matters do not mean much about life *as such* is suggested by the reality whereby many failed suicides live on to look back at the act with horror, seeing it as a sign of their youthful folly rather than as something that was actually reasonable or justified by the experience of living.

A second large category of people who commit suicide is that of the terminally ill, decrepit or elderly. These are frequently people for whom it *makes sense* to wish to cease living, because in their personal lives there is something specific that is bad, such as the approaching prospect of a painful death. Many such people also feel that they have had a long and good life, and that "enough is enough", while the rest of their lives could not measure up to the quality of the earlier periods: all sentiments that, again, support the idea that life is, often, good, and indeed that – under half decent social conditions, in reasonably good health and without severe mental problems – the baseline of life is good.

When we go deeper, we indeed see that most people who kill themselves in fact do so because of the *absence* of something: life is good unless crippled by severe ill-health, or by the prospect of decline into dementia and lack of control towards the end of their life, for example. And so, to summarize this point, that so few people kill themselves, and that those who do, do so either during stages of immaturity or when they have good reasons to do so (particular reasons not shared by most people during most of their lives), does not support Benatar's claims. Moreover, suicide due to the absence of the good aspects of life goes some way to *support* the goodness of life, showing how life is typically full of good things, while usually it is only the *absence* of such goodness which leads (relatively few) people to take their lives. *If suicide is typically a response to the absence of something good that usually prevails among the common features of life, then this suggests that life tends to be good.*

In itself, the importance of some things in order for people to have a sense that living is worthwhile implies a vulnerability to loss, and therefore opens the door for badness. But when we note the relative rarity of suicide, and see that much of it follows from the absence of things which, for most people, exist and suffice to make life reasonably good, we see that any general claims about the badness of life become quite weak.

### 3. Suicide and not being born:

Benatar reasonably seeks to distinguish wanting not to have been born from wanting to kill oneself. I myself have sought to do so in one context (Smilansky 2007b), when trying to show Bernard Williams's mistake in thinking that if one thinks one's life is worth living then one cannot wish not to have been born. Yet the two are close enough to be worrisome for the idea that life is bad. After all, one indeed does not control whether one was born, but one does almost always control whether one continues living: if life is so bad, the badness can be stopped. So the relative rarity of suicide prima facie indicates that most people are happy enough living, and do not wish to not have been born. Indeed, it does not seem unreasonable to infer that most people thereby affirm that it was fine for their parents to have brought them into existence. There can hardly be a very big problem with having been born if so few people take up the obvious solution to this problem.

Another way of thinking about this concerns risk. If one produces children, then in a sense they come to exist at the mercy of fortune. Yet typically people in economically advanced countries can do a great deal to make it probable that their children will live a good life, and thereby to limit the risks. But alongside this probability there is also the knowledge that if things really work out terribly, there is, almost always, a way out. Death is bad, but some things are worse than death, and in case the gamble of life fails, death too is an option. So taking the risk of generating life seems reasonable, when coupled with the existence of a possible exit strategy. The existence of this option is not painless, yet it limits the moral problem of bringing people into the world, and puts into relief the significance of the relative rarity of taking it.

Of course matters are more complicated. It will not do to reply that, after being alive, people find life gripping and so it is emotionally "too late" for them to end up with the result of not existing. If they find life so gripping, this supports the "pro-goodness" case rather than the evils of having been born. The attachment to others is a stronger point here. Some people indeed find little joy in living, but do not kill themselves because this would greatly sadden their close relatives or friends. Yet even here we must take care: if personal attachments and concern for others prove *so* meaningful and powerful in preventing suicide, then either this adds fuel to the "life is good" stance (since there are things worth living for), or the badness of life which pushes against the force of such concern and towards suicide is not that strong; it is difficult to deny both claims.

Moreover, if this issue would be general and prevail beyond relatively few individuals, then we could expect mass suicides of the closely interconnected: if all members of some circle would see themselves as *victimized by their very existence*, what stops them from liberating themselves from this predicament? Killing themselves *together* will then not leave any of them alone, without their relatives, saddened by the loss. Yet this sort of action – and even the thought of it as a live option, as far as we can tell – seems to be so rare as to be negligible. Nor does Benatar himself seem to recommend it.[1] Some individuals indeed refrain from killing themselves only for the sake of others, but this (a) shows the strength of some of the good things in life (love, friendship and care for close others), (b) is unusual (and not shared by those relatives and friends who do not themselves wish to kill themselves as well), and (c) often happens, as we saw, when there is some *particular* strong, but unusual, reason for doing so.

It also seems significant that there is so little expression of the wish not to have been born, or at least this is so with most people who live under objectively tolerable conditions. If life were so bad, then – even if we bracket the possibility of suicide – we could expect much more expression of the Job-like wish not to have been born, in common sentiments, literature and the like. The idea is culturally available. Yet the sentiment is hardly to be found, except with those who are by temperament unusually melancholy, or are in depression, or, like Job, have some good reason for feeling so.

### 4. The benefits of apparent badness:

Mature people often view hardships and difficulties in their past as challenges that helped them to grow and to make more of their lives: while it would be silly to claim that all bad features of lives turn out to be useful and "worth it", we should also not fall into the opposite trap of seeing every difficulty as a blot upon life. In extreme but not rare cases we might even want to speak of "Fortunate Misfortune" (Smilansky 2007a). Much of what makes life good builds upon what may seem as purely negative. While being denied immediate success may be disappointing, it often builds character, allows for the development of talent, pushes us to improve our performance and become better, and enhances satisfaction and self-respect when things work out. We may fantasize on having our magical wishes supplied by some Genie, but in normal life we are better off without it. This means that many things that look as bad features of life are not so, from a broader perspective, and likewise that many of the frustrations and complaints of life also need not be taken at face value. We saw above that there are

---

1　The claim that on Benatar's view of the badness of life he should call for suicide and not merely for non-procreation has been forcefully made by Elizabeth Harman (2009). I find this line convincing, but have tried to develop other arguments here.

surprising indications that most people are quite happy; it is instructive to note that even when they are not, this may often just be short-sighted.

More broadly, the unhappy are often misperceiving good actual features of their surroundings and condition, missing out on much of the good that is there, passing over cues that the less pessimistic or melancholy are able to catch.[2] Other people do care about them, opportunities are open, and pursuing some goal will prove to be personally worthwhile if done wholeheartedly; life, in short, is good, yet this is not recognized. Likewise, given events or circumstances may be interpreted in different ways, and often it is only if a negative interpretation is chosen that matters will seem grim or unrewarding. So again, it is often not so much that life is bad, but that certain people filter out the goodness.

## 5. Illusion:

Benatar also deploys the counter-claim that, even when people say that they are happy, most of this is but an illusion, a product of irrational bias: "In fact, however, there is very good reason to doubt that these self-assessments are a reliable indicator of a life's quality" (Benatar 2006: 64). Here I think two replies can be made. The first is to cast some doubt over the claim for the extreme prevalence or importance of illusion, as a factor pertinent to our topic. There is admittedly plenty of evidence in social psychology that people over-estimate their abilities, and often hope unreasonably. Unfounded beliefs and superstitions also play a substantial role. Moreover, many people respond to adversity by adaptation, "moving the goal posts" of their aspiration. Benatar does a good job of pointing all this out. So with all this undeniably going on, I will not have a simple, decisive reply. Yet it seems to me that much of what we saw above supports the view that illusion is not, in fact, the dominant factor here. The prevalence of suicide by the irrational (e.g., unstable young people) puts into relief the norm, whereby most people do not do so. And the suicides rather than the rest of us are often those for whom a case of living under illusion would more plausibly be made: love is blind, and love sometimes leads people to kill themselves, while regular life and more calm relationships are less deluded, and only rarely lead people to suicide.[3]

Likewise, the consistent correlation between good personal and social conditions and reports of well-being, e.g., the difference in reported happiness between people in poorer and wealthier countries, indicates that reality matters here a great deal. People tend to be happier when they have good reasons to be so and less happy when they have good reasons to be less happy, and for all its helpfulness, the important role of illusion does not undermine the thought that people can be sensible concerning the goodness and badness of their lives. Recent research in fact seems to have scaled back the sanguine perception among past researchers of the ability of people who have been severely harmed (spinal-cord accident victims or people with multiple or chronic problems) to quickly return to their previously high levels of happiness (Diener 1999: 287).

Moreover, even the (indubitable) role played by illusion should not obviously play into the "anti-goodness" side. Insofar as life tends to be quite good (at least for the mentally stable and moderately healthy, living in well-ordered societies with decent

---

2    The thought that we are not seeing some good features of life, and the effort to uncover them, has been one of the concerns in my philosophical work; see for example Smilansky (1997) and Smilansky (2012).

3    I cannot be accused of being insensitive to the importance of the role of illusion in our lives; see for example Smilansky (2000) and Smilansky (2004).

living conditions) then illusion is much less needed. But where it is needed more urgently, it comes more into play. That seems to me like a good mechanism, which helps life to be as good as it is.

It is too easy to dismiss the positive role of illusion as a factor that actually does make life better. Consider the "Pollyanna Principle" noted by Benatar (2006: 64-69), where people tend towards optimism. Frequently, this *actually makes life better*, for those under its influence. In other words, to the extent that we live in our hopes and dreams, we live well, even if – indeed, because – we are too optimistic. Benatar focuses on this as a way of undermining prevailing human estimates of their well-being, without sufficiently recognizing how the very mechanisms of illusion in fact make life better, overall, for most people.

Similarly for memories of the past: Benatar makes much of studies that consistently indicate that people remember good aspects of their past lives over bad ones (Benatar 2006: 65). But surely this is *good*, if we seek to understand the quality of life: our memories of the past are, after all, important for our present and future well-being! Illusion can be positive: optimism, for example, can be self-fulfilling, leading to a better reality through inducing greater efforts that result in success, which then justifies the initial optimism. There is a large body of research showing that illusion and self-deception are frequently helpful for people (see for example Goleman 1985; Taylor 1989, Taylor and Brown 1994).

Perhaps we are biologically determined to some extent to deceive ourselves about our happiness. But perhaps things go deeper, and we are biologically determined to do as much as we can with difficulty and misfortune, not let them get us down or even turn them to good use. Or perhaps even most of us are simply biologically determined to be quite happy, much of the time, to experience life as good. And even when maintaining the level of happiness requires self-deception, that as well may just be a way for life to be good.

## 6. Value:

So far I have focused, like Benatar, upon happiness. But another and highly significant way in which life can be good concerns value. The very features emphasized by Benatar as making people biased and therefore unreasonably satisfied with their lives arguably push in the direction of making the whole issue of happiness less important (see Liszka 2005). In any case, even where people are not very happy, they can be filled with a sense of the *significance* of their lives, whereby they respect, appreciate and enhance value. Freud famously eschewed painkilling medication at the end of his life in order to be able to think clearly and further his valuable life-project. Many and perhaps most people see room both for happiness and for values (moral goodness, knowledge, beauty, respect), which are not necessarily understood in terms of experiential well-being. Admittedly this may be a source of disappointment, for some people who are otherwise happy may become despondent because they come to have doubts about the meaning of their lives (Benatar 2006: 82ff). Yet this does not in fact seem to make life not worth living for most people. In a way it seems that there are two distinct (if related) paths to the good life – happiness and value (cf. Wolf 1997). I may find great pleasure in watching my favorite team triumph in a football match, but not think that there is any value in the experience; I am just having a good time. On another occasion I may see value in doing things – helping students think more clearly, or helping injured or ill relatives – which in themselves I may not enjoy. This allows people some leeway in living good lives, which will typically combine happiness and value, but could be worth living due to the second, even for those who are deprived of the first.

Albert Camus (1975) famously suggested that the question whether to kill oneself was the most important question a person should confront. Yet in order to confront it, one must already be alive. The potential for existential meaning in one's life is granted only when one has been brought into existence.

It is perhaps especially important in our context to see that value comes forth in procreation. As I have argued elsewhere (Smilansky 1995), continuing the generations may not only make some people happy (say, your parents), but may enhance value in the world. Sometimes there are special circumstances involved. Consider one example: Hitler wanted to eradicate the Jews from the face of the earth, and every Jewish child born is like a finger in his eye, a moral enhancement of value and affirmation that evil has not triumphed. More generally, having children is itself often a contribution in terms of value. One's children might well create value (moral goodness, love, knowledge, beauty), and are very likely to be consumers and appreciators of value. Having children is hence prima facie valuable.

## 7. The future:

The future is shrouded in mystery, yet we can say some things about it, albeit in probabilistic terms rather than with certainty. To the extent that life is bad for reasons inherent to human existence, then it is doubtful how much hope the future holds – although the prospects of genetic modification and the like might hold forth promise even here. But in any case we did not see good reason to feel that life was bad, as distinct from particular lives burdened by individual or social misfortune. If that is indeed the case, then this supports the hope that at least the sources of social misfortune can be overcome, and life may become better in the future. Losing children to disease or hunger, or being persecuted by the secret police serving the dictators who rule over one can indeed make one's life considerably less good, but to the extent that historical tendencies to limit and overcome such evils will prevail, the argument that life is bad will further weaken.

It is instructive that many of the complaints people have over "life" are that life is too short: they want more of what they take to be a good thing. As knowledge and technology progress, the average life span increases, and the goodness of life should increase. That central element of the badness of life which consists of the feeling that there is not enough "living time" should then decrease. There is a question as to what makes death bad. This issue lies beyond my scope, yet note only that at least one of the leading views, according to which the main problem presented by death is its life-depriving aspect (see, e.g., Nagel 1988), does not support Benatar's general view. If the main problem with death is that it deprives the victim of death from more years of living, this suggests that life is good.

Global warming, nuclear escalation and other calamities may prove such optimism wrong, but induction from history supports a modest optimism about the future of humanity, while at the very least showing that there is very little wrong with life as such, that life can be, and often is, good.

## 8. What we should worry about:

So, in Benatarian territory, what *should* we worry about? Not, if I am right, so much about life itself, and – clearly much less than Benatar thinks – about bringing people into this world. But this does not mean that we need not worry about procreative decisions, or about the general situation which procreation produces. The following concerns seem to me to be particularly worth pursuing:

a. Which people are about to be born into more or less hopeless conditions? Singling them out, rather than a general focus on all people who are brought into existence, makes more sense. Difficult questions will need to be asked here, but my point is that in order to do so we need to re-focus away from the general pessimistic Benatarian viewpoint.

b. Anyone who (undeservedly) happens to have a bad life, overall, concerns us, for he or she would have not had it were he or she not born. So there is much to regret in *those* cases, and perhaps even blame accruing to those who brought them into existence. Yet the fact that this badness is not the given lot of humanity opens up possibilities to lower the number of people who will end up as having had bad lives – not through avoiding procreation – and trying to improve the lot of those who have had particularly bad deals in their lives.

c. This brings up the issue of the reasonableness of risk, a topic largely neglected in Benatar's discussion. People take upon themselves considerable physical and emotional risk, in where they live, at what they work, with whom they live, and even with what they do in their leisure time. So the fact that life is full of risk (risk which would not exist were the living not born) does not, in itself, prove much. This issue as well calls for further exploration.

d. Since life is so good for so many, but bad for some, this makes life's goodness as such problematic, as it increases the inequality among people. Inequality is a well-worn topic, yet it receives much of its cosmic sting particularly from the goodness of life.

All these problems are worth discussing further. Yet note that many of them are created not because life is uniformly or even typically bad, but rather because it is often very good. We should all be grateful to David Benatar for forcing us to look more closely at the moral problem of procreation. However, it seems to me that the most philosophically and practically useful ways of doing so might well come out of a more moderate and positive perspective on the goodness of life.[4]

## References

Benatar, David (2006). *Better Never to Have Been.* Oxford: Oxford University Press.

Camus, Albert (1975). *The Myth of Sisyphus.* Justin O'Brien, trans. London: Penguin.

---

4   I am thankful to Thad Metz for the invitation to the conference on David Benatar's work held at the University of Johannesburg in November 2011. I am grateful to David Benatar for his reply to my talk, and to other participants at the conference for their thoughts; as well as to Iddo Landau, Ariel Meirav, Thad Metz, and Daniel Statman, for comments on written drafts of this paper.

Diener, Ed et al. (1999). "Subjective Well-Being: Three Decades of Progress", *Psychological Bulletin* 125: 276-302.

Goleman, Daniel (1985). *Vital Lies, Simple Truths*. New York: Simon & Schuster.

Harman, Elizabeth (2009). "Critical Notice of *Better Never to Have Been*", *Nous* 43: 776-785.

Liszka, James (2005). "Why Happiness is of Marginal Value in Ethical Decision-Making", *Journal of Value Inquiry* 39: 325-344.

Nagel, Thomas (1988). "Death", in *Mortal Questions*. Cambridge: Cambridge University Press.

Smilansky, Saul (1995). "Is There a Moral Obligation to Have Children?", *Journal of Applied Philosophy* 12: 41-53.

Smilansky, Saul (1997). "Should I Be Grateful to You for Not Harming Me?", *Philosophy and Phenomenological Research* 42: 585-597.

Smilansky, Saul (2000). *Free Will and Illusion*. Oxford: Oxford University Press.

Smilansky. Saul (2004). "Terrorism, Justification, and Illusion", *Ethics* 114: 790-805.

Smilansky, Saul (2007a). "Fortunate Misfortune", in *Ten Moral Paradoxes*. Malden: Blackwell Publications.

Smilansky, Saul (2007b). "Preferring Not to Have Been Born", in *Ten Moral Paradoxes*. Malden: Blackwell Publications.

Smilansky, Saul (2012). "On the Common Lament, That a Person Cannot Make Much Difference in This World", *Philosophy* 87: 109-122.

Taylor, Shelley E. (1989). *Positive Illusions*. New York: Basic Books.

Taylor, Shelley E. and Jonathon D. Brown (1994). "Positive Illusions and Well-Being Revisited: Separating Fact From Fiction", *Psychological Bulletin* 116: 21-27.

Wasserman, Danuta et al. (2005). "Global Suicide Rates Among Young People Aged 15-19", *World Psychiatry* 4: 114-120.

Wolf, Susan (1997). "Happiness and Meaning: Two Aspects of the Good Life", *Social Philosophy and Policy* 14: 207-225.

# How Best to Prevent Future Persons from Suffering: A Reply to Benatar[1]

## Brooke Alan Trisel

**Abstract**

David Benatar claims that everyone was seriously harmed by coming into existence. To spare future persons from this suffering, we should cease having children, Benatar argues, with the result that humanity would gradually go extinct. Benatar's claim of universal serious harm is baseless. Each year, an estimated 94% of children born throughout the world do not have a serious birth defect. Furthermore, studies show that most people do not experience chronic pain. Although nearly everyone experiences acute pain and discomforts, such as thirst, these experiences have instrumental value. For example, when a person picks up a hot object, in response to the pain, the person releases the object, thereby preventing serious harm. The standard that Benatar uses to evaluate the quality of our lives is arbitrary, as I will demonstrate. His proposal that we phase humanity out of existence by ceasing to have children is misguided and an overreaction to the problem of human suffering. The 'threshold conception of harm', which is a targeted approach for preventing future persons from suffering, is a more sensible approach.

## 1. Introduction

There are billions of potential people we could bring into existence. How many additional people should we create? 'Zero' is the response given by David Benatar. In his provocative book, Benatar (2006) claims that everyone was seriously harmed by coming into existence. To spare future persons from this suffering, he argues that it would be best if we ceased having children, with the result that humanity would gradually go extinct.

Because the quality of our lives is very bad, Benatar claims, he argues that it is generally, all things considered, morally wrong to procreate. I will dispute both of these claims. I will argue that the quality of our lives, on average, is good according to an objective list account of well-being. This paper will contribute to the literature on this

---

1    Thanks to Thaddeus Metz for helpful comments. Also, thanks to David Benatar and to the other participants at the November 2011 workshop on anti-natalism at the University of Johannesburg for their comments.

topic by demonstrating that pain and discomforts have instrumental value and that we are better off having the capacity to feel pain than we would be without this capacity.

Also, I will point out similarities between Benatar's envisioned ideal world and the idea of heaven, and will demonstrate that such a standard for judging the quality of our lives is arbitrary. Benatar's universal anti-natalism can be thought of as a proposed solution to the problem of human suffering, but this solution is an overreaction to the problem. To prevent future persons from suffering, some philosophers have argued that prospective parents should refrain from bringing a new person into existence unless the life of that new person would be worth living or above some other specified level of well-being – the so-called 'threshold conception of harm'. This view can be thought of as an alternative approach for preventing future persons from suffering. I will argue that this approach makes more sense than universal anti-natalism.

## 2. The 'Procreational Russian Roulette'

Before discussing Benatar's arguments, it is important to provide context for understanding the arguments. Benatar writes: 'procreation is usually the consequence of sex rather than the result of a decision to bring people into existence' (2006: 2). Benatar's claim is substantiated by studies. For example, it is estimated that 49% of all births in the United States (U.S.) in 2001 were unintended (Finer & Henshaw 2006: 90).

Thus, in almost half of these births, new people were brought into existence and no consideration was given to the quality of their lives. Nonetheless, after they entered the world, many of these individuals were embraced, loved, and taken well care of by their parents. In contrast, some new people were born into extreme poverty. Others entered the world infected with HIV or addicted to cocaine. Benatar refers to people's procreational habits as a 'procreational Russian roulette'. The loaded gun is aimed, not at their own heads, 'but at those of their future offspring' (2006: 92).

Although an estimated 51% of the births in the U.S. were intended, this does not necessarily mean that the parents gave any consideration to the quality of life that would be experienced by the future persons. When deciding whether to have a child, sometimes the prospective parents do consider that the future person may be born with a serious congenital disorder, such as Down syndrome. However, when they consider this risk, I suspect that many of them are thinking of how the birth of the child with the disorder would affect the quality of *their own* lives, as opposed to how it would affect the quality of life of the new person.

Over the last forty years, there has been extensive debate regarding whether non-existent future persons have rights and what, if any, obligations we have to future persons. Some philosophers have argued that prospective parents have an obligation to refrain from bringing a child into existence unless the quality of that child's life would be above a certain threshold.[2] For example, Jeff McMahan contends that parents should refrain from bringing a child into existence unless the life of that child would be 'objectively worth living' (1998: 226-228). More recently, Eduardo Rivera-López has proposed a higher threshold by arguing that it is prima facie wrong for prospective parents to bring a child into existence if that child 'will suffer a non-trivial disability or disadvantage, even if we also know that her life will be worth living' (2009: 352).

To spare future persons from suffering, Benatar argues that it would be best not to bring any additional human beings into existence. Those philosophers who support the threshold conception of harm are also seeking a way to prevent future persons from

---

2    For more background on the threshold conception of harm, see Meyer 2010.

suffering. With this targeted approach, prospective parents would refrain from bringing into existence a select group of future persons – those whose lives would not be worth living or who would fall below some other threshold of well-being. This approach is a form of selective anti-natalism, which contrasts with Benatar's universal anti-natalism.

*Some* future persons do experience serious harm by coming into existence and so it is understandable why the threshold conception of harm would be proposed as an approach to prevent suffering. In contrast, Benatar goes well beyond this by arguing that we should voluntarily phase humanity out of existence. As discussed next, Benatar believes that everyone was seriously harmed by coming into existence, not just those who are born with a serious congenital disorder or those who are born into severe poverty.

## 3.   Introducing Benatar's Two Arguments

Benatar makes two independent arguments for his conclusion that it is generally, all things considered, morally wrong to procreate. His first argument, in rough form, is that we seriously harm potential persons by bringing them into existence, but that we do not benefit them in any way. This 'asymmetry argument' will not be discussed here.[3]

Benatar makes a second argument – the one that I will dispute - for his conclusion that we are wrong to procreate and that it would be better if we had never been born. Taking into account the good and bad features of our lives, as well as other factors such as the order of the good and bad in our lives, he claims that everyone was seriously harmed by coming into existence. Because all of our lives are very bad, it is generally wrong, he argues, to bring additional human beings into existence. Benatar paints a gloomy picture of human life. He points out that there are wars, natural disasters, and incidences of murder and starvation throughout the world. He also argues that everyone experiences 'negative mental states daily or more often. These include hunger, thirst, bowel and bladder distention (as these organs become filled), tiredness, stress, thermal discomfort (that is, feeling either too hot or too cold), and itch' (2006: 71).

Despite the pain and discomfort that we experience, most people do not think that their lives are bad, as Benatar acknowledges. On the contrary, they think that their lives 'go quite well' (2006: 64). If our lives are bad, as Benatar contends, then why do most people think that their lives are good? How do we explain this glaring discrepancy? Has one person, namely Benatar, misjudged that all of our lives are bad, as I will argue, or have vast numbers of people from different cultures throughout the world all misjudged that their lives are good, as Benatar argues?

Benatar claims that there are three psychological phenomena that explain these favorable assessments of our lives. He argues that the most influential of these phenomena is a tendency towards optimism – what psychologists refer to as the Pollyanna[4] Principle, unrealistic optimism, or optimistic bias. Benatar points to studies suggesting that people have a tendency to remember positive rather than negative experiences. People ignore or downplay the bad in their lives, Benatar argues.

---

3    Earlier commentators on this argument include Belshaw 2007, Smilansky 2008, Harman 2009, DeGrazia 2010, Spurrett 2011, and Metz 2011.

4    Pollyanna is a child from fictional literature who looked on the bright side of everything, including every misfortune.

Benatar discusses two other psychological phenomena (2006: 67-68), but indicates that they may lead one to overstate or understate the quality of one's life. Thus, Benatar concludes that 'it is only Pollyannaism that inclines people unequivocally towards more positive assessments of how well their life is going' (2006: 68).

Earlier commentators have not challenged Benatar's claim that people have a tendency towards optimism. To convince us that our positive assessments of our lives are inaccurate because of optimistic bias, Benatar relies heavily on psychological studies. It is important that we take a closer look at these studies to see whether the study populations were representative of 'people' in general. Reginald Smart (1966) points out that most psychological studies used college undergraduates as the study population. He also points out that the college population differs considerably from the adult non-college population in many characteristics such as age, social class, and learning ability. In a systematic review of psychological studies that Benatar points to as evidence that 'people' have an optimistic bias, Shelley Taylor and Jonathon Brown do indicate that many studies did find that 'most people' have an optimistic bias. However, they also indicate that 'much of the evidence' for optimistic bias comes from research with college students (1988: 194). Benatar also refers to the book *The Pollyanna Principle* by Margaret Matlin and David Stang. In a study of Pollyannaism by Matlin and Valerie Gawron, they indicate that their study population consisted of 'young, white, middle-class students from Upstate New York and Long Island' (1979b: 412).[5]

Despite earlier warnings from Smart and others about sample selection bias in psychological studies, the problem has persisted.[6] The psychologist Jeffrey Arnett analyzed studies published from 2003 through 2007 in six premier journals of the American Psychological Association. Although the U.S. accounts for less than 5% of the world's population, the study populations were predominantly American, according to Arnett. As part of his analysis, Arnett analyzed the study populations from studies published in the *Journal of Personality and Social Psychology*. He found that 67% of the samples from the American studies, and 80% of the samples from the studies performed in other countries, consisted solely of undergraduate psychology students (2008: 604).

In pointing to research findings discussed by Ronald Inglehart (1990: 243), Benatar notes that self-assessments of happiness vary between countries, but that 'everywhere there is a tendency towards optimism'. (2006: 66). Later research has raised doubt about the universality of optimistic bias.[7] For example, regarding their findings in a cross-cultural study of Canadian and Japanese psychology students, Steven Heine and Darrin Lehman conclude: 'This cultural difference suggests that the "normality" of self-enhancing biases might be specific to Western cultures' (1995: 605).

As demonstrated, because of sample selection bias, the findings from the studies on optimistic bias cannot be generalized to 'people' in general. Furthermore, studies have found that many Japanese students have a pessimistic bias, which is the tendency to expect that negative events are more likely to occur to oneself than to others.[8] For these reasons, the most that can be concluded from the studies of optimistic bias is that many undergraduate psychology students in Western countries have such a bias.

---

5    For additional examples of studies on Pollyannaism by Matlin where undergraduate students were the study population, see Matlin and Stang 1975 and Matlin et al. 1979a.
6    See Peterson 2001, Arnett 2008, and Henrich et al. 2010.
7    See Markus and Kitayama 1991.
8    See, for example, Chang and Asakawa 2003.

### 4.  Why We Are Better Off Having the Capacity to Experience Pain

Benatar purportedly considers the good and bad in our lives in his evaluation of the quality of our lives. However, in his book, there is little discussion of love, family, friendship, aesthetic enrichment, accomplishment, and autonomy – some of the positive features of life that make life worth living.[9] One approach to responding to Benatar's argument would be to provide a more balanced picture by pointing out all of the objective goods in life. Another approach would be to argue, as Elizabeth Harman does, that 'some features of a life are very valuable, and can easily outweigh many mundane discomforts' (2009: 783). Instead of pursuing these approaches, I will dispute Benatar's claim regarding the *amount of bad* in our lives and will do so for the following reason. Most people already recognize the positive features in life. However, very few people realize that many of the experiences that Benatar counts as 'bad', such as acute pain and thirst, are beneficial, as I will demonstrate.

Benatar believes that pain is *intrinsically* bad, meaning that pain is bad 'in itself'.[10] Many people share this view. Are pain and discomforts something that we would be better off without, as most people assume, or do pain and discomforts have an important *instrumental* value, meaning that they have value as a *means* for realizing certain desirable ends?

To help determine whether we would be better off without pain, we can look at a summation of clinical case studies of individuals who experience no pain – those born with the rare condition of 'congenital insensitivity to pain'.[11] It might be thought that these individuals are fortunate to live their lives without pain, but this is far from the truth. Ronald Melzack and Patrick Wall describe the lives of individuals who are born without the ability to feel pain: 'Many of these people sustain extensive burns, bruises and lacerations during childhood, frequently bite deep into the tongue while chewing food, and learn only with difficulty to avoid inflicting severe wounds on themselves' (1996: 3-4).

Elna Nagasako has indicated that 'the observation that these people often die in childhood because they fail to notice injuries and illnesses has been viewed as compelling evidence that the ability to perceive pain has great survival value' (2003: 213). Pain serves three valuable purposes (Melzack and Wall 1996: 3). First, pain alerts a person to the threat of harm. Upon feeling pain, one immediately reacts by avoiding the source of the pain, which prevents serious injury. For example, when one picks up a hot object and feels pain, one reacts by immediately releasing the object, which prevents the object from burning the skin and underlying tissue. When we experience certain types of pain, such as the pain that occurs from touching a hot object, we learn to avoid such experiences in the future, which is a second valuable purpose served by pain. When a person sustains a serious injury, such as a leg fracture, the pain limits the person's activity and promotes a period of rest, which is important for the body's natural repair system to work effectively. This is a third valuable purpose served by pain.

A distinction should be made between acute pain and chronic pain. Acute pain, such as that which occurs by spraining an ankle, has a brief duration. In contrast, chronic pain has a duration of many months and, in some cases, can last for years. Acute pain

---

9   Benatar does include some discussion about meaning in life (2006: 83).

10  A distinction is typically made between the following four types of value: final value, instrumental value, intrinsic value, and extrinsic value. For further discussion, see Korsgaard 1983.

11  This condition has in the past been referred to by various other names such as 'congenital analgesia'. See Nagasako 2003.

has value from a biological perspective whereas chronic pain no longer serves a bio-logically useful purpose. A person who has an arm or leg amputated may continue to experience severe 'phantom' limb pain for years. However, as Melzack and Wall write, they gain 'nothing from the pain. Pain such as this now becomes a problem in its own right' (12). The late philosopher Nikola Grahek (2007), and the renowned physician Paul Brand (1997), had argued that our capacity to feel pain is a gift. How-ever, they were also well aware that pain is a gift that nobody wants. At this point, one might agree that acute pain is valuable for warning us of threats, but think that it would be better if these threat warnings were experienced, not as pain, but as pleasure or some other pain-free sensation. Suppose that the threat warnings were felt, not as pain, but as a mild squeezing sensation. What would occur in this scenario? Many people would ignore the mild squeezing sensations and would be badly injured as a re-sult.[12] Even when the threat warnings are felt as pain, some people ignore them. For example, some athletes who have sustained an injury, and are eager to return to their sport, will play despite the pain, which often delays healing.

If threat warnings were experienced as pleasure, we would not ignore them, but what would happen under this scenario? With our current physiology, when one picks up a hot object, the pain deters one from holding on to the object, which prevents seri-ous harm. If the threat warnings were experienced as pleasure, when one picks up a hot object, the pleasure would provide an incentive to hold on to the hot object as long as possible, with the result that serious harm would occur. As the object burned through more and more tissue, the pleasure would intensify.

One might respond that we, as rational beings, would begin to recognize that plea-sure precedes harm and so, to avoid being harmed, we would try to resist the tempta-tion of pleasure. When we feel pain, we immediately react, without thinking about it, by withdrawing from the source of the pain. If we experienced the threat warnings in the form of pleasure instead of pain, we would not react as quickly. The pain-free warning systems that were examined above would not be nearly as effective in pro-tecting us from harm as the warning system that we have.

As noted earlier, Benatar argues that discomforts such as thirst, feeling too hot or too cold, and the feeling of bladder distention contribute to making our lives bad. Re-garding these discomforts, Harman writes: 'I think these experiences are often neutral or even good' (2009: 782). Harman does not expand on this thought. There is, how-ever, strong scientific support for the belief that these discomforts have instrumental value. These discomforts *alert* a person to a threat to his or her body. For example, if one did not feel bladder fullness, the bladder would continue to fill with urine and eventually rupture, with the result that urine – a waste product - would leak into areas of the body where it can cause serious harm.[13] Of all the discomforts that we experi-ence, we should perhaps be the most grateful for the feeling of thirst. Michael McKin-ley and Alan Johnson write: 'Thirst is a subjective perception that provides the urge for human and animals to drink fluids. It is a component of the regulatory mechanisms that maintain body fluid homeostasis and ultimately is essential for survival' (2004: 1).

Homeostasis refers to the ability of the human body to maintain a relatively constant internal environment - which is needed for cells to function properly - despite poten-

---

12   Brand (1997: 191-197), who treated patients who lacked the ability to feel pain, attempted to devise 'a practical substitute for pain' that would alert his patients to threats. This warning system consisted of artificial sensors that would trigger a piercing sound or blinking lights. Brand indicates that the patients simply ignored or manually interrupted this warning system.
13   See Parker et al. 2009.

tially large fluctuations in the external environment. Benatar argues that feeling too hold or too cold contribute to the bad in our lives. One way that the body maintains homeostasis is by providing us with feedback. When one feels too hot or too cold, one adjusts to this feedback by, for example, sitting in the shade when it is hot or putting on a coat when it is cold. Thus, the feedback, in the form of thermal discomfort, is of critical importance for helping to protect us from serious harm.[14]

After reading *Better Never to Have Been*, one might assume that the quality of our lives would be much better if we were unable to experience pain or discomforts. However, this is a false assumption, as demonstrated above. Because acute pain and discomforts are essential for protecting us from serious harm, the quality of our lives, on the whole, could not be much better than what it is today. In the next section, I will argue that the quality of our lives is high enough such that it will often be morally permissible for prospective parents to bring a new person into existence.

## 5. Do the Benefits to Parents Outweigh the Potential Harm to Future Persons?

Despite his anti-natalism, Benatar acknowledges that having children can yield benefits to the parents of the new person and to other people. He notes that parents find fulfillment in raising children, that children are an insurance policy for old age, and that children provide parents with quasi-immortality (1997: 351; 2006: 88, 98).[15] Because he understands the benefits to parents and others from procreating, he also recognizes that his proposal for a phased extinction would be detrimental to some existent people. For example, in discussing the question of how quickly extinction should occur, he writes: 'in some situations failing to bring people into existence can make the lives of existent people a lot worse than they would otherwise have been' (2006: 184). Benatar has indicated that: 'One way, then, to defend the having of children, even if one accepts my view that existence is a harm, is to deny that that harm is great. One could then argue that the harm is outweighed by the benefits to the parents' (1997: 351).

It is undeniable that serious congenital anomalies are harmful to persons coming into existence. However, in assessing *how much* harm is experienced by new persons, we must ask ourselves the following question. What percentage of new persons have a serious congenital anomaly? The geneticist Arnold Christianson et al. estimate that, each year, 6% of children born throughout the world have a serious birth defect (2006: 2). Regarding Benatar's claim that everyone is seriously harmed by coming into existence, if the 6% figure is correct, then this indicates that 94% of new people do not have a serious birth defect. Furthermore, many children throughout the world are born into good conditions, are well cared for by their parents, and never experience serious harm in their lives.

In contrast to acute pain, chronic or persistent pain has no instrumental value. A World Health Organization study found that 22% of primary care patients experienced persistent pain in the prior year.[16] In other words, 78% of the primary care patients in the study did not experience persistent pain in the prior year.

---

14   For a discussion of thermoregulation, see Blatteis 1998.

15   For discussion of whether there is a duty to procreate and how having children can enrich our lives, see Smilansky 1995 and Spurrett 2011.

16   Gureje et al. 1998. Persistent pain was defined as pain that was present most of the time for six months or more during the prior year. The study was conducted at 15 centers throughout the world. Other studies may report lower or higher percentages of people who experience chronic pain. There are often in-

Serious birth defects and chronic pain are bad, but most people do not experience these problems. Furthermore, as demonstrated earlier, we are better off having the capacity to experience acute pain and discomforts than we would be without this capacity. As mentioned, individuals who are born without the capacity to feel pain often die during childhood. Benatar asserts that everyone was seriously harmed by coming into existence, but an examination of this claim has revealed that it is baseless. For Benatar to conclude that everyone was seriously harmed, he must be conceiving of 'serious harm' in a very broad and unusual way. If a person who experiences nothing more than common pains and discomforts would file a 'wrongful life' lawsuit and claim that he had been seriously harmed by being brought into existence, the lawsuit would be dismissed for being unfounded and frivolous. The judge would rightly wonder 'Where is the alleged serious harm?'

If the quality of our lives is very bad, as Benatar claims, then it would be difficult to imagine that they could be worse. However, we can easily imagine that the quality of our lives could be *much worse*. We could live in caves and be without the modern conveniences that we take for granted, such as clean running water and electrically powered lights. We could spend all of our time hunting for food and not have time to pursue other interests. We could be without antibiotics and other medicines to fight disease. We could have an average life expectancy of 25 years and children could go without a decent education.

As suggested, the quality of our lives is much better than that of our distant ancestors. We are fortunate to be living at a time in human history where the quality of life is good for large numbers of people.

Because Benatar overstates how many people are harmed by coming into existence, the argument that the benefits to parents (and others) from having children outweigh the potential harm to new persons is much stronger than Benatar had assumed. In many instances, the benefits to prospective parents from having a child will outweigh the potential harm to the new person.

## 6.   The Desire for Heaven on Earth

Pessimists and religious apologists often disagree about whether God exists. However, there is one thing that pessimists and some religious apologists have in common. They both use unreasonable (i.e., extreme and unfair) standards. Some religious apologists claim, for example, that life is meaningless or is not 'truly' meaningful unless God exists and there is everlasting bliss in heaven.[17] There is a striking similarity between Benatar's envisioned ideal world, in which there are human beings but no suffering, and the idea of heaven, as I will show.

According to Colleen McDannell and Bernhard Lang (2001), there are two accounts of heaven, one that is anthropocentric and one that is theocentric. In the theocentric account, heaven is God-oriented and is the timeless experience of contemplating the greatness of God. In contrast, heaven, in the anthropocentric account, is people-oriented. Jerry Walls, a philosopher of religion, writes: 'There the emphasis is upon being reunited with family and friends. In its most fully developed version, heaven is essentially like this life, without, of course, the evil and suffering that mar our present

---

consistencies in how chronic pain is defined and measured, which may explain some of the variation in the findings across studies.

17   Metz (2009: 192) argues that the desire for perfection underlies the standards adopted by proponents of supernaturalism about life's meaning.

happiness' (2002: 7). According to Revelation 21.4 of the Bible (NRSV), 'Death will be no more; mourning and crying and pain will be no more. . .'.

Thus, in the anthropocentric view of heaven, the idea that there will be human beings, but without suffering is a prominent feature. In the ideal world envisioned by Benatar, human beings are also without suffering. Another prominent feature of the idea of heaven is that one's existence in heaven is *everlasting*. Benatar argues that 'Coming into existence is bad in part because it invariably leads to the harm of ceasing to exist' (2006: 213). Thus, Benatar's standard for judging whether a life is worth starting seems to demand that life be everlasting. If it were not everlasting, then the harm of ceasing to exist would occur, which would mean that the person's life would not have been worth starting.

The idea of heaven has been fading. As McDannell and Lang explain: 'The modern heaven . . . has become the minority perspective during the twentieth century. Rich and detailed accounts of the afterlife, accepted in the nineteenth century, are labelled as absurd, crude, materialistic, or sheer nonsense' (322). Walls attempts to resurrect the idea of heaven. He is concerned that because the universe may end billions of years from now that this somehow makes our lives pointless. He writes: 'If the universe will conclude in this fashion, everything can finally seem pointless' (175).[18]

Benatar makes a useful distinction between whether a life is worth starting and whether a life is worth continuing (2000: 176; 2006: 22). He argues that a higher standard should be used to judge whether future lives are worth starting than should be used to judge whether our lives are worth continuing (2006: 213). Our lives are very bad, he argues, but they might not be so bad that we should seek to end our lives.

Benatar argues, in the context of the 'asymmetry' rationale, that even a small amount of bad would make a future person's life not worth starting (2006: 48). Thus, according to Benatar's standard, perfection, in the form of the complete absence of any amount of bad, is required for a life to be worth starting. Once started, for a person's life to be 'good', it would have to be better than the lives of nearly everyone in existence today. Benatar claims that high quality lives are 'exceedingly uncommon' (2006: 92).

There is nothing wrong with having a desire for a post-life heaven or a desire to live our current lives everlastingly and without any bad in them – a heaven on Earth. However, as I will argue in the following section, it is inappropriate to turn these desires into standards for judging whether life is meaningful (as Walls does) or whether future lives are worth starting (as Benatar does).

## 7.  Benatar's Arbitrary Standard

Benatar argues that it is sometimes appropriate to appeal to a human perspective when making certain kinds of judgments, such as those related to distributive justice (2006: 86). However, he argues that it is more appropriate to assess the quality of our lives *sub specie aeternitatis* or from the point of view of the universe.[19] This latter phrase, which originated with Henry Sidgwick, is a bit misleading because, if taken literally, it suggests that the universe has a perspective independent of sentient beings. Without sentient beings, the universe would not have a perspective. What Benatar means by 'perspective of the universe' is that *we* can view ourselves from a detached external

---

18   In Trisel (2002) and (2004), I respond to this argument.
19   In response, Metz (2011: 252-253) argues that the human perspective would be what is most likely to have enabled human beings to evolve and hence to have grounded value judgments.

standpoint – one that encompasses times long before humanity existed and long after humanity will be extinct. From this objective view, our lives are meaningless, Benatar argues (2006: 83).

In trying to convince us that our lives are very bad, Benatar argues that human beings endure a period of frustration before fulfilling a desire. He writes: 'It is logically possible for desires to be fulfilled very soon after they arise, but given the way the world is, this does not usually happen' (2006: 74-75). Also, he indicates: 'From the human perspective, what we take to be worthwhile is very much determined by the limits of what we can expect. For instance, since none of us lives until age 240, people tend not to think that failing to reach that age makes one's life go less well' (2006: 82). Benatar indicates that 'Perhaps the good life is something that is impossible to attain. It certainly sounds as though a life that is devoid of any discomfort, pain, suffering, distress, stress, anxiety, frustration, and boredom, that lasts for much longer than ninety years . . . would be better than the sort of life the luckiest humans have' (2006: 82).

Standards must be context specific. Benatar considers and rejects this possible objection to his argument that we should judge the quality of our lives *sub specie aeternitatis*. He argues that 'we sometimes do and should judge the brightest people by supra-human standards' (2006: 86). However, he fails to provide any examples where this has occurred. Furthermore, even if this has occurred, it does not necessarily mean that it was appropriate.

### The Extreme Standard

Benatar does not explicitly outline a standard for judging the quality of our lives, but based on his comments, his standard is as high as, if not higher than, the following Extreme (E) standard:

(E) A human's life is good only if: (1) there is no pain or negative mental states; (2) one's desires, as they arise, are fulfilled in 15 minutes or less; and (3) one will have a lifespan of at least 240 years.[20]

If one adopts such an extreme standard, then one will conclude that the quality of our lives is very bad. This raises the question of whether it is appropriate to adopt such a high standard. Should we should assess the quality of our lives based on what is logically possible, as Benatar does, or based on what is nomologically (i.e., physically) possible given the actual laws and limitations of the universe? An outcome might be logically possible, but physically impossible. For example, suppose a person has a desire to become a renowned novelist. To avoid any frustration in fulfilling this desire, she hopes to achieve the goal in five minutes. However, before doing so, she must think of an interesting story, write her novel, find a publisher, and then have it read by people – all in a matter of five minutes. This would be physically impossible. There are limits on how quickly a person can think and write.

Although we can *imagine* a world that is devoid of frustration, stress, pain, and discomforts, it would be inappropriate to judge the quality of our lives by that standard. Standards must be based on what is nomologically possible, not on logically possible, but nomologically impossible, conditions. When standards are based on logically pos-

20  I have not sought to include all of the values/disvalues that might be included in a standard. I selected three that were discussed by Benatar: absence of pain, desire fulfillment, and length of life.

sible, but nomologically impossible, conditions, arbitrariness is the result, as I will demonstrate.

### The Super Extreme Standard

In what follows, I will be comparing the Extreme standard to two other standards. Suppose that someone proposes the following Super Extreme (SE) standard:

(SE) A human's life is good only if: (1) there is no pain or negative mental states; (2) one's desires, as they arise, are fulfilled in a minute or less; and (3) one will have a lifespan of at least 50,000 years.

Of the Extreme and Super Extreme standards, which one is more appropriate to judge the quality of our lives? Both of the standards are logically possible, but nomologically impossible, given the known actual laws of the universe. *Without being grounded in the context of what is nomologically possible,* there is no way to determine which of these standards is more appropriate than the other, which is what I mean when I indicate that the standards become *arbitrary.* One might try to argue that the Extreme standard is more appropriate because it is not as far out of our reach as the Super Extreme standard, but this would be invoking the concept of nomological possibility.

Because the Extreme and Super Extreme standards disregard the actual laws of the universe, they end up being arbitrary and simply reflect the personal preferences of various individuals. Thus, the standards become arbitrary and relative.

### The Perfection Standard

If the standard for assessing the quality of our lives is based on logically possible, but nomologically impossible, conditions, then whatever a person happens to desire, no matter how outlandish, could be proposed as a standard for judging the quality of our lives, as long as it was logically possible. For example, one might propose the following Perfection (P) standard.

(P) A human's life is good only if: (1) there is no pain or negative mental states; (2) one's desires, as they arise, are fulfilled instantaneously; and (3) one will live forever.

As argued earlier, Benatar uses the Perfection standard to assess whether the lives of *future persons* are worth starting. If a person proposed that the Perfection standard should be used to judge the quality of *our lives,* Benatar would have no basis on which to argue that the Extreme or Super Extreme standards are more appropriate than the Perfection standard. As shown, standards which are logically possible, but nomologically impossible, become arbitrary and relative.

As argued, Benatar's standard for judging the quality of *our lives* is at least as high as the Extreme standard. His standard may be as high as the Perfection standard. If he uses the Perfection standard to judge the quality of our lives, then this would be inconsistent with maintaining that a higher standard should be used to judge whether life is worth starting than whether life is worth continuing.

It is logically possible for a species with advanced physical and intellectual capabilities to exist on another planet. Benatar would argue that we should compare the quality of our lives to their lives and that our lives, in comparison, are very bad. Benatar suggests that context matters for some judgments, but not for those related to quality of life (2006: 84-86). Context-free standards become arbitrary. Why compare our lives to the Advanced species? Rather, why not compare our lives to the lives of moles? Moles live underground in tunnels and in solitude. Compared to moles, human beings are extremely intelligent, live long lives, and have a very high quality of life. If context is irrelevant, as Benatar suggests, then judging the quality of human lives based on a comparison with moles *would be appropriate*.

Benatar might argue that it is more appropriate to compare our lives to the Advanced species than to moles, but on what basis? If he argued that our lives are more similar to the Advanced species than to moles, then he would be appealing to context, which would contradict his claim that context is irrelevant. Context is relevant, which explains why we must judge the quality of our lives using human standards.

Benatar judges the quality of our lives based on a *combination* of what is logically possible and from *sub specie aeternitatis*. Is it appropriate to include the totality of what is logically possible as part of *sub specie aeternitatis?* This is unclear. Suppose that we view ourselves from an external standpoint, as if we are looking down on Earth from the Hubble telescope. From this standpoint, our view reflects, not the totality of what was logically possible, but what actually unfolded according to the laws of the universe and what could unfold in the future according to those same laws.

Thomas Nagel's *The View From Nowhere* (1986) is the best known contemporary work regarding the external perspective. In that work, he discusses the capacity of an individual to transcend his or her own 'particular point of view and to conceive of the world as a whole' (3). Thus, Nagel does not refer to all logically possible events or worlds, but to *the world*. Based on this and other comments,[21] it does not appear that Nagel includes the totality of what is logically possible as part of the external perspective, which suggests that philosophers might be conceiving of *sub specie aeternitatis* in different ways. This topic merits further examination in the future.

## 8.  Concluding Remarks

There is a lively debate among demographers regarding whether we are approaching a limit on life expectancy.[22] If we are nearing a limit on life expectancy, then this raises the following question. Taking into account what is nomologically possible, how much better could the quality of our lives be than what they are today? We might find better treatments for some diseases. Also, through lifestyle changes, such as exercising more, we might be able to prevent some chronic diseases and some chronic pain. However, as living organisms, we will still be vulnerable to disease, injury, stress, and natural disasters. Furthermore, even if we could do so through genetic engineering, it would be unwise for us to eliminate our capacity to experience acute pain and discomforts.

Of course, one way to increase the average quality of life for people throughout the world would be to focus on improving the lives of people who have a below average quality of life. Improving the quality of their lives would be physically possible. But could the lives of people who have a high quality of life be much better than what they are today? Based on what is nomologically possible, there is not much room for improvement in the quality of their lives. Future persons could not have a much higher quality of life than a person of today who has a high quality life.

---

21   See also pp. 4-9, 210, 212, and 216.
22   See Olshansky et al. (2001 and 2005) and Oeppen and Vaupel (2002).

Although I have been critical of Benatar's views, I respect his work. Benatar's book is important for challenging us to reflect more deeply about why we have children and for bringing attention to current procreational practices that sometimes harm new people. Regarding the question posed in this essay of what is the best approach for preventing future persons from suffering, Benatar would argue that, because the quality of our lives is very bad, the best approach is to not bring any more children into the world. However, as I have demonstrated, Benatar uses an arbitrary and, therefore, inappropriate standard to assess the quality of our lives. In taking into account what is nomologically possible, the quality of our lives, on average, is good from an objective list account of well-being. Universal anti-natalism is an overreaction to the problem of human suffering.

Benatar's recommendation that people stop having children will likely be ignored, as he predicted (2006: 225). Consequently, it is not a viable option for preventing future persons from suffering. Even if it were a viable option, it would not be the best option. The threshold conception of harm is a more sensible approach for preventing future persons from suffering.

## References

Arnett, J. 2008. 'The Neglected 95%: Why American Psychology Needs to Become Less American', *American Psychologist* 63(7), 602-614.

Belshaw, C. 2007. 'Better Never to Have Been: The Harm of Coming into Existence', *Notre Dame Philosophical Reviews*. http://ndpr.nd.edu/review.cfm?id=9983. Accessed May 6, 2011.

Benatar, D. 1997. 'Why It is Better Never to Come into Existence', *American Philosophical Quarterly* 34(3), 345-355.

Benatar, D. 2000. 'The Wrong of Wrongful Life', *American Philosophical Quarterly* 37(2), 175-183.

Benatar, D. 2006. *Better Never to Have Been: The Harm of Coming into Existence*. Oxford: Clarendon Press.

Blatteis, C. (ed.) 1998. *Physiology and Pathophysiology of Temperature Regulation*. London: World Scientific Publishing Co.

Brand, P. & Yancey, P. 1997. *The Gift of Pain*. Grand Rapids, MI.: Zondervan.

Chang, E. & Asakawa, K. 2003. 'Cultural Variations on Optimistic and Pessimistic Bias for Self Versus a Sibling: Is There Evidence for Self-Enhancement in the West and for Self-Criticism in the East When the Referent Group is Specified?', *Journal of Personality and Social Psychology* 84(3) 569-581.

Christianson, A., Howson, C., & Modell, B. 2006. *March of Dimes Global Report on Birth Defects: The Hidden Toll of Dying and Disabled Children*. White Plains, N.Y.: March of Dimes Birth Defects Foundation. http://marchofdimes.com/downloads/Birth_Defects_Report-PF.pdf. Accessed July 3, 2011.

DeGrazia, D. 2010. 'Is it Wrong to Impose the Harms of Human Life?: A Reply to Benatar', *Theoretical Medicine and Bioethics* 31, 317-331.

Finer, L. & Henshaw, S. 2006. 'Disparities in Rates of Unintended Pregnancy in the United States, 1994 and 2001', *Perspectives on Sexual and Reproductive Health* 38(2), 90-96.

Grahek, N. 2007. (2nd ed.) *Feeling Pain and Being in Pain*. Cambridge: MIT Press.

Gureje, O., Von Korff, M., Simon, G., & Gater, R. 1998. 'Persistent Pain and Well-Being', *JAMA* 280(2), 147-151.

Harman, E. 2009. 'Critical Study. David Benatar. *Better Never to Have Been: The Harm of Coming into Existence*', *Nous* 43(4) 776-785.

Heine, S. & Lehman, D. 1995. 'Cultural Variation in Unrealistic Optimism: Does the West Feel More Invulnerable Than the East?', *Journal of Personality and Social Psychology* 68(4), 595-607.

Henrich, J., Heine, S., & Norenzayan, A. 2010. 'The Weirdest People in the World?', *Behavioral and Brain Sciences* 33(2/3), 1-75.

Inglehart, R. 1990. *Culture Shift in Advanced Industrial Society*. Princeton: Princeton University Press.

Korsgaard, C. 1983. 'Two Distinctions in Goodness', *The Philosophical Review* 92(2), 169-195.

Markus, H. & Kitayama, S. 1991. 'Culture and the Self: Implications for Cognition, Emotion, and Motivation', *Psychological Review* 98(2), 224-253.

Matlin, M. & Stang, D. 1975. 'Some Determinants of Word-Frequency Estimates', *Perceptual and Motor Skills* 40(3), 923-929.

Matlin, M. & Stang, D. 1978. *The Pollyanna Principle: Selectivity in Language, Memory and Thought*. Cambridge MA: Schenkman Publishing.

Matlin, M., Stang, D., Gawron, V., Freedman, A., & Derby, P. 1979a. 'Evaluative Meaning as a Determinant of Spew Position', *The Journal of General Psychology* 100, 3-11.

Matlin, M. & Gawron, V. 1979b. 'Individual Differences in Pollyannaism', *Journal of Personality Assessment* 43(4), 411-412.

McDannell, C. & Lang, B. 2001. (2nd ed.) *Heaven: A History*. New Haven: Yale University Press.

McKinley, M. & Johnson, A. 2004. 'The Physiological Regulation of Thirst and Fluid Intake', *News in Physiological Sciences* 19, 1-6.

McMahan, J. 1998. 'Wrongful Life: Paradoxes in the Morality of Causing People to Exist' in *Rational Commitment and Social Justice: Essays for Gregory Kavka*, ed. J. Coleman. Cambridge: Cambridge University Press, 208-247.

Melzack, R. & Wall, P. 1996. (2nd ed.) *The Challenge of Pain*. London: Penguin Books. Originally published 1982.

Metz, T. 2009. 'Imperfection as Sufficient for a Meaningful Life: How Much is Enough?' in *New Waves in Philosophy of Religion*, ed. Y. Nagasawa & E. Wielenberg. New York: Palgrave Macmillan, 192-214.

Metz, T. 2011. 'Are Lives Worth Creating?', *Philosophical Papers* 40(2), 233-255.

Meyer, L. 2010. 'Intergenerational Justice' in *The Stanford Encyclopedia of Philosophy*, ed. E. Zalta. http://plato.stanford.edu/archives/spr2010/entries/justice-intergenerational/.

Nagasako, E., Oaklander, A., & Dworkin, R. 2003. 'Congenital Insensitivity to Pain: An Update', *Pain* 101(3), 213-219.

Nagel, T. 1986. *The View From Nowhere*. Oxford: Oxford University Press.

Oeppen, J., Vaupel, J. 2002. 'Broken Limits to Life Expectancy', *Science* 296(5570), 1029-1031.

Olshansky, S. J., Carnes, B., Désesquelles, A., 2001. 'Prospects for Human Longevity', *Science* 291(5508), 1491-1492.

Olshansky, S. J., Passaro, D., Hershow, R., Layden, J., Carnes, B., Brody, J., Hayflick, L., Butler, R., Allison, D., & Ludwig, D., 2005. 'A Potential Decline in Life Expectancy in the United States in the 21st Century', *The New England Journal of Medicine* 352(11), 1138-1145.

Parker, H., Hoonpongsimanont, W., Vaca, F., & Lotfipour, S. 2009. 'Spontaneous Bladder Rupture in Association with Alcoholic Binge: A Case Report and Review of the Literature', *The Journal of Emergency Medicine* 37(4) 386-389.

Peterson, R. 2001. 'On the Use of College Students in Social Science Research: Insights from a Second-Order Meta-analysis', *Journal of Consumer Research* 28, 450-461.

Rivera-López, E. 2009. 'Individual Procreative Responsibility and the Non-Identity Problem', *Pacific Philosophical Quarterly* 90, 336-363.

Smart, R. 1966. 'Subject Selection Bias in Psychological Research', *Canadian Psychology* 7a(2), 115- 121.

Smilansky, S. 1995. 'Is There a Moral Obligation to Have Children?', *Journal of Applied Philosophy* 12(1), 41-53.

Smilansky, S. 2008. 'Better Never to Have Been: The Harm of Coming into Existence. By David Benatar', *The Philosophical Quarterly* 58(232), 569-571.

Spurrett, D. 2011. 'Hooray for Babies', *South African Journal of Philosophy* 30(2), 197-206.

Swenson, W. 1980. 'Sample Selection Bias in Clinical Research', *Psychosomatics* 21(4), 291-292.

Taylor, S. & Brown, J. 1988. 'Illusion and Well-Being: A Social Psychological Perspective on Mental Health', *Psychological Bulletin* 103(2), 193-210.

Trisel, B.A., 2002. 'Futility and the Meaning of Life Debate', *Sorites* 14, 70-84.

Trisel, B.A., 2004. 'Human Extinction and the Value of Our Efforts', *The Philosophical Forum* 35(3), 371-391.

Walls, J. 2002. *Heaven: The Logic of Eternal Joy*. Oxford: Oxford University Press.

# Antinatalism, Asymmetry, and an Ethic of *Prima Facie* Duties[1]

## Gerald Harrison

**Abstract**

Benatar's central argument for antinatalism develops an asymmetry between the pain and pleasure in a potential life. I am going to present an alternative route to the antinatalist conclusion. I argue that duties require victims and that as a result there is no duty to create the pleasures contained within a prospective life but a duty not to create any of its sufferings. My argument can supplement Benatar's, but it also enjoys some advantages: it achieves a better fit with our intuitions; it does not require us to acknowledge that life is a harm, or that a world devoid of life is a good thing; and it is easy to see why it does not have any pro-mortalist implications.

Benatar (2006) believes that virtually all procreative acts are morally wrong. So do I. However, I arrive at this conclusion via a different route. I argue that duties require victims. As such, we have a duty not to create the suffering contained in any prospective life but we do not have a duty to create the pleasures contained in any prospective life.

My argument is capable of complementing Benatar's, but it does not entail it and enjoys some advantages over it. For instance, Benatar's central case depends on showing that coming into existence is always a harm: a difficult pill to swallow. But my argument shows procreation to be wrong even if being brought into existence confers a considerable benefit to the individual brought into existence.

Benatar wants to respect our intuition that we do nothing wrong in omitting to procreate. However, most of us have the intuition that omitting to procreate is not wrong even if most lives are a benefit to those subject to them (for after all, most people *do* think that lives are a benefit to those subject to them). Benatar, by arguing that we substantially harm anyone we bring into existence, provides us with a *new* reason to think that one does nothing wrong in not procreating. But he does not provide an account of how there could be nothing wrong in not procreating *even if the life one would create*

---

1    Thanks to Thaddeus Metz for comments on an earlier draft and to the other contributors to this volume for their comments on a version of this paper delivered at the antinatalism workshop (University of Johannesburg, 23-24 November 2011).

*would be of great benefit to the exister.* My view does. Finally, my view makes it very clear why suicide is neither obligatory nor supererogatory.[2]

## I.

Benatar argues that there is an important asymmetry between pleasures and pains: a state of affairs in which no pain is being suffered is good, however a state of affairs in which no pleasure is being experienced is not bad unless there is someone for whom the absence of pleasure is a deprivation.

The main support that Benatar gives for this asymmetry is that it explains our intuitions about a range of other cases, the most important being the common-sense moral view that "while there is a duty to avoid bringing suffering people into existence, there is no duty to bring happy people into being" (2006, p. 32; see also McMahan 2002, p. 300). Creating a suffering person would create some pain, and that is bad. But there is no positive duty to create a predominantly pleasurable life, because even though the pleasure it contains would be good if it existed, absent pleasure is not bad unless there is someone for whom it is a deprivation. So if one does not create a life, even a life that one knows for sure will contain more pleasure than pain, one does nothing wrong.

In fact, it is positively wrong to create even a pleasurable life. Even a pleasurable life will contain some suffering. The suffering, if created, would be bad. The absence of the suffering would, however, be good. This is the kernel of Benatar's main case against procreation: non-existence avoids creating any suffering, and so that is good. Non-existence also avoids creating any pleasure, but that is not bad (because absent pleasure is not bad unless it is bad for someone). Thus, non-existence is preferable to existence.

Many find Benatar's asymmetry thesis difficult to accept. "Yes", they will say, "it may well be that absent pleasure is not bad unless there is someone for whom it is a deprivation. But by the same token, absent pain is not good either unless there is someone who benefits by its absence. Similarly though pain is bad when someone is suffering it, pleasure is good when someone is enjoying it. As most lives contain far more pleasurable experiences than painful ones, coming into existence is not a harm: quite the reverse, it is a considerable benefit over non-existence". Alternatively, some might prefer to concede that absent pain is good even when there is no one for whom it is good, but will tmaintain that absent pleasure is bad even when there is no one for whom it is bad.

Anyone who responds like this has to find an alternative explanation for our moral judgements in the wretched life/pleasant life cases. They will have to explain why we must not create lives that will be characterised by great suffering, yet do nothing wrong if we neglect to create lives that will be characterised by great pleasure.

I believe there is an intuitively attractive alternative explanation available if we look to the *prima facie* duty ethical framework and focus on a plausible feature of the concept of duty: that duties presuppose victims.

## II.

The term "*prima facie* duty" was coined by W. D. Ross to refer to a type of action that has a tendency to be right, other things being equal ([1930] 1988, pp. 19-20). Any number of *prima facie* duties can apply to a particular situation, and they can and will

---

2    Benatar's view is often thought to have pro-mortalist implications (see McGregor and Sullivan Bissett in this issue of the journal).

often conflict. When *prima facie* duties conflict, we must judge which consideration trumps. The point about *prima facie* duties is that they "are analogous to 'forces' that pull an action towards rightness or wrongness" (Huemer 2005, pp. 203-204). In the absence of an opposing force – an opposing *prima facie* duty – then the action is pulled all the way to rightness or wrongness.

The list of our *prima facie* duties is a matter of debate. But that need not concern us too much, for in what follows I will focus on some of the most plausible and very general *prima facie* duties.

The objective is to provide a pleasing alternative explanation for our intuition that it is wrong to create suffering people, but not wrong to omit to create happy people. To this end consider two highly plausible *prima facie* duties: the *prima facie* duty to prevent suffering, and the *prima facie* duty to promote pleasure.

The *prima facie* duty to prevent suffering explains why it would be wrong, other things being equal, to create suffering people.[3] Creating a suffering person would be to create some suffering: suffering we have a *prima facie* duty to prevent. To explain why we have no duty to create happy people consider a plausible conceptual claim about duties in general: duties presuppose victims. One can only have a duty to do X, if failing to do X would wrong someone. In other words if one cannot identify some-one who would be wronged by one's failure to fulfil the supposed *prima facie* duty, then the duty does not exist.[4] If this is true (and I will defend it against some objec-tions shortly) then the *prima facie* duty to promote pleasure does *not* generate a duty to create happy people. Why? There is no victim if one does not create a happy person. The happy person who would have been created has not been left frustrated and de-prived in some anteroom to existence. He or she does not exist, never did exist, and never will exist. Without victims who exist, or did exist, or will exist, there can be no duty: and thus there is no duty to create happy people. Compare this with cases of suf-fering people. Preventing suffering is a *prima facie* duty and it generates a duty not to create suffering people, for if one fails to fulfil this duty then there is a victim: the miserable person one created.

So, if duties require victims in the event of non-performance, we can explain why there is a duty not to create suffering people, and why there is no duty to create happy people. Benatar's alternative explanation is that there is a duty not to create happy lives because contrary to most people's assumption, doing so positively harms those who are brought into existence. But mine has the advantage of explaining why we have no duty to create happy people *even if doing so would greatly benefit those we create*. As I suspect most people have the intuition that we have no duty to create

---

3    For the sake of simplicity I am focussing on suffering. But the suffering contained within a life is not all that is objectionable in it.

4    It might be objected that such a claim is obviously false, as there are plenty of cases in which no one has been wronged, yet a wrong has been committed. For instance, the assassin who mistakenly shoots a wax replica of his target in the belief that it is really her. In such a case no one has been wronged, yet intuitively we do not want to let the assassin off the hook. The first point that can be made here is to draw on the distinction between something being bad, and something being wrong. The assassin did noting wrong, but his act was bad as it proceeded from bad motives. The second point is that though no actual wrong was committed this does not mean that the assassin is any less blameworthy for his deed. For what is required for blameworthiness is not 'actual' wrongdoing, but just subjective wrongdoing. If the agent intended to do something that would have been actually wrong had he successfully done it, then the agent is fully blameworthy even though he did not do anything wrong (see Haji 2002 for such an account).

happy people even on the assumption that doing so would greatly benefit them, my explanation has an intuitive edge over Benatar's. So there we have it: the *prima facie* duty view combined with a plausible-sounding claim about duties (that they presuppose victims in the event of non-performance) can get us the result we want.

Nevertheless, it might be objected that my central claim, that duties presuppose victims in the event of non-performance, is false. There are some wrongs that do not seem to wrong anyone. For instance, destroying all the vegetation on a small isolated island in the middle of nowhere seems wrong, even if it is clear that no one is going to be in any way harmed. If one has wronged someone, one is not entitled to his forgiveness, yet it is plausible that there is a duty to forgive. If that is right, then this would seem to be a duty that has no victim in the event of non-performance. Finally, perhaps there is a *prima facie* duty to create good states of affairs. Failing to create a good state of affairs need not involve wronging anyone, and so we have another counterexample.[5]

Regarding the putative *prima facie* duty to create valuable states of affairs: I agree that it is plausible there is such a duty when failure to fulfil it would wrong someone. But it is far less plausible that there is such a duty when there would be no victim of non-performance: when there would be no one who would be wronged by the failure. And consider that if one insists otherwise – if one insists that there *is* a *prima facie* duty to create valuable states of affairs even when no one would be wronged by one's failure to do so – then one generates a presumptive positive duty to create happy people. And that is counterintuitive.

I will not dispute that the other cases mentioned involve the violation of duties (though I believe there is room to do so). However, I do not think it is too difficult to locate someone who has been wronged in such cases and thus do not think the cases provide devastating counter-examples to my thesis. For instance, if there are circumstances where someone has a *prima facie* duty to forgive someone (rather than it being something supererogatory), I would find it plausible to think that the other person *was* entitled to forgiveness and would thus be wronged if it was not given (though it may be entirely inappropriate for him to demand it or resent its absence). Plus a general duty to cultivate a forgiving nature can be understood as a duty one owes to oneself. I wrong myself – let myself down – if I fail to cultivate that disposition in myself; similar remarks could apply to cases of wanton destruction of isolated island vegetation.

These are not knockdown replies and so there will be some who are unconvinced. But even if there are some duties that have no victims in the event of non-performance, this does not really pose a significant threat to the plausibility of the explanation I am offering. It would have to be conceded that not all duties presuppose victims, but it would remain plausible that *in general* the failure to find a victim strongly suggests that there is no duty to be violated, especially in the case of the two *prima facie* duties mentioned: the duty to promote pleasure and the duty to prevent suffering (and perhaps many others). We have seen how this delivers the right verdict in the happy life/suffering life cases. This is in itself a powerful source of support for the view. And in further support, we often conclude that there is nothing wrong with an activity once it becomes apparent that there is no victim. We often draw this conclusion even in light of quite powerful countervailing intuitions that the said activity is wrong. For instance, some have an intuition that there is something wrong with homosexual sex between consenting adults; and virtually all of us have the intuition that there is some-

---

5    Thanks to Thaddeus Metz for suggesting these sorts of case.

thing morally wrong with acts of incest, even between consenting adult siblings above the agent of consent and who have no prior familial relationship with one another. But if, when we inspect these cases more closely, we come to think that these activities do not wrong anyone we, or many of us, will take this to provide powerful *pro tanto* reason to think the activities are not wrong after all and that our intuitions to the contrary are simply misguided.

So, an independently plausible claim about duties – that they presuppose victims – can explain why there is a duty not to create miserable people yet no positive duty to create happy people. The account is simple, and importantly, it achieves the right result even if it is true that one greatly benefits someone by creating him. Given that most people do believe that being created confers a great benefit yet still do not consider it a duty to create such lives, this result is intuitively satisfying.

## III.

The absence of a positive duty to procreate does not yet show procreation to be positively *wrong*. However, I believe closer inspection reveals that there is a positive duty *not* to procreate, other things being equal.[6] Consider, we have already seen that the pleasures contained in a potential life are not pleasures anyone has a *prima facie* duty to create: no one would be wronged by the failure to create him. But there is a *prima facie* duty to prevent the (inevitable) pains contained in any potential life. Thus, when it comes to creating a new life, even a very happy one, there is a *prima facie* duty to prevent the suffering it contains but no *prima facie* duty to create the pleasures. And so the *prima facie* duty to prevent the suffering is unopposed and thus decisive. In the absence of any special reason to think otherwise, we have a duty not to procreate: a duty derived from the *prima facie* duty to prevent the suffering contained in any life.

A common objection to Benatar's antinatalist position is that being created does not harm us. Our lives contain far more pleasures than pains and thus we have been positively benefited. Better to be. A similar objection might now be made to my view. The pleasures of a life eclipse its sufferings, at least in the bulk of cases, and therefore the duty to prevent suffering does not apply to most prospective lives. The *prima facie* duty to prevent suffering applies to net suffering. And most lives contain no net suffering.

It is easy to see why such a reply will not work. The type of moral consideration that conflicts with, and so can potentially trump, a *prima facie* moral duty is another *prima facie* moral duty. The claim that there is no net suffering resulting from a procreative act, presupposes that the potential pleasures in a life can be used to trump some lesser

---

6    It might be objected that this detracts from my account's intuitive attractiveness. For while most people have the intuition that there is no positive duty to create happy people, most people also have the intuition that there is nothing wrong in creating happy people (although I should mention that by no means everyone has this intuition – I do not). If the name of the game is uncritical respect of as many intuitions as possible, then the objector would have a point. However, I do not think it is. Not all intuitions are equal. I cannot argue the point in detail here, but intuitions it would have been adaptive for people to be disposed to have; that are hard to accommodate in one's body of other intuitions; and that concern matters over which we have strong emotions; are intuitions whose credibility I consider to have been placed in doubt (on this see Huemer, 2008). I believe the intuition that there is nothing wrong with procreation satisfies *all* of these criteria and so is not one I think any great effort should be made to accommodate. Furthermore, it is worth noting that historically remarkably little philosophical attention has been given to the morality of procreation, despite its obvious significance. The antinatalist conclusion is a surprising one. But when an issue has been neglected we should not be surprised by a surprising result when we cease to neglect it.

quantity of suffering it contains. But that presupposes there is a prima facie duty to promote the potential pleasures in a life by creating a new person. There is not.

Certainly there are circumstances under which it is plausible that we might be justified in subjecting someone to some suffering in order to promote some greater quantity of pleasure. For instance, perhaps it can be right to subject an existing person to 10 units of suffering if doing so is the only way to gain him 1000 units of pleasure. But that is because in such cases there is a conflict between the *prima facie* duty to prevent suffering, and the *prima facie* duty to promote pleasure. When it comes to procreative acts the pleasures contained within a potential life are not ones we have a *prima facie* duty to promote. So if the potential life contains 10 units of suffering and 1000 units of pleasure, there is no *prima facie* duty to create those 1000 units of pleasure, though there *is* still a *prima facie* duty to prevent the creation of those 10 units of suffering. Thus the pleasures contained within a potential life cannot trump its pains.[7]

Our actual duties are determined by the sum total of *prima facie* duties operative in any given situation. And so far I have focussed on two, albeit very significant and widely agreed-upon *prima facie* duties: the duty to prevent pain and the duty to promote pleasure. My object here is not to offer any kind of exhaustive list of *prima facie* duties. But I will briefly mention one more very plausible *prima facie* duty because it too yields a *prima facie* duty not to procreate.

It is plausible there is a *prima facie* duty not to do anything that will seriously affect another without gaining his prior consent. To create someone is to profoundly affect him.[8] And clearly one cannot give prior consent to be created. To create someone is to *subject* someone to a life. Thus, the *prima facie* duty not to seriously affect another without his prior consent also generates a *prima facie* duty not to procreate.[9] Of course, it is often right to do things to others without their prior consent (pushing someone out of the way of an oncoming truck; making children go to school etc.) But in such cases there is always some other *prima facie* duty (or duties) that conflicts with and plausibly trumps the duty in question.[10] When it comes to potential lives there are no duty *prima facie* duties to create the lives in question (not if we are focussing on

---

7    The example might give the misleading impression I consider the disvalue of the suffering contained in a life to be a simplistic function of its quality and quantity. I do not. The badness of some suffering for the person suffering it is affected by a range of considerations, including how it is distributed in a person's life and the quality and quantity of pleasures contained in the life among other things (for instance, see Benatar 2006, pp. 61-64). A small amount of suffering in a life that contains little else is worse than a larger amount of suffering in a life that contains much pleasure besides. We have no *prima facie* duty to promote pleasures contained in a potential life and so such pleasures cannot be offered up as possible trumps for the suffering it contains (unlike in an actual life), but that most certainly does not mean that the pleasures have no bearing on the badness of the suffering, and thus on the weight of the duty to prevent them. After all, it would be absurd to say that it would be more wrong to create a life that contained 20 units of suffering and 100 of pleasure than a life that contained 10 units of suffering and 10 units of pleasure!

8    A proponent of a strong person-affecting view would object that one cannot be affected either for the better or worse through being created as one can be made better or worse off if one already exists. I follow Benatar and Feinberg in rejecting this view and holding that someone can be harmed or benefited even if they are not made better or worse off (Benatar 2006, p. 20-33; Feinberg, 1992).

9    Seanna Shiffrin has also highlighted the moral significance of the fact it is impossible to consent to be created and that as such procreation is not a "straightforward, morally innocent endeavor" (1999, p. 118). Shiffrin's views are discussed in Asheel Singh's article in this issue of the journal.

10   It might be objected that there are other accounts available here. For instance, perhaps what explains why it is right to push someone out of the way of an oncoming truck is that the person would have consented to action if they had been informed and rational. I believe such accounts are flawed for a num-

duties owed to the potential exister). Just as the duty to prevent the pains in a potential life went unopposed, so too does the duty to not seriously affect another without his prior consent.

It therefore seems there are at least two *prima facie* duties that push towards making procreative acts wrong overall: our *prima facie* duty to prevent pain and our *prima facie* duty not to seriously affect someone else without his prior consent. Other things being equal, these generate a duty not to procreate. Fulfilling this duty will mean that no more lives are created and this, I am allowing, is a bad state of affairs, even if it is not bad *for* anyone. However, it is not a state of affairs we can have any duty to prevent obtaining, for preventing it would mean subjecting people to lives and creating pains we have a duty to prevent, while not preventing it would not wrong anyone.

Nevertheless, some are going to have difficulty accepting that someone can be *wronged* by a deed that greatly benefits him. If life is a benefit to the exister, how can it be wrong to have bestowed such a benefit? If we are happy to be alive, and grateful to our parents for having created us and would not want things to be another way, can we really take the idea that we have been wronged seriously? Is it plausible that we could be wronged yet happy for having been so wronged? Grateful even? Yes, there is nothing odd about this: there are many such cases. For example, most would agree that lying is *prima facie* wrong. But one can benefit from being lied to. Someone can break a promise to us, and this can work to our benefit, yet we have been wronged nevertheless. Or take another plausible *prima facie* duty: the *prima facie* duty not to do something that seriously affects another without first gaining his consent. If someone hacks into someone else's bank account and places a bet on a horse on his behalf, but without first gaining his consent, then that person has been wronged even if the horse wins and they are considerably better off, as a result. If someone did that to me, I would be very pleased and grateful – but I would still think I had been wronged. I may think it would be inappropriate for me to complain about it, but that is different. In short then, there is nothing remotely incoherent or surprising in the idea that someone can be wronged, even wronged quite seriously, yet benefit by the wrong, be happy that the wrong was committed, and not want things to have been otherwise.

In summary then, one can have a duty to do X (or omit to do X) if failure to fulfil the duty would wrong someone. If this is correct, then there cannot be a *prima facie* duty to procreate deriving from a *prima facie* duty to promote pleasure. But the sufferings a potential life contains are sufferings we have a *prima facie* duty to prevent. Added to this it is plausible we have a *prima facie* duty not to subject others to lives without first gaining their consent.

There are important parallels with Benatar's view. My view, like his, entails that it is the sufferings contained in a potential life that count, and not its pleasures. But unlike Benatar this is not because absent pleasures are not bad unless there is someone for whom they are a deprivation. Rather, it is because the pleasures we have a duty to promote are those that we would have wronged someone by not promoting, and none of the pleasures contained within a prospective life are of this kind.

---

ber of reasons, in part because such accounts would seem to resurrect the duty to procreate, and would also deliver counter-intuitive verdicts about other cases. However, it would be beyond the scope of this paper to argue the matter. The point I wish to make in this paper is that the *prima facie* view I have outlined delivers intuitively attractive verdicts about creating happy people versus creating miserable people and also yields the antinatalist conclusion.

Whatever the ingenuity of Benatar's argument, it is difficult to accept that one has been harmed by being brought into existence only if the life one has been subject to is one that contains far more pleasure than suffering. It is difficult to accept that it would have been better never to have been born. The case I have made above does not require accepting such things. For my argument is consistent with us having been benefited by being created: with it being better to be.

## IV.

It is often thought that antinatalism yields pro-mortalism. It is easy to understand why. If an antinatalist argues that being created harms us, it is natural enough to think it best for us to cease living as soon as possible in order to limit the harm in question.[11] My route to antinatalism in no way implies a duty to commit suicide, nor any special reason to think suicide supererogatory or prudent.

I have argued we have no duty to promote the pleasures contained in a potential life. That does not mean we lack a duty to promote the pleasures contained in an actual life. Quite the reverse: we have a duty to promote the pleasures in any actual life, for if we fail to do so there certainly *is* someone whom would be wronged by our failure.

The fact that we have a duty to prevent the pains contained in a potential life by not bringing it into being, does *not* mean that we have a duty to prevent the pains contained within our actual lives by ceasing to live them. Suicide would certainly prevent any further suffering in that life. But it would also prevent any further pleasures, and as mentioned above, those pleasures are ones we have a duty to promote.

Existence transforms the situation from one in which life's pleasures count for nothing morally, to one in which they count for a great deal. Once someone exists then we certainly have *prima facie* duties to promote his pleasures, prevent his sufferings and not do anything that will seriously affect him without his prior consent. If we have duties to ourselves, then we have *prima facie* duties to ourselves to promote our own pleasures and prevent our own suffering. Assuming that in most circumstances suicide would not be the best way of promoting our pleasures, then far from having a duty to kill ourselves, (and even farther from it being supererogatory) we have a duty to stay alive as long as possible, other things being equal.  And if we do not have duties to ourselves, then it remains highly imprudent to commit suicide in most circumstances.

Of course, there may be many circumstances in which suicide *is* the right or permissible and prudent course of action: situations in which one is suffering and where there is no prospect of the suffering ending or being adequately compensated for by future pleasures. However, we can leave the details of when exactly suicide is permissible, prudent, or (perhaps) positively obligatory to one side. For the point here is that my particular way of arriving at the antinatalist conclusion does not in any way provide a reason to commit suicide nor does it do anything, in itself, to suggest that suicide might be obligatory or prudent. Whether one is always entitled to kill oneself; to what degree (if at all) the *prima facie* duty to promote pleasure applies to oneself; to what degree (if at all) the *prima facie* duty to prevent pain applies to oneself: all of these

---

11  Benatar does devote considerable space to explaining why his view does "not imply that death is better than continuing to exist, and a fortiori that suicide is (always) desirable" (2006, p. 212). Absent pleasure is not bad unless there is someone for whom it is a deprivation, and clearly there is someone for whom it is a deprivation when someone is already up and running. So denying yourself future pleasures by killing yourself is bad, other things being equal. To think that Benatar's main argument for antinatalism implies pro-mortalism is just to ignore the asymmetry thesis that is central to it.

matters are left open. So whatever one's view on the permissibility or otherwise of suicidal acts, the case for antinatalism that I have presented should leave it untouched.[12]

## V.

So far I have focussed exclusively on duties to the one who will be created and have argued that such duties generate a duty not to procreate (but no duty to commit suicide). However, that does not imply that it would *always* be wrong to procreate.[13] Duties to third parties can, and sometimes will, generate a permission or duty to procreate. For instance, the *prima facie* duty to prevent harm could generate a duty to create a new life if creating a new person would prevent another from coming to some very significant harm (for instance, creating a source of bone marrow for a relative who would otherwise suffer terribly). But there are good reasons to think that such occasions will be very rare, and that procreation will generally be wrong.

Most would agree that the duty against creating harm is more stringent than the duty to prevent harm. The harm one's procreative act might prevent would therefore need to be greater in significance than the suffering it creates. It would be even more rare for there to be a situation in which procreating could bring benefits to others substantial enough to overcome the duty not to create the suffering in that new life. The typical benefits associated with procreative acts – enhancing one's happiness; providing a playmate for a son or daughter; ensuring the family line continues and so on - do not seem likely to have the clout necessary. Intuitively it would normally be morally impermissible to subject someone to suffering of the same significance as that contained in the average life in order to enhance someone else's happiness or to provide someone else with the benefit of a playmate, or to continue the family line.[14]

Smilansky suggests that "the existence of *promises* to have children can also be a moral consideration towards a possible duty to have them" (1995, p. 46). But it is implausible that any *prima facie* duty to keep that promise could have the clout necessary to trump the *prima facie* duty not to create the suffering contained in a life or the *prima facie* duty to avoid seriously affecting another without his consent. To borrow an example from earlier: if John has made a promise to Jane to hack into Tom's bank account and place all his savings on a horse (one he is fairly sure will win), then I think most of us would still consider John's act wrong overall. The fact he was fulfilling a promise to Jane does little, if anything, to alter that judgement.

## VI.

The antinatalist view I have presented in this paper is compatible with Benatar's, is as robust as Benatar's, and owes a great deal to it. But it is not the same view. It does not require one to believe that life is not a benefit to the procreated, nor does it require that one accept that a world devoid of life is a better place than one with life. Nevertheless,

---

12  An exception would be if one holds that killing oneself is obligatory when doing so is the only way of ensuring that a new life is created. Of course, such an act would not strictly speaking be a 'suicide' given that it would be performed with the intention of benefiting someone else. But, the fact remains that if one held this kind of view, then the realisation that duties are asymmetrical in the way I have outlined would alter matters such that one could no longer consider killing oneself for the sake of creating a new life to be a duty.

13  Nor does Benatar's view (see 2006, pp. 98-99; 191-193).

14  I am assuming that the sufferings contained in a life are nearly always very significant. But of course, I am not claiming that the sufferings nearly always eclipse the pleasures. The point, rather, is that it is only the sufferings that we can consider, given that we have a *prima facie* duty not to create them, but no *prima facie* duty to create the pleasures.

my view yields the same substantial moral conclusion: that there is a duty not to procreate, but does so while respecting our intuition that we do no wrong in not procreating even if the lives we would have created would have been ones brimming with pleasure and that would have massively benefited those subject to them.

## References

Benatar, D. 2006: *Better Never to Have Been.* Oxford: Clarendon Press.

Feinberg, J. 1992: "Wrongful Life and the Counterfactual Element in Harming", pp. 3-36, in *Freedom and Fulfillment.* Princeton: Princeton University Press.

Haji, I. 2002: *Deontic Morality and Control.* Cambridge: Cambridge University Press.

Huemer, M. 2005: *Ethical Intuitionism.* Basingstoke: Palgrave Macmillan.

Huemer, M. 2008: "Revisionary Intuitionism" *Social Philosophy and Policy,* 25/1, pp. 368-392.

McGregor, R. and Sullivan-Bissett, E. 2012: "Better No Longer To Be: The Harm of Continued Existence" *The South African Journal of Philosophy* (present issue).

McMahan, J. 2002: *The Ethics of Killing: Problems at the Margins of Life.* Oxford: Oxford University Press.

Ross, W. D. [1930] 1988: *The Right and the Good.* Indianapolis: Hackett.

Shiffrin, S. 1999: "Wrongful Life, Procreative Responsibility, and the Significance of Harm" *Legal Theory,* 5, pp. 117-148.

Singh, A. 2012: "Furthering the Case for Anti-natalism: Seana Shiffrin and the Limits of Permissible Harm" *The South African Journal of Philosophy* (present issue).

Smilansky, S. 1995: "Is There a Moral Obligation to Have Children?" *Journal of Applied Philosophy,* 12/1, pp. 41-53.

# Furthering the Case for Anti-Natalism: Seana Shiffrin and the Limits of Permissible Harm

## Asheel Singh

### 1) Introduction

Anti-natalism is the view that it is (almost) always wrong to bring people (and perhaps all sentient beings) into existence. This view is most famously defended by David Benatar (1997, 2006). There are, however, other routes to an anti-natal conclusion. In this respect, Seana Shiffrin's paper, "Wrongful Life, Procreative Responsibility, and the Significance of Harm" (1999), has been rather neglected in the natal debate. Though she appears unwilling to conclude that procreation is always wrong, I believe that she in fact puts forth a case for anti-natalism no less compelling than Benatar's. My overall aim here is to demonstrate the force of her argument by defending a Shiffrin-esque route to anti-natalism from a powerful objection. This objection appeals to the common belief that because most people endorse their creation, procreation often is all-things-considered permissible. I will show how this objection fails, and why Shiffrin's rationale for anti-natalism, as I will be representing it, ought to be taken seriously.

I will proceed by briefly explaining Shiffrin's argument, pointing out some key differences between her views and Benatar's, and illustrating how her argument can be employed to construct and defend a principle of permissible harm that supports anti-natalism. The key feature of this principle is that it is impermissible for one to impose serious, ongoing and inescapable (without great cost) harm upon an unconsenting individual purely for the sake of granting that individual benefits. I will test this principle against a strong objection that appeals to a view many people hold, and that David DeGrazia (2011) has recently put forward.[1] This objection, which I will be referring to as the objection from "endorsement", holds that it is permissible to bring persons into existence if we have good reasons for presuming that these persons will be, without delusion, glad to have been created. On the behalf of the anti-natalist, I in turn advance four replies to this view. I conclude with a brief discussion of three other objections that could be made to Shiffrin's arguments.

### 2) Shiffrin's (Reluctant) "Anti-natalism"

Shiffrin is aware of Benatar's early (1997) statement of his anti-natal views, though she does not respond to them. There are, as she acknowledges,[2] similarities between her views and Benatar's. To my mind, the most crucial similarities are both authors'

---

1     NB: As of time of writing, all references to DeGrazia are to an unpublished version of his work, and the cited page numbers are thus likely to differ from the published version of his text.

2     In a footnote, Shiffrin (1999:136) mentions that Benatar, "[i]ndependently...has advanced some related arguments that causing to exist imposes burdens on children..."

intuitions that we have stronger obligations not to harm than to benefit, their emphasis on the moral relevance of the fact that if we do not procreate, then no one will face the harms of existence, and their emphasis on the seriousness of the harms to which procreation exposes children. A crucial difference between their views is that Shiffrin grants that creation might in fact often result in an overall benefit to children—though she entertains the possibility that it might nevertheless always be impermissible to act to bestow this benefit.

Both Benatar and Shiffrin are clear about not viewing procreation as a morally innocent activity. Shiffrin advances what she terms the "equivocal view" (Shiffrin 1999:136), which sees procreation as an intrinsically morally problematic endeavour, as it always involves "serious moral hazards" (Shiffrin 1999:136).[3] What all procreators must realise, she asserts, is that by creating new people they are *imposing* significant harm upon these persons (Shiffrin 1999:136-7). This is an "imposition" not only because non-existent persons cannot give their consent to be harmed, but also because it is indeed the very nature of harm to transform the agent experiencing it into an "endurer" as opposed to an actively willing agent (Shiffrin 1999:123-4).

Furthermore, the standard defence for the harms of creation—namely that they are offset by the greater benefits of being in existence—does not work, says Shiffrin. On her account of harm, procreation appears generally impermissible because it imposes a (serious) harm to nonconsenting individuals that is not for a suitably important end—which apparently is, for Shiffrin, only the prevention of greater harm (Shiffrin 1999:128-9). Here she argues that whilst we consider it morally permissible to harm someone in order to prevent a greater harm befalling her—for example, when rescuers or surgeons must injure persons in order to rescue them from far worse harms—we do not consider it similarly morally permissible to harm an unconsenting person in order to secure her a greater "pure benefit" (Shiffrin 1999:126-7). These kinds of benefits impart (non-essential) improvements—sensual pleasure, material enrichment, and the like—to our lives, and do not derive their "beneficial" status from the removal or prevention of harm (Shiffrin 1999:124-5). As examples of pure benefits that we would deem it wrong to break an unconsenting patient's arm for, Shiffrin lists "supernormal memory, a useful store of encyclopedic knowledge, twenty IQ points worth of extra intellectual ability, or the ability to consume immoderate amounts of alcohol or fat without side effects" (Shiffrin 1999:127).

Shiffrin (1999:127) employs a parable to presumably suggest that creation represents the bestowal of pure benefits (among other things), which appear impermissible to bestow. I summarise this parable below:

*Wealthy/Unlucky Case*

*Wealthy* is a very wealthy individual. One day he decides to share some of his wealth with his neighbours, who live on a nearby island. They are in no need of extra money. Wealthy gets into his plane with a hundred cubes of gold bullion. His intention is to drop these gold cubes from the sky. He goes about doing this, taking care not to hit anyone. He is aware that his actions could maim, or even kill, but he has no other means of distributing his wealth. Most of the recipients of gold cubes are surprised but happy to receive their unexpected gifts.

---

3   Benatar emphasises that there is a sort of gamble one takes when deciding to conceive a child, something he calls "procreational Russian roulette" (Benatar 2006:92).

One person, *Unlucky*, does in fact get hit, and the impact breaks his arm. Unlucky is glad to have the extra money—a life-changing fortune, in fact—but he is unsure as to whether he would have consented beforehand to have been placed in harm's way to receive it.

Wealthy might have delivered an all-things-considered benefit to Unlucky, but in doing so he placed Unlucky at great risk where no such risk previously existed, and indeed inflicted a serious injury upon Unlucky. Similarly, even when parents create persons who come to consider their lives to be all-things-considered beneficial, parents expose their offspring to potentially serious harms:

> Even if [Wealthy] took the greatest care, he imposed risk of harm and injury on another without consent and without the justification that it was necessary to avoid a more substantial harm. Everyday procreation may be described in similar terms (Shiffrin 1999:136).

All lives—even the best ones—contain harms. Shiffrin stresses that parents *impose* these harms upon their offspring, in the sense that their offspring are not available to give their consent to be placed in harm's way. Furthermore, whilst a rescuer can be excused from liability for the harm he causes due to the fact that he acts to alleviate a greater harm, neither Wealthy nor parents can say that their actions were in aid of alleviating a greater harm.[4] Unlucky and the other members of his community—and, by analogy, the unborn—are in no need of rescuing. To clarify, the reason it is justifiable for a rescuer to harm his rescuee is not available to the procreator. Being created, on Shiffrin's view, is thus not comparable to being saved from a greater harm (for non-existers cannot suffer harm), nor is it the bestowal of a pure benefit; being created is, in effect, a "burden-riddled mixed benefit" (Shiffrin 1999:140).[5]

To my mind, Shiffrin is appealing to the following sort of principle:

Shiffrin's Principle of Permissible Harm (Principle A):

*It is permissible for one to knowingly harm unconsenting patient A to a non-trivial degree if, and only if, the following conditions are met: a) one imposes the harm with the reasonable expectation of thereby alleviating or saving patient A from a pre-existing or anticipated harm; and b) the imposed harm is a lesser harm than the harm one aims to alleviate.*

I think Principle A takes into account the most salient features of Shiffrin's position regarding permissible harm. Shiffrin does not think it is (ordinarily) permissible to harm a patient in order to bestow a pure benefit upon this patient. I have thus not seen it necessary to mention the bestowal of pure benefits in constructing the above principle; only features necessary to justify harm to an unconsenting patient are included, and, as can be seen, there aren't many such features on Shiffrin's viewpoint.

As I have noted, Shiffrin does not intend to argue for anti-natalism, strictly speaking. She is explicit about this:

---

4   I set aside the possible "harm" of (intentional) extinction.
5   Benatar (2006:1) makes the stronger judgement of creation as a "net harm". Briefly, what Benatar means here is that there is a fundamental asymmetry between harms and benefits, such that the benefits of coming into existence never outweigh the harms. I am unclear as to why Shiffrin calls creation a sort of "benefit" (as opposed to a "burden-riddled *action* or *event*", say). In any case, recall that Benatar (2006:1) makes the stronger judgement of creation as a "net harm". Briefly, what Benatar means here is that there is a fundamental asymmetry between harms and benefits, such that the benefits of coming into existence never outweigh the harms.

I am not advancing the claim that procreation is all-things-considered wrong. It is consistent with these arguments to regard nonconsensual, burden-imposing actions as morally problematic but not always impermissible, or to regard procreation as a special case. All I mean to advance is the claim that because procreation involves a nonconsensual imposition of significant burdens, it is morally problematic and its imposer may justifiably be held responsible for its harmful results (Shiffrin 1999:139).

Perhaps she fears that an anti-natal conclusion will be considered a *reductio* of her arguments. In any case, I am of the view that it is in fact *not* consistent with Shiffrin's arguments to consider avoidable, nonconsensual burden-imposing actions—specifically procreative actions—permissible. Consider the fact that Shiffrin argues that Wealthy should compensate Unlucky. She gives two possible positions one could adopt to explain this judgement. The first, stronger position holds that Wealthy's actions were morally wrong, all things considered, because his actions violated something like my Principle A: Wealthy's action "risked and inflicted serious harm on nonconsenting individuals but was not in the service of a suitably important end (such as the prevention of greater harm to them)" (Shiffrin 1999:128-9).

The second, weaker position holds that Wealthy's actions were (merely) *pro tanto* wrong, but all-things-considered permissible as long as he adequately compensated for any "incidental harm" he inflicted (Shiffrin 1999:129). Shiffrin is explicit about which position one ought to adopt: "I am inclined toward the stronger position and believe that Wealthy acted immorally" (Shiffrin 1999:129). I submit that if she intends the Wealthy/Unlucky parable to be analogous with procreation, and she believes that Wealthy acts impermissibly, then she must conclude that procreators act impermissibly. To be clear, parents, on this hard version of Shiffrin, act immorally when they impose the harms of existence upon their offspring.

I have mentioned compensation as a possible strategy to defend creation. I further explore the objection from compensation elsewhere.[6] This objection, to be clear, holds that it is permissible for one to bring individuals into existence if one intends to offer adequate compensation for the harms to which one exposes these individuals. In my view, a stronger case can be made for the permissibility of creation from another objection. According to this popular and initially appealing objection, procreation is all-things-considered permissible if there is a high probability of parents' procreative actions garnering the subsequent *endorsement* of their offspring. Many people, if not most, do indeed appear to endorse their parents' pro-natal decisions. According to the current line of reasoning, procreation is thus ordinarily permissible.[7]

## 3) The Endorsement Objection
It is important to note that endorsement is not equivalent to hypothetical consent, nor is it the same as subsequent consent. Consent is a relational property, in the sense that consent always entails a sort of tacit agreement or contractual relationship between two or more individuals or institutions. Endorsement is different. Endorsement is

---

6   *Assessing Anti-Natalism: A Philosophical Examination of the Morality of Procreation* (unpublished MA dissertation, University of Johannesburg, 2012).

7   Where it is known that an individual will be born with terrible disadvantages—where individuals will be born into a life of slavery, for instance, or into a life characterised by terrible suffering due to a genetic disease—the friend of endorsement can concede that it would be wrong to procreate in such cases.

purely internal to the individual; even if it is about another's actions, it does not essentially involve a relationship with her. She can consent to another's actions; whether or not she endorses them is another matter. This distinction is particularly evident in cases where "consent" is given under duress.

As I will be characterising its (mis)use, the spirit of "endorsement" is often thought to be captured by the phrase, "I'm *glad* you did that for me." To my mind, this is the sense in which most people seem to understand endorsement when talking about their creation; most people say something like, "I'm glad to be alive." This appears to be the sense in which DeGrazia understands endorsement as well. The fact[8] that the majority of people appear to endorse their existence, and what this fact means for the morality of procreation, need to be examined in detail.

What is the best explanation for the prevalence of this gladness? Benatar and DeGrazia have very different views, whilst Shiffrin is mostly silent on the issue.[9] According to DeGrazia (2011:34), the best explanation for the prevalence of gladness at being alive is that most people, contra Benatar, are undeluded in their life assessments. DeGrazia is interested in factors that *may* justify procreation: he understands the "undeluded gladness factor" (2011:34) to be a necessary, but not obviously sufficient, condition for judging when procreation may be permissible (2011:35, 38). When I refer to "the friend of endorsement", I am thus not referring exclusively to DeGrazia, whose own estimation of the force of the undeluded gladness factor is weaker than I think it can plausibly be represented. After all, many, if not most, people appear to be pro-natal friends of endorsement![10]

The friend of endorsement, as I will be representing him, says that though some acts of procreation are wrong—namely, where it is almost certain that children will be born into lives not worth living—many (if not most) acts of procreation lead to lives deemed to be worth living by their bearers. On this view, all Shiffrin does, at best, is provide reasons for why procreation might be considered a *pro tanto* wrong.[11] In other words, procreation, though normally wrong (to some degree), might be an act that can be rendered permissible due to other moral considerations. The friend of endorsement wants to say that the reasonable expectation of endorsement renders the *pro tanto* wrongness of procreation permissible. He claims that many people consider their lives to be worth living, are glad to have been born, and, crucially, are not deluded about their life assessments. And so, if a person truly is glad to have been born—such gladness signifying an endorsement of her creation—her parents surely could not be said to have acted wrongly in creating her. Thus, not all lives, contra anti-natalism, are wrong to start, for many people seem to have lives they are without delusion glad for.

---

8    I concede, for the sake of argument, that this is a fact, but I am not sure that it really is. On the face of it, high suicide rates seem to temper optimistic estimations of the prevalence of gladness.

9    Apart from saying that most recipients of Wealthy's gold bullion are "delighted" (1999:127), Shiffrin also opines that "most children experience their imposed lives as miraculous benefits" (1999:141).

10   A quick note on my usage of the words "deluded" and "delusional". I use these words to be consistent with the style adopted by DeGrazia. He appears to use these words in a loose, non-technical sense, and so do I. Briefly, I take it that we both mean that judgements which are undeluded are not so adversely affected or motivated by non-rational psychological mechanisms—adaptation, etc.—as to render them dubious or inadmissible.

11   DeGrazia (2011:23-4, 27) also advances this reading of Shiffrin. I think that he is correct both in asserting that Shiffrin herself only intends to defend this claim, and that Shiffrin's arguments can easily be read as motivating the stronger claim that procreation is always wrong.

As I will be characterising him, the friend of endorsement wants endorsement to be sufficient to render procreation permissible. He concedes that procreation might be *pro tanto wrong*, but permissible if there are good reasons for assuming the (future) undeluded endorsement of the one acted upon. For instance, it might appear *pro tanto* wrong, albeit in a weaker sense than in the case of creation, to deceive someone, but nonetheless permissible in light of other considerations. Consider the following example of deception in order to promote what appears to be a pure benefit:

*Surprise Party Case*

Janet and Yoko are friends. Janet wants to throw Yoko a surprise party to celebrate Yoko's big promotion at work, and so she goes to some length to distract, misinform, mislead and generally lie to Yoko. On the day of the party, Janet even goes to the extent of preventing Yoko from fulfilling Yoko's own plans for the day, hiding her car keys and telling the sulking Yoko that she must come along to a friend's house "for a party". Janet goes to these lengths because she is sure that Yoko will be immensely glad that Janet managed to keep the party a surprise from her: Yoko loves surprises just as much as she loves parties.

Janet's actions appear permissible, because, for one thing, she is not trying to harm Yoko, and, further, she has good reasons for assuming that Yoko will endorse her actions. It can thus be suggested that the friend of endorsement is appealing to the following sort of principle:

The Friend of Endorsement's Principle of Permissible Harm (Principle B):

*It is permissible for one to knowingly harm unconsenting patient A to a non-trivial degree if, and only if, the following conditions are met: a) one has good reasons for presuming patient A's subsequent and undeluded endorsement of one's action; and b) though one foresees this harm, one does not intend it.*[12]

It is usually thought that procreators often have good reasons for presuming that their offspring will be glad to have been born. Furthermore, (most) procreators do not intend to harm their offspring by conceiving them. Appealing to something like Principle B, the friend of endorsement puts forward an initially plausible case for the permissibility of procreation. But I believe that his view is mistaken, and, in the following section, I show how it can be defeated.

## 4) Replies to the Endorsement Objection

I have four replies to the friend of endorsement on behalf of the anti-natalist. I group these four replies under two levels. On the first level, I grant Principle B but show that it doesn't give the friend of endorsement what he needs to defend procreation. Here I argue (in 4.1) that what might be motivating B is various conflations; none is equiva-

---

12   David Boonin has opined that Principle B seems to imply that one must have some prior view of what is right in order to know what would be endorsed, and that, if this is indeed the case, endorsement isn't doing the justificatory work. If my act is permissible according to some endorsement-independent standard, then that standard, and not endorsement, is what renders my action permissible. We ought thus to reject Principle B. I could well agree with Boonin. As I will make clear in the main text, despite its intuitive appeal, there is something extraordinary about appealing to endorsement as a sufficient condition for justifying harmful actions.

lent to an endorsement of one's creation. I then (again) suggest (in 4.2) that the delusion criterion in Principle B is not satisfied in the case of procreation. On the second level, I cast doubt upon the principle itself and conclude that it lacks justification. Here, I first discuss (in 4.3) a counterexample to Principle B, and then argue (in 4.4) that the friend of endorsement ultimately does not put forward a legitimate moral argument in the sense that no prominent moral theory supports it.

### 4.1. Should Endorsement Be Equated with Gladness?

When assessing the morality of procreation, the friend of endorsement may equate endorsement with an alleged undeluded gladness at being alive. But if this is indeed what he does, then it does not look like Principle B can motivate a defence of procreation. The friend of endorsement should want (undeluded) judgment and not gladness. The two are not equivalent. Consider this revealing but neglected distinction between two understandings of "an endorsement of one's creation":

*E1. Endorsement, emotional:*
"I am glad to have been born. Therefore (or, "in other words"), I endorse my creation."

*E2. Endorsement, rational:*
"I think that my parents were all-things-considered justified in creating me. I therefore endorse my creation."

I am doubtful of the move of considering endorsement primarily as an emotional phenomenon. It appears to me that the friend of endorsement, DeGrazia included, sees endorsement like this. On the friend of endorsement's view, E1, to be *glad* that one was created is to *endorse* one's creation. This picture of endorsement can be contrasted with another. On this alternative picture, E2, one examines one's creation rationally, and deems one's parents to have acted, all things considered, permissibly.

For me, the latter construal of endorsement—as more of a cognitive evaluation than a purely emotional appraisal—is the more appealing. After all, when it comes to judgments regarding matters of great importance—specifically those that impact upon others—we are not usually satisfied with conclusions that stem exclusively, or even primarily, from the emotions. For instance, we would prefer a society where people carefully considered their options at election time, and not a society where people voted out of blind (that is, emotional) allegiance to particular political parties. Even if excellent reasons do in fact exist for adopting a certain position, holding that position entirely for emotive reasons surely isn't desirable or morally commendable. I assert that we ought to require rational, measured views, especially when we intend to rely on these views to make monumental decisions with far-ranging consequences. Procreative acts are paradigm cases of such decisions.

The friend of endorsement could object that I propose too strict a standard for actual endorsement, in that I neglect the fact that we sometimes do seek type-E1 endorsements. For instance, I might decide to give my young niece a birthday gift. Suppose that I do not know her very well, and am thus unsure as to what gift to give her. I do some research into the sort of gifts she will most likely be glad to receive. I present her my gift, and, in order to confirm that I have made the right choice, I will look for an immediate emotional response—signs of "gladness".

However, this gift-giving case backfires against the endorsement-as-gladness view. My niece might appear glad to have received my gift, but it would be strange for her to say, "I *endorse* your gift," or, "I endorse your act of gift-giving." This lends credence to my view that gladness and endorsement are not synonymous or co-referential.

It might seem that people typically E1-endorse their creation. To my mind, this may have something to do with the fact that most people avoid philosophical deliberation—especially about their creation. Adopting a revised view of procreative endorsement like E2, or even understanding the need for it, seems to require considerable reflection to satisfy. If we accept my claim that endorsement as rational appraisal (E2) ought to be our standard, then we can see that, in addition to Benatar and DeGrazia, it is plausible to posit a third (Benatar-esque) explanation for the prevalence of gladness: most people are putatively glad to have been born due to a lack of philosophical reflection. And in the absence of such, they do not often "endorse" their creation in the relevant sense.

Furthermore, people do not even clearly endorse their creation if we adopt E1 as our standard. The reason is that people often confuse, for instance, gladness *at being alive* with gladness *at being born*—which are not equivalent.[13] The friend of endorsement is, I suspect, often conflating these two states. (To my mind, DeGrazia makes this conflation.) There are many components to being "glad to be alive", and being "glad to be born" need not be one of them. For instance, near-death experiences often cause people to reassess the value of their lives and gain a new appreciation for being alive. Often, though, such experiences motivate these people to assess their lives in terms of their mortality—that is, death (the end of life) and not birth (the commencement of life).[14]

To be clear, for Principle B to justify procreation, we need endorsement of—which (for the sake of argument) might be gladness about—*the act that caused one to exist*, and not just *the contents or quality of one's life*. To see the point, return to the case of my niece. Perhaps my niece is initially glad to receive my gift, but, after reflection, thinks that it was wrong of me to present it to her. Perhaps she suspects some ulterior motive on my part. Maybe I have presented her the gift partly, or entirely, to impress other people, to present myself in a more favourable light. Perhaps she is glad to have the gift (it brings her joy), but she might well not be glad that I gave it to her; she does not, that is to say, endorse my actions. By analogy, one might be glad to exist, but that does not mean that one is glad that one was created.

Consider the following two cases where the two come apart. First, think of a person who is glad for having had the experiences she's had in life, and is glad to be alive, but would still choose not to have had her life started, given certain intolerably harmful events, perhaps, she's had to endure.[15] Here, "glad to be alive" alone doesn't get us to "glad to have been born"—let alone to an endorsement of being born in the reflective sense I think is relevant. Second, there seems to me to be a difference between being glad for *the way one's life has gone* (it could have been *worse*, after all), and being glad that *one's life was started*. It seems eminently plausible to me that people could express an outlook that makes the latter distinction.

---

13  For my purposes, "being born" is synonymous with "being created".

14  On a related point, though a near-death event—such as a narrow escape from being murdered by one's hostage takers, for instance—can perhaps make one monumentally glad to be alive, and though one indeed might recognise that this gladness would not have arisen without this event, one might nevertheless wish that one never had to endure the harm of this perspective-shifting event.

15  This is a modification of an idea expressed by David Blumenfeld (2009). Blumenfeld claims that it is plausible to think that a person would refuse to live her life again, were it possible, due to certain harmful experiences she would once again have to endure.

To summarise, there are two issues here. First, people often adopt the incorrect understanding of endorsement as gladness. If I am correct in asserting that E2 is instead the appropriate standard, then Principle B doesn't justify procreation, because endorsement then involves reflection of a kind in which people rarely engage. Second, even if E1 is the correct conception of endorsement, pro-natalists regularly conflate different objects of gladness, and thus illegitimately presume endorsement of procreation. People make the leap from being glad to be alive, on the one hand, which might well be frequent, to being glad about their creation (and creation in general), on the other, which perhaps is not. I have argued that, despite its commonness, this leap is without justification.

## 4.2. Can Endorsement Arise without Delusion?

For the sake of argument, grant the claim that gladness and endorsement are equivalent. Suppose that E1—endorsement as gladness—is an adequate standard. This still might not give the friend of endorsement what he needs. I am going to suggest that there are compelling reasons for believing that gladness at one's creation might rarely arise without delusion.

Adherents to endorsement, along with DeGrazia, should want to exclude "endorsement" that arises due to the adaptive mechanisms Benatar (2006:64-8) discusses. In other words, friends of endorsement should want to say that, despite the adaptive mechanisms we do in fact have, our (life-affirming) life assessments are nevertheless reliable. However, in support of a Benatarian claim, it strikes me that *coming into existence might be the ultimate test of our rationality in the face of our adaptive mechanisms*. I submit that there is much to impede the (for the sake of argument, deliberative) formation of anti-natal conclusions. Consider the fact that so many people, even those with seemingly terrible lives, find anti-natal ideas unintuitive—unspeakable, even. Many unhappy people try to find happiness in sexual activities—either for exclusively pleasurable or procreative ends. Think about the problem of overpopulation and hungry babies in poverty-stricken societies. Closing off such avenues for finding fulfilment (or simply for escape) might understandably meet with considerable resistance.

Consider also how foreign the ideas of anti-natalism are: they seem to make a mockery of centuries of human evolution, struggle and endeavour, the search for meaning, the "natural goodness" of the family unit, the "purity" of the mother-child union, and so on. In this respect, I find similarities between anti-natalism and atheism. As with the idea that it is always wrong to procreate, many people find the idea that there is no god deeply unintuitive. This is at least in part because the idea goes against centuries of human tradition, and many atheists still face ridicule and/or persecution for their beliefs. Anti-natalism says that all people are wrongfully created, must endure serious harms they ought not to have been exposed to, and must face, and fall to, (arguably) the most serious of all harms: death. And this apparently absurd cycle of birth and death has been going on for millennia! But, similarly, the atheist is struck by the absurdity of religious persecution and violence—which has also been going on for millennia, and shows no signs of going extinct. Many people think that the removal of god means that life ceases to have any meaning and that all morality falls away. Atheism makes no sense to such people. To many atheists, on the other hand, atheism is the most, or perhaps *only* rational position, and it does not somehow destroy ethics or render life meaningless. In my view at least, atheism is with good reason the default position of the Academy; but it remains, revealingly, a minority view in wider society. It would be naïve to suggest that this is because most people (read: non-academics) have a better idea of what's what. On the contrary. Most people, though, will continue to hold theistic views, for mostly untenable reasons. Similarly, anti-natalism might never gain widespread support, given the conceptual challenges and courage required to make sense of such an uncommon and seemingly cheerless view.

Given these considerations regarding the unpalatability of, and steep intellectual challenge offered by, anti-natal views, I suggest that it is no wonder that these ideas are resisted by so many. But there are *arguments* (in my view, good ones) for these "unintuitive" ideas. The same cannot be said for many of the other debunked positions to which masses of people cling. It is not enough to show, as the friend of endorsement tries to do, that a view held by many (namely endorsement as gladness) sufficiently justifies holding that view. To my mind, the preceding strongly suggests that pro-natal beliefs arise from, and thrive under, much the same circumstances as theistic beliefs. As such, there are, I assert, strong reasons to believe that the popularity of pro-natalism may be due to widespread delusion.

### 4.3. Some Harms Remain Impermissible Despite Endorsement

It is possible to grant that i) gladness can be equated with endorsement, and that ii) endorsement without delusion is possible, whilst denying that an appeal to endorsement is a sound moral strategy—that is, whilst rejecting Principle B. Apart from the degree of harm involved, some actions continue to appear impermissible despite apparently good reasons to assume that they will be endorsed.

For example, imagine that someone who is sexually assaulted comes to endorse the actions of her assailant. Perhaps she sees this as an expression of his affection for her—and she is glad to have his affection—or his actions result in her bearing children she comes to love dearly. Assume her assailant, for whatever reason, does not judge his actions to involve any serious harm. Furthermore, assume that he is perhaps motivated to act in this harmful manner because he believes that his partner will be glad that he decided to so vigorously display his attraction to her. For most of human history, conceivably, many marriages contained (and unfortunately continue to contain) such scenarios.

The obvious reply on behalf of the friend of endorsement is that sexual assault remains wrong, because despite the assailant having an intention to benefit his partner, she is glad that he acted in this manner toward her due to faulty reasoning. What is more, he ought to know that her gladness arises in this deluded manner. The reply, to be clear, is that procreation is disanalogous with this example: procreators, though they foresee harm, do not intend this harm; rather, they intend to benefit their offspring, and their offspring are, without delusion, glad to have been created.

However, this reply assumes that sexual assault is wrong in a way that procreation is not. It assumes that sexual assault is perhaps always wrong, and that there is a *prima facie* case for believing that those who think otherwise do so due to deluded reasons, but that procreation is merely *pro tanto* wrong, with a *prima facie* case for believing that there are good reasons for assuming its permissibility. I think that it is possible to contest this reply. Apart from noting that anti-natalism challenges precisely the notion that there is a *prima facie* case for the permissibility of procreation, I must emphasise that many factors are taken into account when deciding whether something is "reasonable" not. One factor that could motivate the view that a judgement is reasonable is its consistency with received wisdom. It could be argued that both the victim and perpetrator in the above example were not being unreasonable: it was not unreasonable for them to believe the things they did, because, traditionally, the sort of action they were reviewing was considered permissible. Similarly, would-be parents are not necessarily unreasonable, or deluded, to appeal to the traditional view of procreation as a morally innocent activity.

But the point I want to emphasise here is that there is a difference between a correct and a reasonable judgement—a distinction the friend of endorsement's view apparently neglects. It strikes me that something is amiss with his strategy. Post-Benatar, we cannot, without controversy, presume a certain view of what's right in the case of procreation. To my mind, seeing as significant harm is at stake only if we do act, we ought to refrain from acting until we are sure not merely that it is reasonable to consider our actions permissible—anti-natalism, as with atheism or environmental ethics, turns received wisdom on its head!—but that they are all-things-considered correct. In other words, we have to concern ourselves with ascertaining what is right, as opposed to what is merely reasonable to believe will be endorsed. I therefore believe that the sexual assault counterexample to Principle B withstands criticism that the adherent to endorsement would proffer.

### 4.4. No Moral Theory Underwrites Endorsement

In my view, what follows is the strongest way of objecting to the friend of endorsement's view. I argue that the friend of endorsement does not give good reasons for why either the consequentialist or the deontologist should care about his claims. This is because an appeal to endorsement doesn't naturally fit into either of the two dominant moral theories. And thus, because we can't make sense of appeals to endorsement in light of our best moral theories, I conclude that we ought to reject this strategy, that is, we ought to favour Principle A over Principle B.

Moral theorists are often concerned with giving an account of what's right in general. When it comes to assessing the morality of actions—that is, whether an action is permissible or not—there are two dominant theories moral philosophers adopt. On one theory, an action is permissible, roughly, if that action promotes the good. This perspective, focusing on the outcomes or consequences of an action, is known as "consequentialism". On the other moral theory, an action is permissible roughly if that action accords with some moral principle or norm. This perspective, "deontology", denies that an action can be justified solely by its consequences. So, even if an action will in fact produce certain goods, this action, according to the deontologist, ought not to be performed if it violates certain moral principles or norms. Deontology thus defines the right independently of promoting the good.

An anti-natalist could either be a consequentialist or a deontologist: he could say either that procreation does not in fact ever promote the good, or that even though good might result, it is all things considered wrong to procreate. To be clear, the anti-natal deontologist claims that the act of procreation is (nearly) always wrong, and that this judgement does not rest solely upon any putative good produced by the act of procreation. Thus, whilst genuine (undeluded, cognitive) endorsement of creation by those who are in fact created would be (no more than) *nice*, this would not undo the wrong of creation. Put in other words, setting aside for now claims about adaptive preferences and other varieties of delusion, the fact that a person comes into existence and truly experiences her life as a benefit ought not to matter to the deontologist, as the putative good of endorsement, which comes long after procreative action, is irrelevant to the question of wrongness. The deontologist, depending on her stance, cares about whether procreation is a violation of dignity or of rights (etc.); the post-creative feeling of gladness does not naturally fit into her moral view.

To the consequentialist, an action is right or wrong depending on whether it promotes intrinsic goods. The consequentialist need not, and invariably does not, care whether or not her actions are endorsed. What if it were argued, though, that the consequentialist ought to care—that genuine endorsement is good for its own sake, a value that we ought to promote because our actions would increase happiness were they to be endorsed? In reply, imagine two possible outcomes of some act $x$. On Outcome 1, act $x$ successfully promotes the good, but this good is not endorsed by its intended beneficiaries. On outcome 2, the same act successfully promotes the same good, but this time the good *is* endorsed by its intended beneficiaries. Outcome 2 seems better, as there is more good (as happiness). But the fact that she can only hope for Outcome 1 does not give the consequentialist less cause to perform act $x$: if she deems that Outcome 1 is a good worth promoting, and that action $x$ has an excellent chance of promoting it, it is permissible for her to promote Outcome 1. Her aim is to promote some definitive good via act $x$; any additional "good" would be a bonus. Of course, Outcome 2 would be preferable, but if the consequentialist considers Outcome 1 a satisfactory consequence worthy of promotion, this is all she needs. Moreover, though the lack of endorsement of her actions is regrettable, it is not a determining factor, on consequentialist grounds, for the permissibility of her actions.

## 5) Conclusion

I have tried to present Principle B as the most plausible representation of the friend of endorsement's moral intuitions. I have argued that even if Principle B is tenable, it cannot be used to justify procreation. But I have argued further that Principle B in fact lacks justification. It appears as though an endorsement-independent standard is required in order to justify procreation; contrary to the friend of endorsement's claims, endorsement alone will not suffice. This is a significant revelation, as many people are inclined to believe that "endorsement" is sufficient to render procreation permissible.

Beyond the endorsement objection, Shiffrin's anti-natalism can be tested against at least three other objections. Procreation might be all-things-considered permissible because it is permissible: (1) for one to knowingly harm an unconsenting patient non-trivially if one has good reasons for assuming her *hypothetical consent*, and procreators can indeed reasonably rely on some notion of hypothetical consent; (2) for parents to harm a child by having created her if they subsequently offer her *adequate compensation*; and (3) for parents to impose the harms of life upon their offspring if some *intended benefit (or prevention of harm) to third parties* is subsequently realised.[16] Of these objections, I think the last one is the most promising. But I am of the view that Shiffrin's "anti-natalism" is sturdy enough to withstand even this Mill-inspired objection. Shiffrin's route to anti-natalism, as with Benatar's, thus constitutes a considerable moral position.

---

16 I examine these objections in *Assessing Anti-Natalism: A Philosophical Examination of the Morality of Procreation* (unpublished MA, University of Johannesburg), from which the present article is taken. I argue there that none of these objections is successful.

**References**

Benatar, D. 1997. "Why It Is Better Never To Have Come Into Existence," *American Philosophical Quarterly* 34: 345-55. Reprinted in: Benatar, D. (ed.) (2004). *Life, Death, & Meaning: Key Philosophical Readings on the Big Questions.* Maryland: Rowman & Littlefield Publishing Group: 155-168.

Benatar, D. 2006. *Better Never To Have Been: The Harm of Coming Into Existence.* Oxford: Clarendon Press.

Blumenfeld, D. 2009. "Living Life Over Again," *Philosophy and Phenomenological Research* LXXIX: 357-386.

DeGrazia, D. 2011. "Bearing Children in Wrongful Life Cases," in his *Creation Ethics: Reproduction, Genetics, and Quality of Life.* Oxford: Oxford University Press, ch. 5 (forthcoming).

Shiffrin, S. 1999. "Wrongful Life, Procreative Responsibility, and the Significance of Harm," *Legal Theory* 5: 117-148.

Singh, A. 2011. *Assessing Anti-Natalism: A Philosophical Examination of the Morality of Procreation* (unpublished MA dissertation, University of Johannesburg, 2012).

# A New Argument for Anti-Natalism

## Christopher Belshaw

Arguments for anti-natalism – the view that it's better never to have been born and hence that procreation is wrong– excite more curiosity than approval. The claim is strongly counterintuitive: there are some desperately bad lives but in general it's hard to believe we do anything wrong in bringing new people into the world, in prolonging the existence of those already here, or in thinking that life is worth living.

David Benatar's position is, of course, not quite so radical as it might at first seem, or as that suggested here. He's against starting new lives, but not against continuing those lives already under way. He's down on birth, but far from up on death.[1] But this softening of the view hasn't won him many friends. The view now may be more acceptable but it is, the suspicion has it, less consistent.

I don't intend here to look at Benatar's claims in any detail. Rather I want to offer a new argument for this seemingly unstable anti-natalist and anti-mortalist mix. No human lives should be started. But once they're properly under way, we usually do well to continue them. I begin on this argument in Section II. But first some preliminary scene-setting. And I want to pick out three points on which Benatar I are in agreement, before moving on to one where we start to come apart.

I

Why should anyone be even so much as tempted by anti-natalism? If it's better that we never come into existence, this is most likely going to be in virtue of what's in store for us when do exist.[2] And what's in store is, in fact, some measure of frustration, distress, pain. It's a contingent matter as to just how much pain some life will contain, and it's a contingent matter too as to whether it contains pain at all. As a matter of fact all of us living anything like a normal life will undergo some degree of pain, but we can perhaps imagine for ourselves a pain-free existence, or even persuade ourselves we'll have such an existence in the afterlife. So anti-natalism will be at best contingently true. First, then, Benatar and I are in agreement on that.[3]

Most of us will agree that there is pain, but object that only rarely is it so bad as to make non-existence preferable. Typically, the anti-natalist argues not about the detail of the amounts, but insists that any painful episode is enough to warrant the downbeat stance. And now there is already available a familiar position, and a straightforwardly

---

1    Benatar (1997) 349-350, (2006) 22-24, 211ff.
2    'Most likely' as we can perhaps imagine that the transition from non-existence to existence is itself very bad. Somewhat analogously, someone might think ceasing to exist is bad, even while once having ceased there is no further bad to come.
3    Benatar (1997) 345, (2006) 29.

valid argument for the anti-natalist conclusion. We need simply to buy into that version of negative utilitarianism that acknowledges that there are both pleasures and pains but counts the former for nothing. So the smallest amount of pain is sufficient to make our lives not worth living, and cannot be countered by any degree of pleasure. Were this true, then, given that there is pain, the anti-natalist is home. Unfortunately, there's more to a good argument than validity. Negative utilitarianism can be plucked from the shelf, but there is no good reason to suppose it true. And were it true, it would take us too far, generating not only anti-natalism but straightaway also its pro-mortalist neighbour. For if pain is really that bad and the only way to minimise it is by death, then death it is. Unsurprisingly, then, neither Benatar nor I appeal to it, and we both have need for less straightforward arguments.

What negative utilitarianism involves, and introduces now into the discussion, is an asymmetric approach to pleasure and pain. Pain counts – pleasure doesn't. This we can characterise as a strongly asymmetric position. But there are available some weaker asymmetries – ones that venture less and are thus perhaps easier to defend. Both Benatar and I appeal to such asymmetries.[4] Can we appeal? Most people hold to there being an important asymmetry here. For most people hold, first, that there are some lives that are, others that are not, worth living and, second, while there is an obligation not to start bad lives there is no corresponding obligation to start good lives. (Either there is no obligation here at all, or any obligation is noticeably less strong than its negative counterpart.) There's a closely related asymmetry. Most of us think that while there is no obligation to start good lives, there is an obligation to preserve such lives, at least once they're well under way. This isn't always an overriding obligation, but if someone close to hand is dying for want of food I ought at least to sacrifice a slice of pizza to help him. But with bad lives, this second asymmetry doesn't obtain. If I am forbidden to start such lives, I am, or so it might seem, required to end them. Now I'm not fully defending any of this here, and it is by no means uncontroversial – the point is only that asymmetry is already so well into this general ball park that it is far from eccentric for anti-natalists to want in some way to draw upon it.[5]

This second point connects intimately with a third. I'll assume that we can coherently claim that not existing, either through being dead or through never being born, might be better or worse for someone than existing. The anti-natalist's claim isn't that it would be better for other creatures, or for the environment, or for the universe, or in itself (whatever that means) if we didn't exist. It would be better for us. Even if his opponent isn't claiming that it would be worse for us not to exist, but is merely denying that it would be better, he appears to fully understand, rather than reject as incoherent, the anti-natalist's position. The assumption being made here is, then, extremely widespread. Doubts about it, right now, just have to be set aside.[6]

---

4    Benatar (1997) 346, (2006) 32. I should point out that these particular and well-known asymmetries referenced here are not the starting point of Benatar's argument but rather figure as relevant data that are allegedly best explained by appeal to further asymmetries. See note 27 below.

5    The asymmetry here is famously identified by Jan Narveson, in his claim that 'We are in favour of making people happy, but neutral about making happy people' (1976) 73. And it is challenged, though less famously, by John Broome (1994) 228ff.

6    See, for example, David Heyd (1992) for sustained doubts about whether the non-existent can be assigned any level of well-being. I'm with Benatar here: 'I shall not claim that the never-existent literally are better off...' (2006) 4. But though not literally better off, still meaningful comparisons can, we both think, be made.

So far, so harmonious. But I want to turn now to that most troubling aspect of Benatar's position – the mix of anti-natalism on the one hand, and a rejection of pro-mortalism on the other. In some ways this isn't troubling at all, but not, I'll suggest, in ways that offer Benatar any comfort.

Why isn't it troubling? Surely this can be true – someone can reasonably wish they'd never been born, reasonably judge their life to have been best not lived, even while they have now no wish to die, and want now to live on. Why never born? Perhaps twenty years ago they were ordered to kill all the people in some village. Or, and here more relevant, perhaps for their first twenty years there was nothing to their life but the enduring of a series of painful operations. But what's done is done, the past is the past and right now, and for foreseeable times ahead, life promises to be more than merely tolerable. We might be untroubled, then, simply by noting that even if the value of a whole life is the sum of its parts, those parts are unlikely to be uniform. So a life might be overall not worth living, worse than nothing, while parts of it are worth living, are better than nothing. And when those parts are present and future it's perfectly clear how someone might regret having been born, yet have no wish to die. Could something like this be true of all of us? Suppose our lives are really bad for the first ten years, and then get much better. Then it could be true of all of us (all of us over ten) that death would be bad for us, even though it was bad for us to be born.[7] And I'll appeal to something like this in my argument below.

It doesn't help Benatar. His argument doesn't depend on there being any more than a minimal amount of pain.[8] And it doesn't depend on where, in life, that pain occurs. So how does he avoid pro-mortalism, holding that in spite of our almost all of us having considerable amounts of pain to come there is no reason to throw in the towel? He appeals to what has called the dual-benchmark view,[9] the idea that different standards apply in thinking about tolerable shortcomings in first future, second present lives. So, for example, while we might properly decide not to bring someone into existence if they will be lacking a limb, a similar disability wouldn't be reason to end a life. And, more generally, 'We require stronger justification for ending a life than for not starting one'.[10] Pursue this, and we can have our cake and also eat it, holding that our lives are so bad – in virtue of containing some pain – as to be best not started, but even though they are not now less bad, are still not bad enough to warrant their being ended.

The limb example is Benatar's own.[11] And it fails on a number of counts. Certainly, if someone is in danger of being born without a limb, and this can be fixed *in utero* then we should fix it. It's better to have all four limbs. If we can choose between two possible children, one with four limbs, the other with three then it may well be reasonable to choose the former. If there is no choice, and it's this child or none at all, some will elect for none. It might be reasonable for them to so elect on indirect grounds. But it's hard to see that lacking a limb should make life not worth living.

Suppose we think it does. We need to compare like with like. Because of some inherited disease, a future child will lose a limb at age 30. And a present child will lose a

---

7    Notice that the claim here isn't about the overall balance between pleasure and pain. Even if most of your life has been bad, and there's not much time left, if it's good from hereon then death now is bad. And even if there's more good than bad to come, and indeed more good than bad in total, still, it may be better now to die than to suffer and wait.

8    He says, 'a life filled with good and containing only the most minute quantity of bad – a life of utter bliss adulterated only by the pain of a single pin prick – is worse than no life at all' (2006) 48.

9    See in particular Archard and Benatar (2010) 37-42.

10    Benatar (2006) 23.

11    Benatar (2006) 23-24.

limb at age 30. As there clearly isn't reason to kill this child now, so there isn't reason to prevent the other child, at least if we're thinking only of his good, from being born. Suppose the future child will be born without a limb. If we think this will make his life not worth living, we should think of a present child, who was born without a limb, that his life is not worth living, even if we decline to kill him.

So, as there can be value differences between lives overall and the parts that make them up, there can similarly be value differences between being always limbless, or blind or what have you, and meeting with these conditions in the course of your life. There's a further difference. We might be obligated to make some sacrifice, pay some price, in order to preserve the life of someone with a disability, but won't need to make such a sacrifice in order to start a life. But, as I've said, we're not obligated to start even the best of lives. It's quite another matter to claim we are obligated to prevent them from starting.

To summarise this: Consider good lives. There is no reason to start such lives, but if started, there is reason to continue them. Consider bad lives. I said earlier that we might think that if there is reason not to start such lives, then there is reason to end them. We can now see where there is truth in this. If the part of a life that provides us reason not to start it remains in the future, then there is reason to end it. Once that part is in the past, the reason disappears. And we can see where Benatar might have a problem. Pain is a reason not to start a life. But for almost all of us, there is pain to come in the future. Thus there is reason to end our lives.

## II

The focus has been, and will be, on human lives. But to get to anti-natalism I need a detour. So, consider now those non-human animals like rabbits, sheep, giraffes and so on, about which, surely, we have good reasons to believe they feel pleasure and pain,[12] but lack good reasons to raise the complicating question of whether they are persons. Set aside, then, corals, worms, insects on the one hand, and apes, whales, maybe also dogs and cats on the other. Can such animals live worthwhile lives? I want to suggest they can't. If we are looking just to the well-being of such animals, and not to their instrumental value then, I claim, we should think it better if these animals didn't exist. And so we have reason to end their lives.

We often think it right to put an animal out of its misery. If it is in extreme pain, and there is only more pain to come, then, or so most of us believe, it would be better to end this life now. We might have the same view about human beings in a similar state, and perhaps wish for a change in the law on euthanasia. But now there comes a difference. With an animal, even if there is more pleasure to come, many still think it better to end the life now than have it endure current misery. So even if we can be persuaded that Daphne's parrot, should it survive, will have another year of good parrot life ahead of it, still we might think it better if she lets it die now, rather than subject it to a string of painful operations. And the thought here isn't about what's better financially, or what will be better for Daphne's longer term peace of mind; it's about what's better for the bird. Even if we know there's more long term pleasure than short term pain, still (and for reasons I'll explore) that won't justify us in inflicting upon it this pain. We're unlikely, I suggest, to have the same view about human beings.

---

12   So I want to reject both quasi-Cartesian contentions that there is no pain in animal lives, and also the subtler, although no more convincing, view (as in Carruthers (1992)) that though there is pain, animals are not aware of it.

This points to, and is accounted for by, some important differences between human and animal lives. We typically care a good deal about the future, what happens then, and our place within it. But contrast two sorts of case. Assume I will be alive in the next decade. Maybe it's reasonable for me to endure the dentist now in order to enjoy restaurants then. Assume my future existence is in the balance. I really want to finish Proust, and so want to live on. Maybe it's reasonable for me to have the heart by-pass in order to gain more time. The first sort of case has something of a parallel for animals. It's reasonable to shoe a horse now in order to prevent it from being lame. Not so the second: animals don't have, now, desires about their longer term futures. They don't want to live on. So it's far from clear why we should hurt them so that they can live on. Some of this can usefully be expressed in other terms. Most of us have, regarding the time ahead, both *categorical desires* – desires that give us reason to ensure our future existence, and also *conditional desires* – desires that, assuming we'll have a future existence, this rather than that obtains.[13] So most of us will choose, and it seems we are often not unreasonable in this, to put up with present pain for future benefit, where this benefit is understood either as both providing and shaping the future or as shaping it alone.

I want to deny that animals, at least of the kinds being considered here, have categorical desires. They don't have the sorts of desires regarding the future that provide them with reasons for staying alive. They neither want to live on nor want those things that give them reason to live on.[14] But also, I deny that they have conditional desires. They don't desire the future to be a certain way, on condition that they live to see it. This is why I say the dentist case has only something of a parallel. We can decide to impose some cost on an animal for its future benefit, but it can't decide this for itself. And animals lack both sorts of desires, I suggest, as they lack what they necessarily involve, namely, developed conceptions both of time and of their own identities as persisting through it.[15]

From all this there can be derived some observations about the value of death. Death is bad for us, when it's bad, as it prevents us from doing what we (reasonably) want to, and otherwise would, do. I'm suggesting here a desire-related qualification of the deprivation account – death is bad not simply in depriving us of a good life, but rather of a good life that we desire to live.[16] Animals lack such desires. So a painless death isn't, in the critical sense, bad for them. It isn't something we should regret or seek to avoid. When is death good? In our case it isn't good on every occasion when we would otherwise be in severe pain. Pain is something we can with reason choose to tolerate in order to avoid death. Animals cannot choose to tolerate pain. And as there is no reason for them to avoid death, so we cannot reasonably inflict pain upon them in order to extend their lives. Nor can we, for that reason, reasonably permit them to suffer pain. When it's pain or death we should, on their behalf, choose death.[17]

---

13  See especially Williams (1973) 85ff.
14  For the contrary view, see Bradley (2009) 147-154 and his unpublished paper 'Is Death Bad for Cow?' But see Garner (2005) for reservations about the sorts of evidence appealed to here.
15  See Wittgenstein 'A dog believes his master is at the door. But can he also believe he will come the day after tomorrow?' (1978) 174.
16  This is not uncontroversial. I've argued for the view at greater length in my (2009) 115-121 and also in 'Death, Value and Desire' 2012.
17  I should clarify. My view isn't that whenever an animal experiences any pain whatsoever, then death is to be preferred. Rather, when its life now and in the immediate future is such as to be worse than nothing, then death is to be preferred.

Suppose this isn't quite the choice. An animal has pleasure now. But there is severe pain to come. We can painlessly end its life now, or permit it to live on. Assume we can't end its life at any intermediate time – there just won't be the opportunity for this. Perhaps we should end its life now. Present pains are not justified by future pleasures. And nor can present pleasures compensate for future pain. But the amounts are not critical here. Suppose this animal will have a pleasant life both now and through the medium term future. The pain won't last long before it dies. Still, assuming it's now or never, perhaps we should end its life now. No amount of present or future pleasure can justify the inflicting, or permitting, of future pain.

Very many animals have pain, and in not inconsiderable amounts, ahead. They will suffer from disease, or predation, or they'll be caught in traps, or killed, but less than outright, on roads, or age will make them less able to look after, feed, house themselves. And no one else, neither us nor other animals, will help. Animals are part of nature. They belong, as much as anything does, on this planet. They are useful to us, to each other, to plants. They offer us more than material benefits – we can admire them, study them, enjoy living alongside them, maybe make friends with them.[18] But from none of this does it follow that they lives are worth living, or that it's good for them to be alive. And, I claim, it would be better for them were they not to exist. Best is if they never come into existence. Second best is if they die painless deaths, not as soon as possible, but before they next suffer pain.

An objection permits clarification. Given that I allow animals can experience pleasure and, over their lives, perhaps more pleasure than pain, why is their existence, for them, such a bad thing? An overall pleasant life is usually good for us. It's hard to see what is so different about animals. This objection derives from claims about animal psychology. So too does the reply.

Utilitarians are happy to trade pleasures and pains across different lives. Not so many of us are utilitarians. Many of us think it wrong to subject one human being to pain in order to prevent pain in others. We think torture is wrong, for example. Even more of us think it would be wrong to hurt one human being in order to please another. Rape, for instance.[19] Similarly, it would be wrong to hurt one animal simply in order to generate pleasure in some other animal. Both the amounts and the timing seem irrelevant here. The second animal gets considerable quantities of pleasure now if the first suffers some pain later. This still doesn't justify the pain. Irrelevant too – and this now is the critical claim – is the fact that in these examples different animals are involved. For insofar as they lack categorical desires, and so lack more than a rudimentary notion of their own identity, the psychological parts of an animal's life knit together only weakly. They live in effect fragmented lives. And so the distinction between having the same animal persisting through time, and replacing that animal with another is, in this context, far from profound. As you can't subject one animal to pain for the sake of pleasure for a second animal, so you can't subject this animal to pain at one time for the sake of its own pleasure at some different time. The point here isn't simply about what one can and can't do. Situations in which one animal suffers so others can prosper, or in which it suffers at one time so it can prosper at other times are, I claim, situations we should hope do not obtain.

18   Gruen (2011).
19   See Ryder (2011) for pointed use of this example.

This argument appeals to a lack of integration in animal lives. It doesn't appeal to a negative balance of pleasure over pain. And it claims that both anti-natalism and pro-mortalism are true for animals.

III

Our lives are different. The parts do knit together, and we can reasonably head for pain on the way to pleasure. We can, and often do, have good lives. And those lives remain good even if they have periods of pain within them. There is no reason to end such lives. And it seems there is no reason not to start them. So we can't straightforwardly use the sort of argument above to get to anti-natalism. Nor, given that pro-mortalism falls from it, should we want to. But what are we, that live these different lives?

On one widely held view we are *persons*. Persons, in the quasi-technical sense I mean to evoke here, are characterised by their psychological properties – they are rational self-conscious beings, aware of the distinctions between themselves and other beings, aware of their persisting through time.[20] So, as is often said, the relation between persons and human beings is not one of identity – fetuses, the comatose, the dead are not persons, even if human, while cyborgs, dolphins, gods, may be persons while not belonging to our species. But there's a further strand to the view that I need to pick out. It is uncontroversial, given this understanding of 'person', that most of us go through, and all readers of this are now in, a person phase. It is uncontroversial that as there are teenagers, postmen, psychopaths, so too there are persons. But it is a widely held view that we are persons in a deeper, more fundamental – and indeed more controversial – sense; that persons are the kinds of things we are, that 'person' isn't a phase, but a substance term.[21] As I've just suggested, it is, arguably, a contingent fact that persons are human beings: on the view here it is a contingent fact that we are human beings, or even animals at all. For we, each one of us, might exist without being a human being or an animal at all, if for example we are reduced either to a brain or to a computer programme.

Suppose we are persons, in the substance sense. Then we go out of existence when we lose those psychological properties that are essential to making us what we are. None of us will be, even if we might turn into, a corpse, a victim of brain death, or a hospital patient in PVS. And none of us was ever a human embryo, or a fetus, or a new-born baby, even if we have somehow emerged from those things.[22] For if we are in this sense persons we come into existence when those psychological properties adequately coalesce. There are tricky questions here. There are corpses. If I am never a corpse does the corpse come into existence when I die, or does it somehow exist all along? Does the baby stop existing as I start, or does it manage to continue (but get considerably bigger?) so that there are now two things here – the person I am and the ex-baby from which I somehow derive? There isn't, unsurprisingly, space to pursue all this here, and nothing of critical importance rests upon it. But assume there is something in this person view. And now for a moment forget, more or less, about us, and think about babies.

---

20  Or as Locke put it, 'a thinking intelligent being, that has reason and reflection, and can consider itself as itself, the same thinking thing, in different times and places' (1975) 335; (II, xxvii, 9).
21  For detail on this distinction see especially Wiggins (1980) 24ff.
22  See Olson (1997).

Imagine that our relationship to a baby is like that of a butterfly to a caterpillar. Rather than a piecemeal emergence of complex psychological properties, and thus of the person, imagine instead that a baby is born, lives a baby life for about eighteen months, then falls into some sort of coma. Its life is over. After a year a pretty much fully-fledged person emerges. What should we think of this baby's life? Is it worth living?

A baby is a human animal. And it seems that in many ways we should think of this baby's life as we think about, and as I've argued we should think about, the life of non-human animals such as the rabbit or giraffe. It experiences moments of pleasure, moments of pain. But these moments don't very well knit together. It has no developed notion of itself, or of time, no desire to live on into the future, no ability to think about pain and decide to endure it. Further, if we think seriously about a baby's life we'll probably agree it experiences pain in more than trivial amounts. Even perfectly healthy babies come into the world screaming, cry a lot, suffer colic and teething pains, keep people awake at night. None of us can remember anything about it. Perhaps we've just blanked it out.

Thus construed, this baby's life is, I suggest, not worth living. It might have been instrumental in bringing into existence a wholly worthwhile life – mine – but this is not at all in the interests of, and brings about no compensations or benefits for, the baby. It would have been better for the baby had it never been born. And given there's always more pain to come, it would have been better, at many stages during its miserable existence, had it then died.

Drop the science fiction. Imagine a real baby that because of a condition painless in itself is destined to die at twelve months. And imagine my rather gloomy picture of baby lives is more or less correct. Then whatever short term joys it might bring to the lives of its parents, I think we should believe it would, given the colic, the teething etc. have been better for this baby had it never been born, and better that it die before the twelve months is out. This short life isn't worth living.

Is anything importantly different if we go back to the standard and actual case, where the baby develops gradually into the person? Remember, we are still understanding this as involving a substantial difference – the baby is one being, the person is another. I can't see that gradualism has any bearing here. Even if we come into existence by degrees, the two beings here remain distinct. And so the conclusion still stands. If we value our own lives, want there to be more people in the world, we may well continue to make babies. But what's good for them isn't good for us, and vice versa. We're exploiting them, and exist only because this other creature has suffered. I may be glad that there was a baby. But it would have better for the baby never to have been born.

IV

This is some way from concluding my argument. For on the picture here there's one kind of thing – the baby – about which anti-natalism and pro-mortalism are both true and another – the person – of whom pro-mortalism is false while anti-natalism is seemingly either false or meaningless. Strictly, we are never born. But it wouldn't be better for us never to come into existence. So we're not yet at the position of having one thing for which anti-natalism is true, pro-mortalism false. And that is what I'm after.

Consider now the view that played a critical role in the previous section. Are we persons? Though many think we are, and in the substantial sense, a contrasting and increasingly popular view is that we are animals.[23] We begin as fetuses, if not before, go through baby, teenager, adult and dotage stages, continuing to exist at least until we die. So (and as common sense would have it) we ourselves are born, rather than developing some time after, and depending on, the birth of some other things. Suppose that this is right. What shall we now say? There is on this new picture a considerable difference between a baby and a non-human animal. A baby will develop into an adult human being, and thus become a person (understood here in the phase sense) living, in most cases, a worthwhile life, with a sense of, and desires for, a future. It will become someone who has reasons, on occasion, to suffer pain, and for whom death is bad. It will become someone for whom pro-mortalism is false.

But not yet. Even if it has the potential,[24] this baby isn't so far a person, lacks these desires, these reasons. We can acknowledge what lies ahead but still ask, is death, now, bad for this baby? There are, in broad terms, three responses available – yes, very bad; well, a bit bad; no, not bad at all. The deprivation account insists on the first. Imagine someone dies at 20 rather 80, losing 60 good years. Her death is very bad. But the baby's death is worse: it loses the 60 years along with 19 more. This is a considerably greater loss. A version of a commonsense approach suggests it's a bit bad. If you can save either a baby or its 20 year old mother from a burning car then choose the mother. But of course it's better to save both.[25] I say it's not bad at all. Agreed, having this sort of future ahead is now a difference between a baby and a non-human animal, but it's not a future for which the baby has any desire, in which it has an interest. And it can be contended that if death is bad for babies, then it's bad too for fetuses and embryos and it's bad, further, when conception is close, would have generated a worthwhile life, but is frustrated.[26] Only a handful of those thinking, as altogether naturally most of us do think, that it is a terrible tragedy when a baby dies, want to embrace all this. (I can make a conciliatory gesture. Death is bad for babies in the sense in which it is bad for plants. When they die there are fewer good lives lived. But why care about that?)

Suppose the claim here, that painless death isn't bad for babies, can be defended. Surely it's now only a short step to claim also that it is good for them. For only rarely is death of neutral value.[27] It is, very plausibly, neither good not bad for trees, and it might be argued that it is neither good nor bad for the irreversibly comatose, but where sentient creatures are concerned it's hard to see how it can often hang in the balance. Babies suffer some significant degrees of pain. This doesn't bring them some compensating good. So, if death isn't bad for them then, as it's a means of avoiding this pain, it's good for them.

If it's good for babies to die then it's better for them not to be born in the first place. I mean this in two senses. It's better for them not to be born than to be born and to live. And it's better for them not to be born than to be born and die.

---

23  Snowdon (1990). Olson (1997), (2003).
24  I use this term in something like an Aristotelian sense, to suggest it is more than merely possible for a baby to develop into a person, but rather in its nature or telos to do so.
25  See for interesting discussion of this sort of case, McMahan (1988).
26  See Marquis (1994) for discussion and disagreement on this point. And notice my claim isn't that it is worse when an embryo or fetus dies than when a baby dies, but just that it is, on the deprivation view, equally bad.
27  I mean to distinguish here the state of being dead, which I hold is in itself of neutral value – it is in itself neither good nor bad to be dead – from the event of death which, as it leads to the state, is bad or good depending on whether the life it cuts off would have been good or bad.

What we now have in place is something like the picture I merely began to sketch earlier, where an overall worthwhile life begins more or less disastrously. Imagine we look at creatures on a distant planet. They live for ten years in agony, and thereafter sixty years in bliss. And there are no important psychological connections over this period. We probably think it better if these creatures never come to be, though of course after ten years there's no reason at all to kill them, or wish them dead. This is, I've argued, more or less the picture with human lives.

## V

An ongoing focus has been on mixing anti-natalism with anti-mortalism. We don't easily achieve this. We don't achieve it, I've argued, for animals. From the fairly widespread view that painless death is not bad for them it's not too difficult to conclude, I've suggested, both that coming into existence is bad and death is good for them. If we are persons, distinct from babies, then we get this mix neither for persons – us – or for babies. Babies are now like animals, and it's best they neither start nor continue. And, in most cases, it's neither good for us that we die, nor bad for us that we begin to exist in the first place. Nevertheless, we might think our beginning to exist is an overall bad thing. For on this view we are inevitably free-riding on the several misfortunes of small, helpless and shortlived creatures.

If, however, common sense is right, and we begin with conception or birth, end with death or decay, then though for most of us life is usually good, so that there is no reason now to end it, still, given its condition at the outset, we can believe it would have been better had we not been born.

This is the conclusion Benatar was after. Is my argument really that different? We both appeal to certain asymmetries. But whereas Benatar's discussion here is complex and, as he allows, controversial,[28] I look only to a familiar and widely accepted asymmetry: we are obliged not to start bad lives, but not obliged to start good lives. That there are different standards of acceptability between present and future lives is also controversial. Benatar wants this in order sustain his anti-natalism and anti-mortalism package. My account here is, I think, more straightforward. How straightforward? Where complexities are undeniable I've wanted often to appeal to them. And my argument has drawn on differences between different sorts of lives; it has noted and taken into account the different times at which pain might occur, and it has rested a good deal on observations and claims about the ways in which our psychologies unfold. Benatar makes some reference to such considerations. But they play in his argument at best a marginal role. Finally it should be noted that my argument is less at variance with widely held views than first appears. I start with the claim that a painless death isn't bad for animals. Many people think this. I end with the claim that a painless death is bad for adults, but not for babies. Parts of our lives are not worth living. Benatar holds this is true of all of our lives. Whether he does, maybe he should think death, for the one who dies, is always good. Epicureans believe not this, but that death is never bad. My view is, compared with these, far less extreme.[29]

---

28   As suggested in note 4, the burden of his argument is carried by further alleged asymmetries, discussed at length in (1997) 345-249, and (2009) 30-59.

29   My thanks for comments and discussion to David Benatar, Stephen Holland, Christian Piller, Thaddeus Metz, Jesse Tomalty, Tatjana Visak and to all those taking part in the conference.

**References**

Archard, David and Benatar, David (eds) 2011 *Procreation and Parenthood* Oxford: Oxford University Press.

Belshaw, Christopher 2009 *Annihilation: The Sense and Significance of Death* Chesham: Acumen.

Belshaw, Christopher 2012. Death, Value and Desire. In: Feldman, Fred; Bradley, Ben and Johannsen, Jens eds. *The Oxford Handbook of the Philosophy of Death*. Oxford: OUP.

Benatar, David 1997 'Why it is Better never to Come into Existence' *American Philosophical Quarterly* 14, 3: 345-355.
2006 *Better Never to Have Been: The Harm of Coming into Existence* Oxford: Oxford University Press.

Bradley, Ben 2009 *Well-Being and Death* Oxford: Oxford University Press.
'Is Death Bad for a Cow?' (unpublished paper).

Broome, John 1994 'The Value of a Person' reprinted in Broome *Ethics Out of Economics* Cambridge: Cambridge University Press 1999.

Carruthers, Peter 1992 *The Animals Issue* Cambridge: Cambridge University Press.

Garner, Robert 2005 *Animal Ethics* Cambridge: Polity Press

Gruen, Lori 2011 *Ethics and Animals: An Introduction* Cambridge: Cambridge University Press.

Heyd, David 1992 *Genethics* Berkeley: University of California Press.

Locke, John 1975 *An Essay Concerning Human Understanding* ed. P. Nidditch Oxford: Clarendon Press (from 2$^{nd}$ edition, 1694).

Marquis, Don 1994 'Why Abortion is Immoral' *The Journal of Philosophy* 86: 183-201.

McMahan, Jeff 1988 'Death and the Value of Life' *Ethics* 99.1: 32-61.

Olson, Eric 1997 *The Human Animal* Oxford: Oxford University Press.
2003. 'An Argument for Animalism' in *Personal Identity,* eds. R. Martin and J. Barresi Oxford: Blackwell 318-34.
1997 'Was I Ever a Fetus?' *Philosophy and Phenomenological Research* 57 (1) 95-110.

Ryder, Richard 2011 *Speciesism, Painism and Happiness* Exeter: Societas Imprint-Academic.

Snowdon, Philip 1990 'Persons, Animals and Ourselves' in C. Gill (ed) *The Person and the Human Mind* Oxford: The Clarendon Press.

Wiggins, David 1980 *Sameness and Substance* Oxford: Basil Blackwell.

Williams, Bernard 1973 'The Makropoulos Case: Reflections on the Tedium of Immortality' in Williams, *Problems of the Self* Cambridge: Cambridge University Press.

Wittgenstein, Ludwig 1978 *Philosophical Investigations* Oxford: Basil Blackwell (1$^{st}$ edition, 1953).

# Every Conceivable Harm:
# A Further Defence of Anti-Natalism

## David Benatar

Many people are resistant to the conclusions for which I argued in *Better Never to Have Been*[1]. I have previously responded to most of the published criticisms of my arguments[2]. Here I respond to a new batch of critics (and to some fellow anti-natalists) who gathered for a conference at the University of Johannesburg[3] and whose papers are published in this special issue of the *South African Journal of Philosophy*. I am also taking the opportunity to respond to two other critics whose articles have previously been published in South African philosophy journals[4]. Clearly I cannot respond to all the arguments in each of these papers and thus I shall focus on what I take to be some of the central issues in each. None of the arguments to which I shall respond have caused me to revise my views. However, I am pleased to have the opportunity to show why this is the case.

## Asymmetries

One of my arguments for the conclusion that coming into existence is always a harm appeals to an asymmetry between pleasures and pains (and between benefits and harms more generally):

1) The presence of pain is bad; and
2) The presence of pleasure is good.
3) The absence of pain is good (even if that good is not enjoyed by anyone); but
4) The absence of pleasure is not bad unless there is somebody for whom this absence is a deprivation.

We can employ this asymmetry, which I shall call the *basic asymmetry*, in order to compare existing and never existing:

---

1    David Benatar, *Better Never to Have Been: The Harm of Coming into Existence*, Oxford: Oxford University Press, 2006.
2    A list of comments and responses is being collected here: http://web.uct.ac.za/depts/philosophy/staff_benatar_betternevertohavebeen.htm
3    I am grateful to Thaddeus Metz for conceiving and organizing the conference and for inviting me to participate.
4    Thaddeus Metz, "Are Lives Worth Creating?" in *Philosophical Papers*, Vol. 40, No. 2, July 2011, pp. 233-255, and David Spurrett, "Hooray for babies", *South African Journal of Philosophy*, Vol. 30, No 2, 2011, pp. 197-206.

|                              | Scenario A<br>(X exists)                  | Scenario B<br>(X never exists)              |
|------------------------------|-------------------------------------------|---------------------------------------------|
|                              | (1)<br>Presence of Pain<br>(Bad)          | (3)<br>Absence of Pain<br>(Good)            |
|                              | (2)<br>Presence of Pleasure<br>(Good)     | (4)<br>Absence of Pleasure<br>(Not bad)     |

**Figure 1**

We find that (3) is a real advantage over (1). However, while (2) is good for X in scenario A, it is not an advantage over (4) in scenario B. There are thus no net benefits of coming into existence compared to never existing.

The basic asymmetry strikes me as a fundamental moral truth. I suspect that it is widely accepted – that is, until people see where it leads, namely to the conclusion that coming into existence is always a harm. Once people see this implication they scramble desperately to find some way to avoid having to accept the asymmetry. Because I anticipated this reaction, I did not simply assert the asymmetry. I also argued that we should not abandon it. One reason for retaining it is that it is, I suggested, the best explanation for four other asymmetries that are widely accepted[5]:

*i) The asymmetry of procreational duties:*

While we have a duty to avoid bringing into existence people who would lead miserable lives, we have no duty to bring into existence those who would lead happy lives.

*ii) The prospective beneficence asymmetry:*

It is strange to cite as a reason for having a child that that child will thereby be benefited. It is not similarly strange to cite as a reason for not having a child that that child will suffer.

*iii) The retrospective beneficence asymmetry:*

When one has brought a suffering child into existence, it makes sense to regret having brought that child into existence – and to regret it for the sake of that child. By contrast, when one fails to bring a happy child into existence, one cannot regret that failure for the sake of the person.

---

5    While all the following asymmetries were mentioned in *Better Never to Have Been*, the names I give to them below were not used in the book. I used them for the first time in "Still Better Never to Have Been: A reply to more of my critics", forthcoming in *The Journal of Ethics*. ("Still Better Never to Have Been" was written well before the current response, but it seems that it might only be published afterwards.)

*iv) The asymmetry of distant suffering and absent happy people:*
We are rightly sad for distant people who suffer. By contrast we need not shed any tears for absent happy people on uninhabited planets, or uninhabited islands or other regions on our own planet.

My critics have responded to these asymmetries in various ways.

## David Spurrett:

David Spurrett, denies that the asymmetry of procreational duties is widely accepted[6]. In support of this he cites the many religious people who think that we do have a duty to reproduce – a duty based on the divine command to "be fruitful and multiply" – and nationalists who think that their co-nationals have a duty to procreate for the sake of the nation.

This is a flippant response. First, it should be clear that the procreational duties of which I spoke are duties grounded in the interests of those who would be brought into existence. Neither the religious nor the national case is a counter-example to that. The followers of God's (purported) commandments are reproducing not for the sake of the offspring but because God has commanded them to. And the nationalists are reproducing for the sake of the nation, not for the sake of the children they produce.

Second, almost all the philosophers who have written about ethical issues pertaining to future people have accepted the asymmetry of procreational duties. It is far too glib to ignore this. Even if he were correct that many people deny the asymmetry, it would remain true that the asymmetry is widely accepted by people who have actually thought seriously about it.

Something similar might be said of Professor Spurrett's response to the prospective beneficence asymmetry. Here he says, first, that because there are "plenty of strange truths"[7], the strangeness of citing as a reason for having the child the fact that the child will be benefited, does not mean that we are not warranted in citing such a reason. He then questions whether citing such a reason really is so strange. People do speak in this way, he says.

Both of these responses rely on appeals to the views of those unschooled in these matters. Just as unschooled people do sometimes say that they want to have a child for the child's sake, so people *do* address the deceased in the second-person in death notices and eulogies. That people do speak in these ways does not mean it is not strange – and in a "strange and false" rather than "strange but true" way. Professor Spurrett wants to know what is strange about it. But that is to ask for the explanation – and my answer is that what is strange about it is that it runs counter to the basic asymmetry. This might sound circular, but it is not. It is not circular because I think that people reflecting on the idea of creating a child for that child's sake will discern something odd about it even if they cannot explain it. My basic asymmetry helps them by explaining the oddness.

The same critique can be offered of his response to the retrospective beneficence asymmetry where he again refers to the possibility that somebody might regret "not

---

6    David Spurrett, "Hooray for babies", pp. 200-202.
7    Ibid, p. 202.

having a child because of the benefits that child might have enjoyed"[8]. In defence of this possibility he says that plenty "of people clearly *think* they do things for their *actual* children"[9]. This fact, however, is completely irrelevant. It makes perfect sense to think that one can sometimes benefit actual children by doing things for them. The problem is in thinking that one can benefit somebody by creating him.

Professor Spurrett does not discuss the asymmetry of distant suffering and absent happy people. This is because he restricts himself, for some unknown reason, to a discussion of my early article, "Why it is Better Never to Come into Existence"[10] where I raised only the first three asymmetries that I say are explained by the basic asymmetry. Thus we do not know whether he would accept this asymmetry and, if so, how he would explain it.

Professor Spurrett next turns his attention to the basic asymmetry itself. Here he objects to the fact that I speak only of pains and pleasures. He acknowledges that I treat these as exemplars of harms and benefits but he complains that "being exemplary is far from being exhaustive"[11] and that I need to take account of "harms and benefits besides pleasures and pains"[12]. He thus proposes the addition of at least one further row in my matrix, to yield the following:

| Scenario A<br>(X exists) | Scenario B<br>(X never exists) |
| --- | --- |
| (1)<br>Presence of Pain<br>(Bad) | (3)<br>Absence of Pain<br>(Good) |
| (2)<br>Presence of Pleasure<br>(Good) | (4)<br>Absence of Pleasure<br>(Not bad) |
| (5)<br>Presence of a valuable<br>human life<br>(Good) | (6)<br>Absence of a valuable<br>human life<br>(Bad) |

**Figure 2**

---

8    Ibid.
9    Ibid.
10   David Benatar, "Why it is Better Never to Come into Existence", *American Philosophical Quarterly*, Vol. 34, No. 2, July 1997, pp. 345-55.
11   David Spurrett, "Hooray for babies", p. 203.
12   Ibid, p. 204.

In making this move, Professor Spurrett has completely misunderstood how to make the transition from the exemplary nature of pleasure and pains to the exhaustive categorization of harms and benefits that he desires. This is how one does it:

|  | Scenario A (X exists) | Scenario B (X never exists) |
|---|---|---|
|  | (1)<br>Presence of *Harm*<br>(Bad) | (3)<br>Absence of *Harm*<br>(Good) |
|  | (2)<br>Presence of *Benefit*<br>(Good) | (4)<br>Absence of *Benefit*<br>(Not bad) |

**Figure 3**

There is no need for an additional row in order to capture all benefits and harms. Professor Spurrett anticipates this objection, but his response to it is a non-sequitur: He says that my reasons for the asymmetry "aren't convincing"[13]. But that is an objection to the evaluations of each quadrant and is not relevant to whether there should be the additional quadrants he wants to add.

Moreover, if one does add the additional row, it is far from clear that the evaluations of (5) and (6) should be "Good" and "Bad" respectively. Professor Spurrett thinks that (5) is good because "an individual human life is a valuable thing" and that (6) is bad because the absence of a value is bad. Here he makes a mistake that I shall consider below (when I discuss Skott Brill's discussion of Sick, Healthy and the logic of value).

Thaddeus Metz:

Unlike David Spurrett, Thaddeus Metz accepts the asymmetry of procreational duties. However, he thinks that it is not best explained by my basic asymmetry. Instead, he thinks that the best explanation is "the principle that *it is permissible to start a life if and only if it would be worth continuing.*"[14] He thinks that this is a better explanation because it is simpler – it "appeals solely to the facts about the nature of the lives that

---

13   Ibid.
14   Thaddeus Metz, "Are Lives Worth Creating?", *Philosophical Papers*, Vol. 40, No. 2, July 2011, p. 241.

would exist upon their being created" whereas mine "appeals to those kinds of facts plus facts about non-existence"[15].

One problem for Professor Metz's suggestion is that the principle to which he appeals is not so much an explanation of the asymmetry of procreational duties as another way of stating it. To say that "it is permissible to start a life if only if it would be worth continuing" is to say that one has a duty not to create lives that are not worth continuing, but that one has no duty to create lives that are worth continuing[16]. For this reason, the principle to which Professor Metz appeals lacks explanatory value. The same is not true of my principle.

Moreover, it is *my* explanation that is preferable on the grounds of simplicity. This is because my explanation explains all four of the other asymmetries, whereas Professor Metz has to proffer more than one explanation – and he provides no explanation at all for the asymmetry of distant suffering and absent happy people.

Consider next his explanation for the prospective beneficence asymmetry. He says that the strangeness of citing a benefit to the child as a reason for creating that child, could be explained equally well if we treated the absence of pleasure as being "not good unless there is already a potential bearer of it"[17]. Similarly, he says that the reason why it is not strange to cite the suffering of a prospective child as a reason not to have that child is that "the absence of pain is *not bad* (and that the experience of pain is bad)"[18].

It is difficult to understand how these are explanations of the prospective beneficence asymmetry. I can see how the presence of pain being bad could explain why it is not strange to cite as a reason for not having a child that that child will suffer. I do not see, however, what explanatory work is done by the claim that the absence of pain is "not bad". And why is the purported non-goodness of absent pleasure an explanation why it *is* strange to cite the future possible presence of pleasure as a reason to create the child that will experience that pleasure?

Professor Metz appeals to the same evaluations of absent pain (that is, "not bad") and absent pleasure (that is, "not good") to explain the retrospective beneficence asymmetry. Here too these evaluations fail to explain the *asymmetry*. We can see how the presence of suffering in an existent child can be cause for regret (on the basis of that suffering being bad). However, it is hard to see how the absent pleasures of the happy child that was not brought into existence is not cause for regret if those absent

---

15  Ibid.
16  The asymmetry of procreational duties, as I formulate it, refers to "miserable lives" and "happy lives" rather than to lives that are or are not "worth continuing". However, I presume that Professor Metz understands "miserable lives" as ones that are "not worth continuing" and "happy lives" as ones that "are worth continuing".
17  Thaddeus Metz, "Are Lives Worth Creating?", p. 242. The quoted words are replete with ambiguity. First, the phrase "not good" is ambiguous. On the most reasonable reading of his words here, Professor Metz is providing an alternative to my evaluation of "not bad". I proceed, for the moment, assuming that he is providing an alternative. However, it seems later (as I shall still show) that he may not be disagreeing with me, which only makes his words here more confusing. Second, the phrase "potential bearer" is ambiguous between "an actual bearer who would potentially experience the pleasure" and "a potential but not actual person who, if he were actual, would experience the pleasure". If Professor Metz means the former, as I suspect he does, he should perhaps have said: "unless there is a person who is deprived of the pleasure".
18  Thaddeus Metz, "Are Lives Worth Creating?", p. 242. I am assuming here that when he describes absent pain as "not bad", Professor Metz does not mean that it is good, because then his evaluation of (3) would be equivalent to mine. Thus he must mean "not bad, but not good either".

pleasures are "not good". If the presence of pleasure would be good and its absence is not good, surely we should regret the good that does not exist?

It is not surprising that Professor Metz's alternative evaluations of absent pain and absent pleasure do not explain the prospective and retrospective beneficence asymmetries. His evaluations of absent pain and absent pleasure appear to be symmetrical (both with each other and with the presence of pain and pleasure) and thus it is hard to understand how they could explain an *asymmetry* in prospective and retrospective beneficence.

Part of the problem, I think, is that Professor Metz's evaluations of absent pain and pleasure are unclear. Consider absent pleasure. Although he designates this as "not good", it is not clear that he is actually disagreeing with me. He says that "there is probably no qualitative difference between claiming that the absence of pleasure upon the non-existence of a person is 'not bad' as per asymmetry, and saying that it is 'not good', supposing that the latter is not meant to imply that it is bad, as I have above"[19]. But if that is the case, why complicate matters and not just accept my designation of absent pleasure as "not bad" especially since I have argued that designating it simply as "not good" is insufficiently informative?[20] And why suggest that it is an *alternative* explanation?

Consider next absent pain. Professor Metz says that this is "not bad". I said explicitly that when I evaluated absent pain and absent pleasure of the non-existent I was not making a claim about the intrinsic value of these absent experiences. Instead, I was making a claim about their relative value – that is relative to the scenario in which the person exists. Thus, when I say that absent pain is "good", I mean that it is better than the presence of pain in Scenario A[21]. If that is where Professor Metz disagrees with me, then he is on very weak ground. Surely the absence of pain in Scenario B is better than its presence in Scenario A, when judged with reference to the interests of the person who exists in A. And if he does not disagree with me, and is simply making a point about the intrinsic value of absent pain in Scenario B, then it is not clear how he has undermined my argument for the conclusion that coming into existence is always a harm.

Professor Metz next argues that even if one accepts my basic asymmetry, it does not follow that coming into existence is always a harm. He thinks that before we can reach such a conclusion we need to know something about the magnitude of the goodness and badness. He is aware that I consider and respond to this view, but his reply mischaracterizes my argument.

I argued that (3), the absence of pain in Scenario B (where X does not exist), is an advantage over (1), the presence of pain in Scenario A. By contrast, (2), the presence of pleasure in Scenario A, is not an advantage over (4), the absence of pleasure in Scenario B. Because Scenario B (where X never exists) has an advantage over Scenario A, but Scenario A (where X exists) has no advantage over Scenario B, Scenario A is worse than Scenario B. Scenario A is thus a harm – and it is a harm irrespective of how much pain and pleasure X might experience.

---

19   Thaddeus Metz, "Are Lives Worth Creating?", p. 243.
20   In *Better Never to Have Been* I specifically said that absent pleasure of the non-existent is "not good" and that the question was whether it was therefore "bad" or instead, "not good but not bad either". (pp. 39-40).
21   Ibid, pp. 41-2.

It is hard to see how one can resist this conclusion *if* one accepts the respective evaluations I accord to each quadrant. The claim that absent pain in Scenario B is "good" means, I said, that it is better than the presence of pain in Scenario A. Similarly, the claim that absent pleasure in Scenario B is "not bad" means that it is not worse than the presence of pleasure in Scenario A. Some people, as we have seen, object to those evaluations, but once they are accepted, it follows that coming into existence is always a harm.

Professor Metz attempts to ward off this conclusion but he does so by mischaracterizing my claim that "absent pleasures that do not deprive are 'not bad' in the sense of 'not worse'". He interprets this claim as saying that "if one has not been created yet[22], and so has not been deprived of pleasure, then one is not badly off ... in the sense of worse off than one could have been." He wants to reject the latter claim and asks rhetorically: "Why is one not badly off in the sense of worse off than one could have been *had one existed*?"[23]

If one insists on asking the question that way, the answer is that one is not worse off because although the presence of the pleasures would have been good if one had existed, their absence is not worse if one does not exist. We have already seen - and at this point Professor Metz is accepting for the sake of argument – that *had one existed* the presence of one's pleasures would have been good, but if one *never exists* the absence of those pleasures is not worse. If one accepts that asymmetry it makes no sense to then judge the absence of pleasure for the never existing person by the standards of absent pleasure for an existing person.

## Rivka Weinberg:

Unlike most of my other critics, Rivka Weinberg declares herself "very sympathetic to the intuitions that inspire" my arguments and thinks that my "conclusion is probably right"[24]. However, she says that she has "yet to find an argument to support it"[25]. It seems that my basic asymmetry is not among the intuitions to which she is sympathetic, because she devotes a lot of attention to the arguments I provide for why we should not reject that asymmetry. More specifically, she thinks that the other asymmetries that I say are explained by the basic asymmetry could be explained better by either a "simple and obvious metaphysical fact" or a "common moral principle"[26].

The metaphysical fact is that all "interests are contingent upon existence" – unless "an entity exists at some point, there is no real subject for the interest"[27]. The common moral principle is "the view that our moral obligations are to persons who do or will exist"[28].

Although the metaphysical fact and the moral principle can explain some of the asymmetries, they do not explain all of them. Consider, for example, the asymmetry of procreational duties. Professor Weinberg says that "there may be a duty to avoid

---

22   It is tendentious to include the word "yet". Scenario A is a situation in which a person exists, while Scenario B is a situation in which that person *never exists*.
23   Thaddeus Metz, "Are Lives Worth Creating?", p. 247.
24   Rivka Weinberg, "Is Having Children Always Wrong?", p. 26.
25   Ibid.
26   Ibid, p. 28. In fact, she thinks that the metaphysical fact grounds the moral principle.
27   Ibid.
28   Ibid.

bringing unhappy people into the world because those existent, interested people would be unhappy" but that there is "no corresponding duty to bring would-be-happy people into existence because 'failing' in that 'duty' would not cause anyone's interests to be set back".[29]

The problem is that Professor Weinberg is selective in her invocation of the metaphysical fact and the moral principle. To see how this is so, consider the two duties under examination and the possible outcomes of acting or not acting up on them:

1.    A purported duty not to bring Sad into existence:

   (a)     If violated, there is an existent person whose interests are set back.

   (b)     If fulfilled, there is no existent person whose interests are advanced.

2.    A purported duty to bring Happy into existence:

   (a)     If violated, there is no existent person whose interests are set back.

   (b)     If fulfilled, there is an existent person whose interests are advanced.

In explaining the asymmetry of procreational duties – that is, the existence of the first duty and the absence of the second duty – she appeals only to (a) and (c). However, there is nothing in either the metaphysical fact or the moral principle that requires us to consider only these options and to ignore (b) and (d). If one acted on the duty not to bring miserable people into existence, there would be no existent person. And if one fulfilled the purported duty to bring happy people into existence, there *would* be an existent person[30].

If one *did* appeal to (b) and (d) in applying the metaphysical fact and the moral principle, one would find that the asymmetry of procreational duties, far from being explained, is actually negated.

Exactly the same problem arises for the prospective beneficence asymmetry: If one does create the happy child it will exist, and if one fails to create the miserable child, it will not exist.

Thus, if one wants to use the metaphysical fact and the moral principle to explain asymmetries (i) and (ii), one needs some explanation why only (a) and (c) are relevant and why (b) and (d) can be ignored. My basic asymmetry could provide the necessary explanation, but if Professor Weinberg were to accept that explanation, she would not have provided an alternative to my basic asymmetry. Indeed, she would be deeply dependent on it.

Another possible explanation is the view that avoiding harm is more important than bestowing benefit. However, Professor Weinberg specifically rejects this idea[31]. Her basis for rejecting it is that we often risk harms in order to gain benefits. However, this may be too quick. Perhaps balancing harms and benefits is reasonable within a life, but that when it comes to creating lives avoiding harms takes priority over benefits. If Professor Weinberg accepted this view, however, she would be lead to my anti-natalist conclusion.

---

29   Ibid.
30   Perhaps in response to this thought, Rivka Weinberg says: "We need not do an action in order for its foreseeable results to give us a reason not to do that action." (p. 29). This move does not solve her problems. On one reading this claim actually negates the moral principle. And if it is thought not to negate this principle, a parallel claim could be made: "We need not do an action in order for its foreseeable results to give us a reason to do that action." This claim could lead us to treat the purported duty to bring Happy into existence like the duty not to bring Sad into existence.
31   Rivka Weinberg, "Is Having Children Always Wrong?", p. 33.

In the absence of an explanation why (b) and (d) can be ignored, Rivka Weinberg has not demonstrated how the metaphysical fact and the moral principle can explain asymmetries (i) and (ii). She has thus not provided an alternative to my basic asymmetry.

## David Boonin:

David Boonin's response to my asymmetry argument is a sophisticated one. He recognizes that my basic asymmetry leads to the conclusion that coming into existence is always a harm. This is a conclusion he wants to avoid and thus he seeks a way to reject my basic asymmetry. To do this, he must provide an alternative explanation of the other asymmetries that I suggested are best explained by the basic asymmetry. His solution is a conjunction of two principles – his *Relational Symmetry Principle* and his *Actual Persons Principle*.

According to the *Relational Symmetry Principle*[32]:

(1)   the presence of pain is intrinsically bad

(2)   the presence of pleasure is intrinsically good

(3)   the absence of pain is better than the presence of pain if either

    (a)   there is an actual person whose interests are better served by the absence of the pain or

    (b)   the presence of the pain would require the existence of a person who would not otherwise exist and whose potential interests are better served by the absence of the pain

(4)   the absence of pleasure is worse than the presence of pleasure if either

    (a)   there is an actual person whose interests are better served by the presence of the pleasure or

    (b)   the absence of the pleasure would require the absence of a person who would otherwise exist and whose potential interests are better served by the presence of the pleasure.

The *Actual Persons Principle* says that[33]:

> When choosing between two options, it is prima facie wrong to make the choice the acting on which will result in its being the case that there is an actual person for whom your act made things worse.

There are many things to say in response to this interesting idea. The first is to note that the Relational Symmetry Principle is unhelpful in determining when lives are worth starting. This is because the principle contains two curious clauses, namely the final clauses of 3b) and 4b): "… and whose potential interests are better served by" either "the absence of pain" or "the presence of pleasure".

What 3b) and 4b) say is that the absent pains of non-existence are good only if the life that the person would otherwise had lived would not have been a life worth starting, and that the absence of pleasure is bad if the life that the person would otherwise had lived would have been worth starting. This allows one to insert whatever view one

32   David Boonin, "Better to Be", p. 15.
33   Ibid, p. 16.

has about which lives are worth starting or, put another way, about which lives it is not a harm to create. If we try to use the Relational Symmetry Principle to determine when coming into existence is a harm, we find that we already need to know when coming into existence is a harm in order to use the principle to reach a conclusion. This is question-begging.

The inclusion of these vague clauses in his principle enables Professor Boonin to smuggle in what we might call the orthodox view of procreation ethics – namely, the view that creating people is morally permissible if their lives will be of an acceptable quality. Thus he says that it is acceptable for the Lucky Couple to conceive the Lucky Child – a child that will experience 1 million units of pleasure and only 100 units of pain[34]. Readers who share the orthodox view of procreation and thus accept his assumption that creating such a life is not a harm to the child created, will thus reach the conclusion they want to reach.

But now notice that there is nothing to stop those, such as I, who think that coming into existence is always a harm, to say that the Lucky Child, although he may be lucky relative to other children (who suffer more than he does), is not lucky *enough* if he is actually brought into existence. We can say that in choices between creating and not creating somebody, it is *always* the case that the potential person's interests are better served by the absence of pain[35] and that it is *never* the case that a potential person's interests are better served by the presence of the pleasure that would be attendant upon his existence. Professor Boonin might disagree with me, but his Relational Symmetry Principle provides him with no resources to show that I am wrong.

Now, it might be responded that it is not only Professor Boonin but also I who face the problem of the vague clause in 3b). After all, 3) including 3b) is, according to Professor Boonin, a more precise restatement of the 3) in my basic asymmetry[36]. However, this is exactly what I deny. Professor Boonin has not restated the same claim I made. Instead he has altered my claim. My claim is that absent pain (in a scenario in which somebody does not exist) is *always* better than the presence of pain. That is a very precise statement. To restate my claim in the way that Professor Boonin does is to make it not merely less precise but so vague as to render it open to innumerable interpretations.

My second concern about the combined Relational Symmetry Principle and Actual Persons Principle is that it does not do all the explanatory work that Professor Boonin says it does. It *does* explain the asymmetry of procreational duties. However, contrary to what Professor Boonin says, it fails to explain the other three asymmetries, namely (ii) to (iv). This is because these three asymmetries do not refer to our duties, that is, to what we ought or ought not to do. Instead they are about what is good or bad for people. Not all talk about what is good or bad for people must be cashed out in terms of duties. Some things might be good for people without our being duty-bound to bestow that benefit. And there are some actions that harm people but which are not wrong to

34    Ibid, p. 10.
35    How could the absence of pain in Scenario B not be better than its presence in Scenario A? Professor Boonin's view seems to be that the absence of pain in Scenario B is not better if the presence of the pain in Scenario A is the cost of attaining the pleasures in Scenario A as long as the pleasures are sufficiently plentiful to more than compensate for the pain. I, by contrast, think that it is always an advantage of non-existence that there no pain accompanying it. It is a separate question whether the absence of pleasure in non-existence is a disadvantage.
36    David Boonin, "Better to Be", p.13.

do[37]. Thus, when it comes to asymmetries (ii) to (iv), the Actual Persons Principle, which talks about what it is wrong to do, has no application. The Relational Symmetry Principle does apply, but rather than explaining the three asymmetries it actually negates them.

Consider first the prospective beneficence asymmetry. The Relational Symmetry Principle says that the absence of pleasure is worse than the presence of pleasure if the absence of the pleasure would require the absence of a person who would otherwise exist and whose potential interests are better served by the presence of the pleasure. But if the absence of pleasure is worse (when judged with reference of the interests of the person who would otherwise exist), as the orthodox view would hold about many lives, there is nothing strange about citing, as a reason for having a child that that child will thereby be benefited. Of course the Actual Persons Principle would deny that one had a *duty* to create that child, but the prospective beneficence asymmetry says nothing about our duties. It comments only on the oddity of electing to have a child for that child's sake. The Relational Symmetry Principle, far from explaining that oddity, must deny it.

A similar problem arises when we consider the retrospective beneficence asymmetry. If one fails to bring a happy child into existence – a child that, according to the orthodox view, has a life worth starting – one *does* have a reason to regret the failure to bring that child into existence. The reason is that that child would have been benefited. Again, the Actual Persons Principle will rule out the possibility that one acted *wrongly* in not creating that child and thus one could not regret acting wrongly. But one can regret things one failed to do even if one's failure to do them was not a violation of one's duties.

If we turn to the asymmetry of distant suffering and absent happy people we find, again, that the Relational Symmetry Principle must deny the asymmetry. This is because the principle *does* provide us with grounds for regretting the absent happy people on uninhabited islands or planets. According to that principle, the absence of this pleasure is worse than its presence (because the lives would have been worth living) and that is a basis for regret, even though the situation is not the result of our having acted wrongly.

Perhaps Professor Boonin could respond that an amended version of the Actual Persons Principle could address the above problems and thus, combined with Relational Symmetry Principle, explain asymmetries (ii) to (iv). The Actual Persons Principle could be reformulated to yield the *Reformulated Actual Persons Principle*:

> When comparing existing and never existing people we should only be concerned aboutactual people[38] and that things not be worse for them.

Because this reformulated principle refers not to what is right and wrong but rather to what is good and bad (or better and worse) it might be thought to solve the problems I have described. However, there would be a cost to such a move. Professor Boonin specifically says that a bridging moral principle is needed in order to justify "conclusions about what should or should not be done"[39]. The Reformulated Actual Persons

---

37  For example, incarcerating murders may harm them, but it does not follow that it would be wrong to lock them up.

38  By "actual people", David Boonin means those "who actually exist at some point in time" (p. 16).

39  Ibid, p. 19.

Principle is not a moral principle and thus would fail to do the necessary bridging work if one wants to generate conclusions about what we ought to do.

Perhaps some hybrid of the original and reformulated Actual Persons Principle could do the trick. However, this brings me to a third concern about Professor Boonin's argument – a problem that confronts both this Actual Persons Principle, the reformulated principle or a hybrid of the two[40]. The problem is that while the principle purports to focus our attention on actual people it has another, equally strong focus which is masked by the principle's name. The principle says that it is wrong to make choices that make it the case that (a) there is an actual person (b) for whom your act *made things worse*.

However, there is nothing about (a) the focus on actual persons that necessitates (b) the focus on whether a choice makes things worse, rather than better, for actual persons. Thus we should ask why the Actual Persons Principle should be adopted over the following *Alternative Actual Persons Principle:*

> When choosing between two options, it is prima facie wrong to *fail to* make the choice the acting on which will result in its being the case that there is an actual person for whom your act made things *better*.

Combining this principle with the Relational Symmetry Principle has catastrophic results. Not only does it explain none of the asymmetries (i) to (iv), it actually negates them. Some will favour the Actual Persons Principle over its alternative precisely because the latter has these worse implications. However, we need to ask whether the Actual Persons Principle is just masking problems in the Relational Symmetry Principle – problems that are exposed when that principle is combined with the Alternative Actual Persons Principle. Thus, what we need is a deeper reason to explain why the Actual Persons Principle is to be preferred to its alternative[41]. In other words, we need to know why, in procreational choices, we should make the choice that prevents what is worse for actual persons rather than making the choice that is better for actual persons.

Some might be tempted to respond as follows[42]: If, in procreative decisions, we fail to make the choice that prevents what is worse for actual persons, there will be an actual person who will suffer, whereas if we fail to make the choice that is better for actual persons there will be no actual person to suffer as a result of our choice. The problem with this response is that it begs the question. Why focus on the consequence of failing to do what one should do? Why not focus on the consequence of doing what one should do? If one *did* make the choice that resulted in what was best for an actual person, there *would* be an actual person who benefited. And if one *did* make the choice that prevents what is worse for actual persons there *would not* be an actual person who would benefit.

---

40  I shall discuss the problem as it confronts Professor Boonin's version, but the same objection can be levelled, *mutatis mutandis*, to the reformulated version or to the hybrid.

41  In fact, as before, there is more than one alternative. Consider a hybrid of the Actual Persons Principle and the Alternative Actual Persons Principle:
    When choosing between two options, it is prima facie wrong to, either:
    a) make the choice the acting on which will result in its being the case that there is an actual person for whom your act made things worse; or
    b) *fail to* make the choice the acting on which will result in its being the case that there is an actual person for whom your act made things *better*.

42  David Boonin, "Better to Be", p.24.

Whatever the answer, it must have something to do with an asymmetry of some kind or another between harming and benefiting[43]. One possible suggestion is that, all things being equal, preventing harm takes priority over bestowing benefit, even if not generally, then at least in procreative contexts. However, if anybody were to appeal to an idea of this kind to rescue the Actual Persons Principle, he would have leapt out of the frying pan of the asymmetry argument and into the fire of the quality-of-life argument. Given the amount of harm that can be expected to characterize human life, a principle prioritizing harm avoidance would lead to anti-natalism, albeit via a different route.

## Sick and Healthy, and Intrinsic value

Skott Brill's thoughtful paper is devoted to a critical discussion of the analogy of Sick and Healthy. His paper was written on the assumption that I employed the analogy because it was necessary in order to demonstrate that the absent pleasures of non-existence are not worse than the pleasures of existence - or, in other words, that quadrant (4) is not worse than quadrant (2). However, what I had said about the analogy is that it

> need not be read as proving that quadrant (2) is good and that quadrant (4) is not bad. That asymmetry was established in the previous section. Instead, the analogy could be interpreted as showing how, given the asymmetry, (2) is not an advantage over (4), whereas (1) is a disadvantage relative to (3). It would thereby show that Scenario B is preferable to Scenario A.[44]

While this implies (but does not explicitly say) that the analogy *can* be seen as proving that quadrant (4) is not worse than quadrant (2), it is explicitly saying that it does not *have* to be read that way. In other words, the analogy can be seen as simply an illumination or illustration of what has already been proved. However, even if one does interpret the purpose of the analogy in the first way, one must still distinguish between:

(a)  the analogy being an *additional* way of proving that (4) is not worse than (2); and

(b)  the analogy being *necessary* to proving that (4) is not worse than (2).

Professor Brill seems to assume that (b) is the case. He thinks that without the analogy, I have not demonstrated the basic asymmetry[45]. However, because I take myself to have demonstrated the basic asymmetry without the analogy, my purpose for the analogy is, at most, to provide a further argument (and at least to illuminate and illustrate what I had already demonstrated). If I am correct in thinking that the basic asymmetry is demonstrated without the analogy, then even a successful critique of the anal-

43  There seem to me to be a number of such asymmetries, with which my basic asymmetry is consistent (and thus less surprising).
44  *Better Never to Have Been*, p. 43.
45  He says: "To establish the crucial claim that the non-badness of absent pleasures in non-existence is relative rather than intrinsic, Benatar constructs an analogy involving two people, Sick and Healthy. In this paper, I show the inaptness of the analogy and consequent unsoundness of the argument as it stands." (Skott Brill, "Sick and Healthy: Benatar on the Logic of Value", p. 38.)

ogy would fail to undermine the asymmetry argument. Professor Brill thus overstates the importance of the Sick and Healthy analogy[46].

However, we can set this issue aside and consider Professor Brill's critique of the analogy on its own terms. He suggests that the analogy is in violation of what he calls the *reasonable assumption*, namely that

> in the absence of any countervailing consideration, there is more reason to believe that the logic of intrinsic value that applies to existing things also applies to non-existing things than to believe (as Benatar does) that the logic of instrumental value that applies to existing things becomes part of the logic of intrinsic value when applied to non-existing things.[47]

The so-called reasonable assumption contains a further, unstated assumption – that there is a (single) "logic of intrinsic value". According to Professor Brill's conception, the "logic of intrinsic goodness is such that, unlike the case of an instrumental good, the presence of an intrinsic good is *always* good ... which in turn makes its absence *relatively bad* and *intrinsically value neutral*"[48]. Professor Spurrett, we saw earlier, had the same view about intrinsic goodness.

The crucial problem, however, is that there is not a single logic of intrinsic value and this is because different things might be meant by the phrase "intrinsic value". Consider the claim that "Pleasure is intrinsically good." This is ambiguous between at least the following two claims:

(a)     It is intrinsically good that sentient beings have pleasure.

(b)     It is intrinsically good that there be sentient beings with pleasure.

(a) is the view that pleasure is intrinsically good *for* sentient beings, whereas (b) is the view that pleasure is intrinsically good *simpliciter*. Both of these conceptions satisfy the understanding of intrinsic goodness as non-derivative goodness. However, they have quite different implications for my matrix that compares existence and non-existence. If we adopt (a)[49] then there is nothing stopping us from saying that:

1)     is (intrinsically) bad;

2)     is (intrinsically) good;

3)     is (relatively) good (that is, better than 1); and

4)     is (relatively) not bad (that is, not worse than 4).

---

46   Here is another example of how he overstates the importance of the analogy: In *Better Never to Have Been*, I considered the challenge of those who propose to assign a numerical value of zero to quadrant (4). I said that the best way to see that this is mistaken is to apply the same reasoning to the analogy of Sick and Healthy where its error becomes patent (p. 47). Professor Brill discusses at length whether the analogy really does show the error of assigning a value of zero. However, although I think that the analogy is a particularly lively way of showing the error, we do not actually require the analogy to prove this. The whole point in my original matrix, is that the presence of pleasure in (2) is good for the existent X but does not constitute an advantage over the absent pleasure in (4) of the never-existing X. Assigning a positive charge to (2) and a zero to (4) implies that (2) is an advantage over (4), and thus is clearly an inaccurate way of capturing the relative value "not bad" in (4). The same is true of these quadrants in the Sick and Healthy matrix, but one does not need the analogy to show that absent pleasures in the never existing should not be assigned the value of zero.

47   Skott Brill, "Sick and Healthy: Benatar on the Logic of Value", pp. 44-45.

48   Ibid, p. 53.

49   And extend the conception to include a parallel understanding of intrinsic badness.

The reasonable assumption now becomes unreasonable. This is because the relevant components of the logic of instrumental value that apply to existing things are *the same* as the relevant components of the logic of intrinsic value when applied to non-existing things. More specifically, in both cases, the absence of an intrinsic bad is good, but the absence of either an intrinsic or instrumental good is not bad unless somebody is deprived. It is not that the logic of the one is applied to the other. Instead, it is the case that both logics are the same in the relevant cases.

Perhaps Professor Brill will suggest that we should adopt (b) rather than (a). If we did so, then the logic of instrumental value that applies to existing things would indeed be different from the logic of intrinsic value when applied to non-existing things[50]. However, (b) is problematic. There is a famous distinction between "making people happy" and "making happy people". Most philosophers have thought that any moral reasons or duties we have are restricted to the former. One would have to give up this view if one accepted (b). Because the absence of the sentient beings that would experience pleasure would be relatively bad, there would be some reason to make happy people.

Or consider another implication of accepting (b). Imagine a possible kind of being – we might call them "shmersons". Now imagine that if shmersons existed they would get a lot of pleasure from putting their fingers in their ears, a practice called "shmearing". There are no shmersons, and shmearing means nothing to all beings that do exist. Is it really worse that there are no shmersons because in their absence there is no shmearing-induced pleasure? If one accepted (b) one would have to answer affirmatively, but an affirmative answer seems bizarre. Surely the goodness of shmearing is goodness for shmersons and not goodness simpliciter?

Professor Brill's central argument hinges on the specific interpretation he has of intrinsic value. There is no reason why I need accept his interpretation, and indeed there are good reasons to reject it. I take this to be the most damaging flaw of his argument.

It might now be asked *why* I think that the logic of instrumental value that applies to existing things is the same as the logic of intrinsic value (as I have understood it) when applied to non-existing things. In other words, why is the case of Sick and Healthy a good analogy, even though it embodies an instrumental good, whereas the pleasure of existing people is intrinsically good (albeit in the sense I have said)?

Professor Brill characterizes my answer thus:

1)   Using an analogy involving an exister and a non-exister is inappropriate. (For it is too close to the matter at hand.)

2)   Therefore, (by default) an analogy involving two existers is appropriate.

3)   An analogy involving two existers in conjunction with an intrinsic good is inappropriate. (For, since all existers who lack an intrinsic good *are* deprived, such an analogy would beg the question against the asymmetry argument.)

4)   Therefore, (by default) an analogy involving two existers in conjunction with an instrumental good is appropriate.[51]

---

50   This would not suffice – Professor Brill's argument would still be susceptible to other criticisms – but it would be a response to the particular criticism at hand.

51   Skott Brill, "Sick and Healthy: Benatar on the Logic of Value", p. 45.

He then argues that this argument is "based on two *non sequiturs*" that are "perhaps best identified as instances of the fallacy of Correct by Default".[52]

However, this is a mischaracterization. My argument (or at least the core of it) is better understood as follows:

1) In my matrix comparing X's existence and X's never existing, (4) represents absent pleasures that do not deprive.

2) It is because these absent pleasures do not deprive that (4) is not worse than (2).

3) Therefore, a suitable analogy for such pleasures is another good that does not deprive.

4) The absence of some instrumental goods in an existent person is not a deprivation[53].

5) The absence of the capacity for quick recovery in Healthy is a case in point.

6) Therefore, the absence of the capacity for quick recovery in Healthy is a suitable analogy.

This interpretation of my argument is immune to Professor Brill's objections and it explains why the comparison of Sick and Healthy is analogous to the comparison of X existing and X never existing[54].

While I do not have the space here to respond to all the arguments Skott Brill advances, I do want to clarify some things about where Professor Brill and I disagree in our evaluations of the various quadrants of my matrix and what implications this has for the asymmetries that I say are explained by the basic asymmetry.

Professor Brill seems to think that I deny that the non-badness in quadrant (4) is intrinsic non-badness[55]. However, that is a mistaken account of my view. The absence of pleasure in the non-existent is indeed intrinsically neither good nor bad. It is intrinsically value-neutral. However, the intrinsic value (including value-neutrality) of something does not preclude a different relative value. Thus the pain in (1) is intrinsically bad, but also relatively bad, in comparison with (3) for example. Similarly, I take (3) to be intrinsically neutral, but relatively good – that is, better than (2). And I take the non-badness of (4) to be both intrinsic and relative. The absent pleasure is intrinsically neither good nor bad, but it is also not worse than the presence of pleasure in (2). That said, it is true that when I describe (4) as "not bad" I am not referring to its intrinsic value, and am instead referring to its being "not worse" than (2), as that is what is key to the comparison of existence and non-existence.

Perhaps Professor Brill meant to say that I deny that the non-badness in quadrant (4) is *merely* intrinsic non-badness. That would be an accurate account of my view. (I

---

52 Ibid.

53 The problem with using the absence of an intrinsic good in a non-existent person is not, as Professor Brill says, that it is "too close to the matter at hand". It *is* the matter at hand and is thus not an analogy at all.

54 Professor Brill says that "Benatar needs to give reasons for the legitimacy of using in his analogy two existers in conjunction with an instrumental good" (p. 46). I do give a reason: It is that this is a case of an absent good that is not a deprivation, and is thus like the absent pleasure that does not deprive the non-existent.

55 For example, he says that my asymmetry argument "hinges on the non-badness at issue here[that is, in quadrant 4] being *relative* (no worse than the presence of pleasures in existence) rather than *intrinsic* (value neutral)" (p. 38). And he claims (on p. 46) that I contend "that if non-badness were intrinsic ... it would be better to be S than H ..."

think that it is both intrinsically and relatively not bad.) It seems, then, that Professor Brill and I agree on the intrinsic values of the four quadrants:

1) Presence of pain in the existent is intrinsically bad.

2) Presence of pleasure in the existent is intrinsically good.

3) The absence of pain in the non-existent is intrinsically value-neutral (neither good nor bad)[56].

4) The absence of pleasure in the non-existent is intrinsically value neutral (neither good nor bad).

Since intrinsic values do not preclude relative values, what does Professor Brill think the relative values of each quadrant are – where each quadrant is evaluated relative to its horizontally adjacent quadrant? It seems to me that he is committed to the following:

1) The presence of pain in the existent is (relatively) bad – that is worse than (3).

2) The presence of pleasure in the existent is (relatively) good – that is better than (4).

3) The absence of pain in the non-existent is (relatively) good – that is better than (1).

4) The absence of pleasure in the non-existent is (relatively) bad – that is worse than (2).

The evaluations for (1) and (2) here are inescapable for him. I also cannot see how he could deny that the absence of pain in (3) is better than its presence in (1). Quadrant (4) could be regarded as "not bad" – that is, not worse than (2). That is my evaluation. However, because Professor Brill rejects it, the only other plausible view is that he thinks it *is* worse than (2) – that is, that it is relatively bad.

With these evaluations in hand, we can assess Professor Brill's claim that asymmetries (i) to (iv) do not "support the claim that the absence of pleasures in non-existence is specifically relatively not bad"[57].

Consider (ii) the prospective beneficence asymmetry. Professor Brill says that

> if the absence of pleasures in non-existence is only value neutral (intrinsically not bad), then in view of all the burdens and sacrifices having children places on parents, it is not at all surprising that we do not feel more moral pressure … than we do to have children.[58]

This is a *non-sequitur*. The prospective beneficence asymmetry is not about our duties. It is about whether the interests of a possible child provide us with a reason to create or not create it. Those reasons might be overridden by other factors (such as the burdens or sacrifices of having children), but that has no impact on whether the interests of the child provide a reason for or against having a child. My basic asymmetry explains the prospective beneficence asymmetry. However, if one looks only at the intrinsic values of (1) to (4), which are symmetrical, there is no explanation for the prospective beneficence asymmetry. The presence of pain in (1) is bad, and its absence in

---

56  Professor Brill is not explicit about what intrinsic value he thinks attaches to (3), but I cannot see how it could be anything other than value-neutral.

57  Skott Brill, "Sick and Healthy: Benatar on the Logic of Value", p. 50.

58  Ibid. p. 52.

(3) is neither good nor bad. The presence of pleasure in (2) is good, and its absence in (4) is neither good nor bad. Thus if one has no reason to create a child that will experience more of the good than of the bad, one similarly has no reason to avoid creating a child that will have more of the bad than the good, and *vice versa*.

It will not help Professor Brill if he adds to the above intrinsic evaluations, the relative evaluations that I have said he makes. These too are symmetrical, and adding this symmetry to the symmetry of intrinsic values is not going to explain the prospective beneficence *asymmetry*.

Consider next (iii) the retrospective beneficence asymmetry and (iv) the asymmetry of distant suffering and absent happy people. Professor Brill's response to these is not to show how his symmetrical evaluations can explain the asymmetries, but instead to deny the asymmetries. He suggests that perhaps we should regret that happy people were not created. I shall not here rehearse the various problems with denying these asymmetries and with claiming that we do indeed have a reason to regret the absence of non-existing people (for *their* sakes).

### The Quality of Human Life

The asymmetry argument is the argument in *Better Never to Have Been* that has elicited most response. However, it is not the only argument I provided. Indeed, by itself, the asymmetry argument is insufficient to yield the anti-natalist conclusion. It shows that it is better never to come into existence. It does not show how great a harm it is to come into existence. The second argument – what I shall call the quality-of-life argument – reveals the magnitude of that harm[59]. However, the quality-of-life argument can also be understood as a separate argument for the conclusion that coming into existence is a harm[60].

The first step of the argument establishes that self-assessments of quality of life are extremely unreliable. There is ample empirical evidence that most humans have an optimism bias, which leads them to overestimate the quality of their lives. Quality of life assessments are also corrupted in other ways. First, humans are prone to "adaptation". That is to say, if something bad happens to them, there will be an initial dip in self-assessment of well-being, but this will soon return to close to the original baseline assessment even without any actual improvement in well-being. Second, people's assessments of the quality of their lives are influenced by comparisons with the quality of life of others. Insofar as some harm affects all people it tends not to influence self-assessments of well-being.

The second step of the quality-of-life argument is to show just how many bad things are missed in self-assessments, suggesting that the quality of people's lives is much worse than they typically think. Being brought into existence with such a life is a significant harm.

The third step of the argument is to show that even if the earlier steps are thought to fail, there is nonetheless good reason to criticize procreation. In support of this conclusion I showed just how much suffering there is in the world and how liable any new life is to at least some of these serious harms. Thus any procreators impose the risk of

---

59   The second argument is presented in Chapter 3. The rest of this paragraph and the following three paragraphs, in which I summarize this argument, are drawn from "Still Better Never to Have Been: A reply to more of my critics", forthcoming in *The Journal of Ethics* and are used here with permission of the journal editors.

60   I disagree with Skott Brill, who thinks that I take this argument to be a "fall-back argument". ("Sick and Healthy: Benatar on the Logic of Value", p. 38).

those serious harms on those they bring into existence. They play a procreational "Russian Roulette", in which their children stand to pay the price. If the asymmetry argument works then the gun is fully loaded. But even if the asymmetry argument fails, and the gun is only partly loaded, taking such risks for one's offspring is morally problematic.

## Brooke Trisel:

Brooke Alan Trisel offers a number of criticisms of my quality-of-life argument.

*Questioning the evidence for an optimism bias:*
First, he takes issue with the evidence I cite for a general optimism bias. He refers to two studies[61] that found that the overwhelming majority of psychological studies in the influential journals that were examined had only undergraduate students as research subjects. One of the studies also showed an overwhelming bias towards American research subjects. Neither of the studies to which he refers, however, was specifically about optimism bias, and thus one can ask to what extent *they* provide evidence about a selection bias in studies about optimism bias. Perhaps this is why Mr Trisel then quotes Shelley Taylor and Jonathon Brown, whom I had cited, but who say that "much of the evidence for these positive illusions comes … from research with college students"[62]. However, those same authors note a few lines later that all three of the illusions they discuss "have been documented in noncollege populations as well"[63].

Margaret Matlin and David Stang, whom I also cited, go further. They take specific note of the question about how generalizable the results about disproportionate recall of positive experiences are. They respond

> that the perceived abundance of pleasant events is not limited to upper middle-class college students. A large number of studies included other subject populations, such as children and mill-workers … In all studies conducted on normal populations, the percentage of experiences perceived as pleasant remains remarkably constant… We were able to find only one exception to the rule[64].

When talking about happiness more generally, the same authors refer to studies whose subjects are not undergraduates and not in the United States[65]. Other important works about subjective well-being that I cited also include data on a wide range of subjects[66].

---

61  Reginald Smart, "Subject selection bias in psychological research", *Canadian Psychology*, Vol. 7a. No. 2, 1996, pp. 115-121; Jeffrey Arnett, "The Neglected 95%: Why American Psychology Needs to Become Less American", *American Psychologist*, Vol. 63, No. 7, pp. 602-14.
62  Shelley Taylor & Jonathon Brown, "Illusion and Well-Being: A Social Psychological Perspective on Mental Health", *Psychological Bulletin*, Vol. 103, No. 2, 1988, p. 194.
63  Ibid, p. 195.
64  Margaret Matlin & David Stang, *The Pollyanna Principle: Selectivity in Language, Memory and Thought*, Cambridge MA: Schenkman Publishing Company, 1978, p. 143.
65  Ibid, p. 150-54.
66  For example, Frank M. Andrews and Stephen B Withey, *Social Indicators of Well-Being: American's Perceptions of Life Quality*, New York: Plenum Press, 1976; Angus Campbell, Philip E Converse and Willard L. Rodgers, *The Quality of American Life: Perceptions, Evaluations, and Satisfactions*, New York: Russell Sage Foundation, 1976; Ronald Inglehart, *Culture Shift in Advanced Industrial Society*,

In summary, although psychologists in general have focused disproportionately on undergraduates (and especially undergraduate psychology students) and on Americans, there is plenty of evidence that the optimism bias is characteristic of humanity more generally. Mr Trisel is simply wrong when he says (or implies) otherwise.

To say that an optimism bias is a human tendency is not to say that everybody has this characteristic, or that they have it to the same extent. Mr Trisel goes further and says that some "research has raised doubt about the universality of optimistic bias" and that "the 'normality' of self-enhancing biases might be specific to Western cultures"[67].

There is much that could be said about this research, but I shall restrict myself to a few comments. First, the cited studies examined only one feature of the optimism bias, namely estimation of how well things will go in the future. The optimism bias, however, has many more features, including recall of positive and negative experiences and subjective assessments of current well-being. Thus even if these studies show that the Japanese research subjects in the studies lacked one manifestation of optimism bias (or lacked it to the same extent), the studies do not show that the research subjects lack other features of an optimism bias.

Second, even if it were found that some cultural groups lack an optimism bias entirely, their subjective assessments of well-being might still be unreliable for other reasons, namely the other two psychological phenomena that I said made people's self-assessments unreliable. Mr Trisel does not call those into question[68].

Third, even if a group (or individual) lacked all three of these psychological attributes, it could be that the relevant people's self-assessments of their well-being were reliable but also unfavourable. That is to say, people without these psychological attributes might think that the quality of their lives is not good.

Mr Trisel's paper is an exemplary manifestation of an optimism bias. For example, he says that only "6% of children born throughout the world have a serious birth defect" and this "indicates that 94% of new people do not have a serious birth defect"[69]. However, serious birth defects are only a few of thousands of terrible things that can happen to people in the course of their lives. Even lives that start without serious defect can become laden with other harms. This is why it does not help that Mr Trisel

Princeton: Princeton University Press, 1990; Ed Diener and Carol Diener, "Most People are Happy", *Psychological Science*, Vol. 7, No. 3, 1999, pp. 181-5; and Ed Diener, Eunkook Suh, Richard E. Lucas and Heidi L. Smith, "Subjective Well-Being: Three Decades of Progress", *Psychological Bulletin*, Vol. 125, No. 2, 1999, pp. 276-302.

67    Brooke A. Trisel, "How Best to Prevent Future Persons from Suffering: A Reply to Benatar", p. 82. He cites the following studies: Steven J. Heine and Darrin R Lehman, "Cultural Variation in Unrealistic Optimism: Does the West Feel More Invulnerable than the East?", *Journal of Personality and Social Psychology*, Vol. 68, No. 4, 1995, pp. 595-607; Edward C. Chang and Kiyoshi Asakawa, "Cultural Variations on Optimistic and Pessimistic Bias for Self Versus a Sibling: Is there Evidence for Self-Enhancement in the East when the Referent Group is Specified?", *Journal of Personality and Social Psychology*, Vol. 84, No. 3, 2003, pp. 569-581.

68    In my book I considered three psychological phenomena that provide us with reason not to trust subject assessments of well-being. Mr Trisel considers only Pollyannaism (the optimism bias) because, he notes on p. 82, I say that "it is only Pollyannaism that inclines people unequivocally towards more positive assessments of how well their life is going" (*Better Never to Have* Been, p. 68). But this is not a reason to ignore the other two phenomena because, as I noted on the same page, both of them "operate both from an optimistic baseline and under the influence of optimistic biases" with the result that "in the best cases [they] reinforce Pollyannaism" and in "the worst cases, they mitigate it but do not negate it entirely".

69    Brooke A. Trisel, "How Best to Prevent Future Persons from Suffering: A Reply to Benatar", p. 85.

adds that "many children throughout the world are born into good conditions, are well cared for by their parents, and *never experience serious harm in their lives*"[70]. How many people escape *all* of the following serious harms (among others): severe pain, rape, assault, serious disease or disability, or early death? (Nobody, of course, escapes death entirely, and death is commonly viewed as a serious harm.)

Mr Trisel quotes a World Health Organization study that "found that 22% of primary care patients experienced persistent pain in the prior year"[71]. That sounds like a lot to me. Mr Trisel focuses on the positive and tells us that "78% of primary care patients did not experience persistent pain in the prior year"[72]. But that is only in *the prior year*. Over the course of a lifetime, one's chances of suffering persistent pain are much higher than 22%. The World Health Organization estimates that "each year tens of millions of patients are suffering [moderate to severe pain] without adequate treatment"[73]. This includes "1 million end-stage HIV/AIDS patients" and "5.5 million terminal cancer patients"[74]. In more than 150 countries morphine and codeine are almost not available[75]. Nor is the problem restricted to the developing world. Access to pain relief is better in developed countries, but still inadequate. According to a recent report, more than "116 million Americans have pain that persists for weeks to years"[76]. These figures exclude "pain in children or people in long-term care facilities, the military, or prison"[77]. The treatment for this pain "doesn't fully alleviate Americans' pain"[78].

*The instrumental value of pain:*

A second objection Brooke Trisel levels is that pain can have considerable instrumental value. He devotes many lines to defending this claim, but it is not clear why it constitutes an objection to my views about the quality of life. One possible interpretation is that he thinks this fact undermines my claim that pain is intrinsically bad. This may seem like an extraordinarily uncharitable interpretation but it is not an unreasonable one. This is what he says:

> Benatar believes that pain is *intrinsically* bad … Many people share this view. Are pain and discomforts something that we would be better off without, as most people assume, or do pain and discomforts have *instrumental* value …?[79]

It should be obvious, however, that a pain's having instrumental value does not preclude its being intrinsically bad. If our lives contain lots of pain and discomfort, that is intrinsically very bad even if those pains and discomforts have some instrumental

---

70   Ibid. (Emphasis added.)
71   Ibid.
72   Ibid.
73   "Access to Controlled Medicines Program," World Health Organisation Briefing Note, February 2009, http://www.who.int/medicines/areas/quality_safety/ACMP_BrNoteGenrl_EN_Feb09.pdf (accessed 24 January 2012).
74   Ibid.
75   Sevil Atasoy, Statement by Professor Sevil Atasoy, President of the International Narcotics Control Board (2009) http://www.incb.org/documents/President_statements_09/2009_ECOSOC_Substantive_Session_published.pdf
76   Philip A. Pizzo & Noreen M. Clark, "Alleviating Suffering 101 – Pain Relief in the United States", *New England Journal of Medicine*, 19 January 2012, Vol. 366, No. 3, p. 197.
77   Ibid.
78   Ibid.
79   Brooke A. Trisel, "How Best to Prevent Future Persons from Suffering: A Reply to Benatar", p. 83.

value. The suffering somebody endures might lead to great good, but it does not follow that the suffering is intrinsically any less bad as a result.

Perhaps Mr Trisel means, or could be taken to mean, that intrinsically bad though
pain is, our lives would be much worse without it. This would clearly not be true of *all*
pain. Mr Trisel says as much about chronic pain[80]. But surely it is also true of some
acute pain. What is the instrumental value of labour pains or of the terminal stages of
cancer? And what, for most of human history, was the instrumental value of pain in-
duced by kidney stones, for example? Even those pains that do have instrumental
value may sometimes be gratuitously severe – much more severe than they need to be
in order to get our attention.

However, there are problems even if we focus merely on those pains that not only
have instrumental value but which also have that value without being unnecessarily severe. Perhaps our lives would be even worse without them. That does not mean that
our lives are not already bad. Mr Trisel claims that if "the quality of our lives is very
bad … then it would be difficult to imagine that they could be worse"[81]. He is mistaken. Something's being very bad is not negated by the possibility that things could
be still worse. Losing both one's arms is surely very bad even though things would be
still worse if one also lost both one's legs.

There is a still deeper problem. I agree that without some (but not other) pains and
discomforts our lives would be even worse. But that itself is a terrible feature of sentient life. It would be so much better if some pains were not necessary – if we could
have the benefits that pain sometimes brings but to have those benefits without the
pains. The response to this brings us to Mr Trisel's third criticism of my quality-of-life
argument.

*Perfection is an inappropriate standard:*
Brooke Trisel says that perfection is an inappropriate standard by which to judge the
quality of human life. More specifically, he says that standards "must be based on
what is nomologically possible, not on logically possible, but nomologically impossible conditions"[82].

His main argument for this conclusion appeals to three demanding standards one
might use to judge the quality of life: the Extreme Standard, the Super Extreme Standard, and the Perfection Standard. All of these standards are nomologically impossible, but the Super Extreme Standard is even more demanding than the Extreme Standard, and the Perfection Standard is the most demanding of the three. Mr Trisel says
that if one denies, as I do, that we should judge the quality of life by the standards of
the nomologically possible, then one is unable to choose, in a non-arbitrary way, between the three nomologically impossible standards he discusses.

However, I see no reason why we should not judge the quality of life by the highest
(logically) possible standard. There is nothing arbitrary about choosing perfection over
any standard that approximates but does not reach it.

Mr Trisel thinks that this move is not open to me because if I use "the Perfection
standard to judge the quality of our lives, this would be inconsistent with maintaining

---

80   He says that "chronic pain no longer serves a biologically useful purpose" (p. 84). He may be overstat-
      ing the case here. Perhaps *some* chronic pain does have instrumental value, by preventing one from do-
      ing things that would harm oneself further.
81   Brooke A. Trisel, "How Best to Prevent Future Persons from Suffering: A Reply to Benatar", p. 86.
82   Ibid, p. 88.

that a higher standard should be used to judge whether life is worth starting than whether life is worth continuing"[83], as I suggest we should.

But there is no inconsistency. The quality of both future and current lives could be judged by the Perfection Standard. In using that standard, however, we might think that different conditions need to be met (a) for a life to be worth starting; and (b) for a life to be worth continuing. Thus we might say that only perfect lives are worth starting (in the sense of not being a harm at all), but that even lives that fall significantly short of this standard might be worth continuing even while recognizing how far they are from perfection.

Consider the following analogy. In marking a student's work, we might employ a kind of perfection standard (100%) in judging the student's work. This does not mean that we cannot use one threshold to determine a Pass and another to determine a First Class Pass. Setting a perfection standard is one thing, and benchmarking against that standard is another.

## Thaddeus Metz:

Thaddeus Metz also takes issue with my employing a perfection standard, although his criticism is not framed in the same way. Instead, he objects to my appealing to an objective perspective – *sub specie aeternitatis* – in evaluating the quality of human life.

He advances two arguments. The first refers to the evolutionary origins of our making value judgments and says that for this reason "it is extraordinarily unlikely that" our judgment "would be informed by the point of view of the universe"[84]. His second argument is that I routinely make "judgments of what is immoral and what is harmful … without appealing to the point of the view of the universe"[85]. He says that if I "can know *which* conditions are good or bad without appealing to a non-human standpoint" then I should be able to "make judgments of *how* good or bad something is without appealing to such a standpoint"[86].

The problem with these arguments, however, is that they seem to be based on a mistaken interpretation of what it means to judge the quality of life *sub specie aeternitatis*. Such a perspective does not commit us to the level of abstraction or removal from human evaluation that Professor Metz seems to think. Instead what this perspective does is prevent the limited horizons and imagination of most human beings from getting in the way of reaching conclusions about what would be good for them. Thus, people take sickness, disability, pain, discomfort, frustration, and sadness to be bad. They take intelligence, understanding and vigour to be good. And they want to live as long as possible (unless the life ceases to be worth continuing). What the objective perspective enables us to see is how far short of the ideal we fall on all these things that we value. We get sick, including very sick. We suffer terrible pain, discomfort, frustration and sadness. Our intelligence and understanding, even though they surpass that of other animals, are meagre. We typically live for less than a century. The implication of all this is that our lives are considerably worse than they could be. What stands in the way of people recognizing this is a reigning-in of expectations and a curtailment of imagination in the face of human limitations. The more objective perspective is required to show up these coping mechanisms for what they are and to provide a more

---

83   Ibid, p. 89.
84   Thaddeus Metz, "Are Lives Worth Creating?", p. 252.
85   Ibid, p. 253.
86   Ibid.

reliable view of the quality of human life.

## Rivka Weinberg:

These same points can be made in response to Rivka Weinberg's suggestion that there is no outside perspective from which we can judge human life. She says that because life "is something we are all stuck in ... there seems no 'outside' position from which to assess the preference for human life"[87]. Thus, she says, the "common preference for life is not analogous to standard adaptive preference cases"[88].

For the reasons I have already stated, this seems like a simple failure of imagination. There is a perspective beyond an unreflective subjective perspective – and one that we can access if we think about it. We are not as paralyzed as she seems to think we are in the face of conflicting assessments of life's quality.

She quotes director Roberto Benigni who, in his Academy Award acceptance speech, thanked his parents "for the greatest gift of all: *poverty*"[89], and she refers to Viktor Frankl who "did not regret his excruciating experience in the Nazi death camps because he felt that the experience enriched his understanding and appreciation of the meaning of life"[90]. Commenting on such cases she says:

> One may argue that it is the benefits that are valued in these cases and not the pain that it took to acquire them but that is not how the value is described by the people in the examples above. They describe the pain itself not as an unfortunate yet necessary means to benefit but as itself a benefit.[91]

It is far from clear that this analysis is correct. The pains do seem to be described as instrumentally good. (Note, for example, that Viktor Frankl explains his lack of regret and the explanation consists in the good that arose from it.) However, if it were the case that these and other such people thought that the pain was valuable in itself, we would have excellent grounds to say that they are wrong. Being starved, treated with contempt, and living under the constant threat of death is not intrinsically good, even if it has some instrumental value. If Viktor Frankl could have "enriched his understanding and appreciation of the meaning of life" without having had to endure Nazi death camps, his life would have been that much better. And insofar as people are not able to gain understanding and to appreciate the good in the absence of suffering, that itself is a serious reduction in the quality of human life.

## Saul Smilansky:

Saul Smilansky says that life is good. He does not think that it is *always* good, but he thinks that it is good often enough to exonerate much procreation. He advances a number of arguments for this conclusion. One of his arguments is the now familiar one that the bad things in life can have instrumental value. As I have already pointed to the flaws in this argument in responding to Brooke Trisel and Rivka Weinberg, I shall not

87   Rivka Weinberg, "Is Having Children Always Wrong?", p. 34.
88   Ibid.
89   Ibid.
90   Ibid.
91   Ibid, pp. 34-5.

respond to Professor Smilansky's version of it. Nor shall I reply to his argument that if death is bad, life must be good. My response to this will be implicit in my response to the paper by Rafe McGregor and Ema Sullivan-Bissett. Instead, I shall consider Saul Smilansky's other arguments.

The first of these arguments begins with the observation that most people report being happy, and then claims that "genuine first-personal reports of happiness have strong evidential weight"[92]. But just how much evidentiary weight do they have? Professor Smilansky says that happiness "seems akin to pain" in this regard. Since people cannot be mistaken about whether they are in pain, (truthful) first-personal reports of pain will have massive evidentiary weight. But is happiness really like pain in this way? If by "happiness" one means "pleasure" then I agree that happiness is relevantly similar to pain. One cannot be mistaken about whether one is now in pain or is now feeling pleasure. But this is not what Professor Smilansky means by happiness and it is not what I meant. By happiness we both mean "well-being" – that is, how well one's life is going. People *can* be mistaken about that. Perhaps one cannot be mistaken about how well one's life *seems* to be going, but one can certainly be mistaken about how well it is in fact going. In *Better Never to Have Been*, I showed how irrespective of which account of well-being one adopts, life is much worse than most people think. Professor Smilanksy's claim that happiness "seems akin to pain" does nothing to respond to, let alone undermine those arguments.

I referred to vast empirical evidence that gives us very good reason to doubt that people's self-assessments are a reliable indicator of a life's quality. Professor Smilansky says that I do "a good job of pointing all this out" and that "with all this undeniably going on" he "will not have a simple decisive reply".[93]Thus he attempts to mitigate the significance of the evidence I cited.

For example, he notes that divergences in subjective reports of well-being "tend to make good sense"[94]. More specifically, societies "which report higher levels of happiness are by and large the societies where we would expect this to be so"[95]. But the problem with this argument is that these divergences are entirely compatible with a global illusion. In other words, it is entirely possible that while people in all countries over-estimate the quality of their lives, their overestimations are off an objective baseline. That is to say, people everywhere overestimate, but because their objective conditions do differ, the combination of objective conditions and overestimation yield the result that people report being happier where conditions are better. This can be represented as in Figure 4 on the next page.

The vertical axis represents a range of objective conditions, from worse below to better above. The horizontal axis represents a range of perceptions of life's quality. The A-gradient represents the reports that would be made if reports accurately tracked objective conditions. The B-gradient is one possible representation of reports that are made if reports are subject to the psychological phenomena that cause people to over-estimate the quality of their lives.

---

92    Saul Smilansky, "Life is Good", p. 70.
93    Ibid, p. 74.
94    Ibid, p. 70.
95    Ibid.

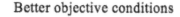

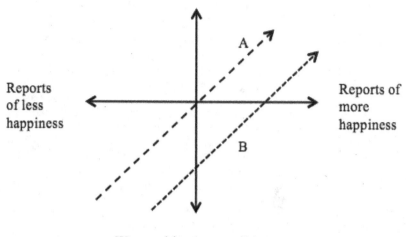

**Figure 4**

What is surprising is not that people report more happiness in societies in which conditions are better (or less bad), but rather that people report as much happiness as they do even in societies where the conditions are objectively among the worst.

Professor Smilanksy seems more confident of his arguments about suicide. He says that suicide is "a great embarrassment" for my claims, because very few people kill themselves[96], which suggests that life is not that bad.

This reasoning is flawed for at least three reasons. First, the fact that coming into existence is a harm does not entail that death (and thus suicide) is preferable. I shall consider challenges to this claim in the next section. Second, if people's self-assessments about the quality of their lives are (generally) unreliable, we should expect that they would want to continue living in many cases when life is no longer worth living. Third, there are good evolutionary reasons why people are generally not inclined towards suicide.

Professor Smilansky claims that "fairly decisive points"[97] can be made against this last point. He says that we find that two categories of people are most likely to take their own lives. The first group is young people, which he attributes to "the temporary instability of hormonal-affected youth"[98]. The other group, he says, is the "terminally ill, decrepit or elderly", who, he says, "are frequently people for whom it *makes sense*

---

96   Ibid, p. 71.
97   Ibid.
98   Ibid.

to wish to cease living"[99]. He claims further that "most people who kill themselves in fact do so because of the *absence* of something: life is good unless crippled"[100] in some way.

These observations fail to ward off my claim that there are good evolutionary reasons why people are generally disinclined to suicide and why we cannot therefore take the yearning to go on living as an indication of life's quality. Even if a more accurate assessment of life's quality would lead many people who currently want to live to instead prefer death, it does not follow that most of those who *have* taken their own lives had lives that were not worth continuing. In other words, it may be irrational for some people to continue living and also be irrational for many of those – including many (but not all) young people – who take their own lives to have done so.

Nor is my position threatened by the suicides of those people, such as the terminally ill, for whom suicide was rational. Indeed, what may be surprising is how bad things have to get before people want to die. Professor Smilansky himself recognizes this when he says that people "typically cling to life even when life objectively seems to be very bad and even hopeless"[101]. If people want to continue living when even a cheery optimist such as Professor Smilansky thinks their condition is hopeless, it is not hard to see how people want to continue living when their condition is seen to be very bad only by those without an optimistic bent.

Professor Smilansky's claim that "most people who kill themselves in fact do so because of the *absence* of something" does not help his case either. Ill-health can be characterized as the *absence* of health, but it can equally be characterized as the *presence* of illness. Whether we phrase it as the presence of bad things or the absence of good things is irrelevant. But perhaps that is not what Professor Smilansky's point rests on. Perhaps he is saying only that life is good unless enough bad intrudes. It is not clear, though, how that assertion undermines the argument that life is not good. This is in part because of how much bad can intrude. Nor is it clear how Professor Smilansky's point undermines the argument that life is merely worth continuing (rather than being good) until enough bad intrudes.

Saul Smilansky invokes suicide in a further way in order to defend procreation. He says that "if life is so bad, the badness can be stopped ... there is, almost always, a way out"[102]. As a result, he says, "taking the risk of generating life seems reasonable"[103].

This strikes me as a callous argument. Taking one's own life, at least when done rationally, is no easy task. Even if one has the physical means to do the job painlessly and effectively, the psychic hurdles are significant. One knows that if one now performs a certain action, one's life will end – one will cease to exist for all eternity. Even when life has become unspeakably bad, the prospective suicide might still face an agonizing choice – even when it is a Hobson's choice. To suggest that it is acceptable to create people because they can take their own lives if things get bad enough, is to underestimate how appalling it is to face the choice of either taking one's own life or endure terrible suffering.

---

99  Ibid.
100  Ibid, p. 72.
101  Ibid.
102  Ibid.
103  Ibid.

The potential suicide also has to consider those who are left behind – bereaved family members and friends. In response to this, Professor Smilansky takes refuge behind logical possibility without considering the practicalities. He considers the possibility of some connected circle of people taking their own lives together so that none is left bereaved. But this simply fails to consider the real world, in which one person may have reached his limit, but others in his circle have not. Nor does it consider the fact that circles of attachment are overlapping. Husband and wife want to end their lives, but they do not want to inflict the suffering of bereavement of their adult children, who in turn do not want to inflict bereavement on their spouses, who in turn do not want to inflict bereavement on their parents and siblings, and so forth. A sufficiently large suicide pact – and one in which coercion were absent – is practically either impossible or at least extremely unlikely. It should thus bring no comfort to those whose practical moral deliberations are rooted in reality.

Professor Smilansky tries some other moves to mitigate the implications of the evidence that self-assessments of well-being are unreliable. He says, for example, that insofar as "life tends to be quite good ... illusion is much less needed"[104]. But that is not a way to show that illusions are less operative. We have evidence that the illusion is present. It is not a proper response to this to assume the antecedent – that life tends to be quite good. And if Professor Smilansky responds that he is not *assuming* that life tends to be quite good, but is instead drawing on conclusions for which he has argued elsewhere in his paper, then it becomes clear that the argument of his that I am now considering adds nothing to his other arguments.

He also says that Pollyannaism often "*actually makes life better* for those under its influence"[105]. I am sure that that is true, but only to a limited degree. Thinking that things are better than they actually are can actually make things better, but it does not follow that things will actually be as good as one thinks they are. In other words, there may well be a feedback loop, but this is not sufficient to obliterate the distinction between one's perceptions of the quality of one's life and one's actual quality of life[106].

Saul Smilansky also argues that "even where people are not very happy, they can be filled with a sense of the significance of their lives"[107]. This is more grasping at straws. All the arguments I provided for why self-assessments of well-being are unreliable, apply equally to self-assessments of significance. Indeed, on some views, significance is part of well-being. And the suggestion that the "potential for existential meaning in one's life is granted only when one has been brought into existence"[108] invites the response that those who never exist have no need for existential meaning and are not deprived by its absence.

In his concluding remarks, Saul Smilansky says that the reasonableness of reproductive risk is largely neglected in my discussion. His response is to note that people "take upon themselves considerable physical and emotional risk" and thus that "the fact that

---

104  Ibid, pp. 74-5.
105  Ibid, p. 75.
106  I discuss this further in David Benatar, "Suicide: A Qualified Defense", in James Stacey Taylor (Ed.), *The Ethics and Metaphysics of Death: New Essays*, New York: Oxford University Press (forthcoming, but pre-printed in David Benatar, *Life, Death and Meaning* (Second Edition), Lanham MD: Rowman & Littlefield, 2010, pp. 307-31).
107  Saul Smilansky, "Life is Good" p. 75..
108  Ibid, p. 76.

life is full of risk ... does not, in itself, prove much"[109]. He says that the matter requires further exploration. In exploring this further, it would be worth recalling that the risks people take upon themselves are importantly different from the risks of procreation, for in the latter the person brought into existence does not decide to assume the risks. Instead, the very considerable risks are thrust upon him by his parents.

## Anti-Natalism and Pro-Mortalism

The paper by Rafe McGregor and Ema Sullivan-Bissett is not directly concerned with the soundness of my asymmetry and quality-of-life arguments. Instead, these authors seek to show that my arguments imply what they call "pro-mortalism"[110], by which they mean the view that suicide is either always or almost always preferable to continued existence[111].

They begin their argument by suggesting that there is a *prima facie* case for thinking that my asymmetry argument entails pro-mortalism. This, they say, is because when somebody

> ceases to exist the result is: an absence of pain, which is good; and an absence of pleasure, which is not bad[112].

However, there is a basic error here that I think precludes a *prima facie* case. I had said that the absence of pleasure is not bad *unless there is somebody for whom this absence is a deprivation*. Now, obviously once somebody dies there is a sense in which that person no longer exists and thus cannot be deprived. However, there is another, at least equally good sense in which there *is* somebody who is deprived. On this interpretation, the person deprived is the ante-mortem person who would have experienced the pleasures had he not died. All those people who think that death does deprive the deceased of the experiences he would otherwise have had – and there are many people who think this – would not apply the "not bad" evaluation to the absent pleasures of the deceased. This is because the absence of these pleasures in the world in which the person dies is worse than the presence of these pleasures in a world in which the person continued living and could thus experience them.

Of course, it is not the case that everybody thinks that death deprives the deceased. Most famously, Epicureans deny that death deprives or otherwise harms the deceased. Mr McGregor and Ms Sullivan-Bissett seem to think that it is crucial that I refute the Epicurean argument. For example they say that it "is important for Benatar that the Epicurean line is mistaken"[113]. They argue at some length that my response to the Epicurean argument fails[114], which is one reason why they think that my anti-natal argument implies pro-mortalism. I have many responses to those arguments, but they can all be bypassed. This is because Mr McGregor and Ms Sullivan-Bissett are mistaken in thinking that refuting the Epicurean argument is crucial.

---

109 Ibid, p. 77.
110 Rafe McGregor & Ema Sullivan-Bissett, "Better No Longer to Be: The Harm of Continued Existence".
111 They begin with the more expansive claim but later consider the slightly restricted claim.
112 Ibid, pp. 56-7.
113 Ibid, p. 59. See also, p. 63.
114 I never set out to provide a refutation of the Epicurean argument. I presented the argument, raised some responses to it and then noted what I take to be an impasse between those who accept and those who reject the argument. (p. 217) While I have my doubts about the Epicurean argument, I am not convinced that there is a decisive refutation of it and am not wedded to its being fallacious.

I made a very limited claim, namely that "the view that coming into existence is always a harm does *not imply* that death is better than continuing to exist, and a fortiori that suicide is (always) desirable".[115] This claim is not undermined if one points out that combining the view that coming into existence is always a harm with some other view yields a pro-mortalist conclusion. To say that view X combined with view Y yields view Z is not to say that X entails or implies Z.

Now this may seem like a mere logical nicety if view Y (the Epicurean view in this case) happens to be true. However, very few people think that the Epicurean view is correct. It is a distinctly minority position. And if the Epicurean view *is* true, anti-natalism is the least of everybody's problems. This is because everybody, and not just those who accept my argument that coming into existence is always a harm, will have to accept that killing somebody does not harm that person. That view seems even harder to accept than mine. However, if one did come to accept it, there would be nothing in the least alarming about pro-mortalism. The claim that suicide is always or almost always preferable to continued existence is alarming only if one thinks that death is a harm. If one thinks that it is not a harm why would one be against death?

It is not evident from their paper, but our discussions in Johannesburg revealed that one of the authors takes their argument to be a *reductio ad absurdum* of my arguments, while the other author thinks that my arguments are sound and simply wishes to point out the purported implications. Clearly the author who thinks the argument is a *reductio* is mistaken: If the Epicurean view is true, there is nothing absurd about pro-mortalism. The other author is mistaken that my view implies pro-mortalism. Some other view has to be added to mine in order to imply pro-mortalism.

Mr McGregor and Ms Sullivan-Bissett also take issue with my argument that we should apply different standards to determining when a life is worth beginning and when it is worth continuing. I had argued that whereas those who do not yet exist have no interest in coming into existence, those who already exist (in the morally relevant sense) have an interest in continuing to exist. While this interest can be defeated if the quality of life is bad enough, it is not the case that the mere existence of harm in a life will be enough to defeat the interest in continuing to live. One conclusion of this argument is that a life may be one that we should not start but that if started it is not one that should be ended.

Mr McGregor and Ms Sullivan-Bissett reject this argument primarily because they think it is incompatible with other things I say (or that they attribute to me). They say that if "(coming into) existence is not only a harm, but a *serious* harm"[116] and if "Pollyannaism is indeed rife amongst human beings … it seems that many interests in continued existence over suicide lack a rational basis"[117]. In other words, if existence is as bad as I say it is and Pollyannaism is as deep and widespread as I say it is, the preference or interest that people have in continued existence may be irrational. They conclude that, following my view, "it is (mostly) rational to commit suicide"[118].

There are many problems with this argument. The first is that although I was explicit in saying that *coming into* existence is always a serious harm, these authors want to attribute to me the view that existence itself is always a serious harm. That more expan-

---

115 *Better Never to Have Been*, p. 212.
116 Rafe McGregor & Ema Sullivan-Bissett, "Better No Longer to Be: The Harm of Continued Existence", p. 64.
117 Ibid.
118 Ibid. p. 65.

sive claim skews their argument in favour pro-mortalism, because if existence itself is a serious harm then ending existence, far from being a harm, is actually a relief from harm and thus a kind of benefit.

However, the evidence Mr McGregor and Ms Sullivan-Bissett provide for attributing the bolder claim to me is flawed. They point[119] to four statements I made:

(1) 'I deny that *any* lives are worth starting' (Benatar 2006: 121, Benatar's italics).

(2) '[I]t would be better if humans (and other species) became extinct' (Benatar 2006: 194).

(3) 'All things being equal, the longer sentient life continues, the more suffering there will be' (Benatar 2006: 209).

(4) 'I have argued that our lives are very bad. There is no reason why we should not try to make them less so, on condition that we do not spread the suffering (including the *harm of existence*)' (Benatar 2006: 210, our italics).

However, none of these claims support their interpretation:

(1) refers to lives that are "worth starting" and thus refers to coming into existence rather than to existence itself.

(2) refers to extinction of the species. Moreover, it is clear from other things I say that it refers to extinction *by non-replacement* of people who die rather than by the killing or death of current people.

(3) also refers to all life and not to individual lives. That is to say, the longer the species lasts *because the more people are brought into existence* the more suffering there will be.

(4) actually rules out many cases of suicide because many cases of suicide will increase the suffering to those left behind.

A second problem is that their argument trades on a vagueness about the relevance of Pollyannaism for the rationality of suicide. To say that most people overestimate the quality of their lives is not to say that if they were to accurately assess their lives they would, here and now, have sufficient reason to end their lives. This is partly because it is possible to overestimate the quality of a life that *is* worth continuing. Such a life may not be as good as one thinks it is but it may nonetheless be good enough to be worth continuing.

Now this might be thought to apply to very few lives if, as I have argued, coming into existence is a *serious* harm. However, that is not necessarily the case. First, it is possible that coming into existence is a serious harm because of the terrible things that will happen later in that life (or that happened earlier in it). Yet, once one exists it might be the case that because those terrible things will only occur in one's future (or because they have already occurred) one is entirely rational in not ending one's life now. It might get bad enough later that it would be rationally preferable to end one's life, but that does not mean that one must end it now.

Second, there is a spectrum of possible standards that one could employ to determine how bad a life must be before it is no longer worth continuing. The more suffering that one thinks is consistent with a life worth continuing, or the more one values continued life, or the greater the harm that one thinks death is, the more serious the suffering that will be consistent with a life worth continuing. Thus, it is possible to be

---

119  Ibid, pp. 58.

experiencing serious harm without it being *serious enough* to make one's life not worth continuing. This is a view many people have about life's suffering. I see no reason why it shouldn't be coupled with the view that coming into existence is always a serious harm.

Moreover, the preference to continue living does not need to be entirely rational in order to have some force in deciding what we should do. If somebody fears death then even if that fear is irrational it may nonetheless be relevant to whether he should take his own life, in just the same way that an irrational fear of heights is relevant to whether one should, for example, take the cableway up Table Mountain.

The kernel of truth in Mr McGregor's and Ms Sullivan-Bissett's paper is that I do think that suicide is both justified and rationally defensible more often than most people think it is[120]. They are wrong, however, in thinking that my anti-natalist arguments commit me to the view that suicide is preferable for most people most of the time.

## Other Routes to Anti-Natalism

The remaining three papers in this special issue all defend anti-natalism. Asheel Singh focuses on defending Seana Shiffrin's (substantially anti-natalist) argument against a possible objection to her argument. Although he refers to my arguments he does so approvingly and thus I shall not respond to his arguments. However, I shall comment briefly on Gerald Harrison's and Christopher Belshaw's anti-natalist arguments.

### Gerald Harrison:

Gerald Harrison proposes an alternative way to reach the anti-natalist conclusion for those who might have difficulty accepting my arguments. His route does not commit him to the view that coming into existence is always a harm. Indeed, he says that his argument is compatible with (but does not assume) the view that coming into existence is sometimes a benefit.

As is the case with my argument, his also rests on an asymmetry. However, he says that instead of it resting on an asymmetry of pain and pleasure, it rests on an asymmetry of duties. Duties, he says, presuppose victims. More specifically he says that one

> can only have a duty to do X, if failing to do X would wrong someone. In other words if one cannot identify someone who would be wronged by one's failure to fulfil the supposed *prima facie* duty, then the duty does not exist[121].

The *asymmetry* is not made explicit here, but it is easy to state it. The asymmetric counterpart to the requirement that there be a victim in the event that the purported duty is breached is the absence of a requirement that there be a beneficiary if the purported duty is fulfilled.

This asymmetry of duties is not enough to generate an anti-natalist conclusion. It is combined with a theory of *prima facie* duties in the tradition of W.D. Ross. A *prima facie* duty not to cause suffering would impose a *prima facie* duty not to procreate be-

---

120  I have discussed these issues only briefly here. A much more extensive discussion can be found in David Benatar, "Suicide: A Qualified Defense", in James Stacey Taylor (Ed.), *The Ethics and Metaphysics of Death: New Essays*, New York: Oxford University Press (forthcoming, but pre-printed in David Benatar, *Life, Death and Meaning* (Second Edition), Lanham MD: Rowman & Littlefield, 2010, pp. 307-31).

121  Gerald Harrison, "Antinatalism, asymmetry, and an ethic of *prima facie* duties", p. 96.

cause procreating brings about a person who will suffer. If this duty is violated, there will be a victim. The same cannot be said of a *prima facie* duty to promote pleasure in procreational contexts. Although procreation causes not only the pain but also the pleasure of those who are brought into existence, there is no victim if, in procreational decisions, one violates the purported duty to promote pleasure. Since a *prima facie* duty not to do X can only be defeated by other (and stronger) *prima facie* duties that pull in the opposite direction, the *prima facie* duty not to cause suffering and thus not to procreate is not defeated. It follows that we should not create new people.

Although Dr Harrison thinks that his argument is compatible with mine, he thinks that his argument has certain advantages. Instead of focusing on whether the purported advantages really are advantages, I shall mention briefly some challenges to his argument.

First, it presupposes a theory of *prima facie* duties. Thus, his argument will have no force against those who reject such a theory. Among the many people who fall into this category are utilitarians, Kantians and virtue theorists. Because my argument does not assume a particular moral theory, it has the advantage of a broader reach.

Second, even if we assume that there can only be duties if, in the event of non-performance, there is a victim, we might ask why this is the case. What explains this asymmetry? Where the absence of a victim is because no person was created, might the duty asymmetry not be explained by my more basic asymmetry? Consider the following procreative options, where a person exists in 1) and 2) but not in 3) and 4):

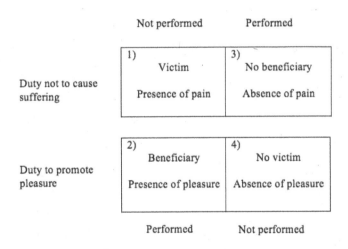

Figure 5

Dr Harrison's duty asymmetry tells us that there can be a duty only if there is a victim in the event that the purported duty is not performed. But why should that be the case? Why should it not be the case that there can be a duty only if there is a *beneficiary* in the event that the purported duty *is* performed? Alternatively, why should it not be the case that there can be a duty only if either (a) there is a victim if the duty is not performed, or (b) there is a beneficiary if the duty is performed? One explanation is that whereas the suffering of the victim in 1) is worse than the absence of that suffering in (3), the pleasure of the beneficiary in 2) is not better than the absence of pleasure in 4).

If my basic asymmetry is what explains the duty asymmetry then Dr Harrison's argument, while indeed an extension of my asymmetry argument (albeit within the limited framework of a theory of *prima facie* duties) could not be an alternative to it. This is because anybody who accepted Dr Harrison's asymmetry argument would also have to accept mine. For this reason, it is a pity that Dr Harrison has not provided an explanation for the duty asymmetry. If there is some explanation other than mine, stating what it is would have shown his argument to be the alternative he says it is.

## Christopher Belshaw:

Christopher Belshaw says that "the most troubling aspect" of my position is "the mix of anti-natalism on the one hand, and the rejection of pro-mortalism on the other"[122]. His argument takes the following form:

1)   If a life is so bad that there is reason not to start it then there is also reason to end the life, as long as "the part of a life that provides us with reason not to start it remains in the future"[123].

2)   David Benatar's argument "doesn't depend on there being any more than a minimal amount of pain"[124] and "for almost all of us, there is pain to come in the future".[125]

3)   Thus, if a life is so bad that it is not worth starting David Benatar should hold that there is also a reason to end it.

Dr Belshaw recognizes that I reject this argument because I deny the first premise. I argue that different standards should be used in determining whether a life is worth starting and in determining whether a life is worth ending. In rejecting this view, Dr Belshaw does not engage my underlying rationale and instead responds to an example I gave. I suggested that while being born without a limb would not make one's life worth ending, it would make one's life not worth starting. Dr Belshaw does not like this example because he says that "it's hard to see that lacking a limb should make life not worth living"[126].

Notice first that he uses the ambiguous "worth living", which I had explicitly disambiguated by distinguishing between "worth starting" and "worth continuing"[127]. Of course it is very hard to see how a life lacking a limb would not be worth continuing. If one fails to distinguish between "a life worth continuing" and "a life worth starting",

---

122   Christopher Belshaw, "A new argument for anti-natalism",p. 119.
123   Ibid. p. 120.
124   Ibid, p. 119.
125   Ibid, p. 120.
126   Ibid. p. 119.
127   *Better Never to Have Been*, pp. 22-24.

by lumping them together under "a life worth living", one will fail to see that such a life may not be worth starting.

Second, there is an obvious response even if we assume that Dr Belshaw thinks that a life with a missing limb is not so bad as to be not worth starting: If life without a limb is nonetheless worth starting, there could still be other conditions that are not worth starting but, once begun, are also worth continuing. In other words, there is nothing in the rejection of the particular example that precludes the possibility that some other condition could do the same work.

Of course, the first premise of Dr Belshaw's argument, as presented above, suggests that he thinks that there are *no* such conditions – that any life worth starting is a life worth continuing. However, Dr Belshaw has not argued for that conclusion (beyond disputing my example). More importantly, he has not shown why my argument for the opposite conclusion is flawed. I had given an account of *why* we apply and should apply different standards in judging which lives are worth starting and which are worth continuing:

> Those who exist … have interests in existing. These interests, once fully developed, are typically very strong and thus, where there is a conflict, they override interests in not being impaired. However, where there are no … interests in existing, causing impairments (by bringing people with defects into being) cannot be warranted by the protection of such interests.[128]

Dr Belshaw provides no argument against this account.

Dr Belshaw thinks that his own argument for anti-natalism[129] fares better than mine. Very little needs to be said to show how implausible that claim is. His argument rests on deeply controversial premises. Some of these are moral claims, such as the claim that pro-mortalism is true for babies[130]. That is to say, his argument requires us to believe that killing human babies never wrongs them. Other claims on which his argument rests are not moral but rather metaphysical. Thus, he thinks that he, and you and I were never babies[131] – that a person and the baby from which he or she grew are metaphysically distinct. These claims are far more controversial than any premise in my argument. Good arguments start from firm premises. Since my premises are much firmer than his, it is very hard to see how his argument for anti-natalism is an improvement over mine.

## Conclusion

Many people think that the conclusions of my arguments are counter-intuitive. They think that it must surely be false that coming into existence is always a harm, or that we should desist from creating new people. I (and other anti-natalists) do not find these views in the least bit counter-intuitive. I can see, of course, why my conclusions do run counter to most people's intuitions. There are, after all, good psychological explanations why people tend to be resistant to anti-natalism. Moreover, procreation is

---

128  Ibid, p. 25.
129  Dr Belshaw mistakenly suggests that anti-natalism "is the view that it's better never to have been born" (p. 117). In fact, anti-natalism is the view that procreation – creating new people – is wrong. One way to reach this conclusion is by arguing that it is better never to be born. But there are other routes to this conclusion. For example, one could note, as I did in *Better Never to Have Been*, that one could oppose the creation of new people because of how destructive a species *Homo sapiens* is.
130  Christopher Belshaw, "A new argument for anti-natalism", p.124.
131  Ibid, p. 123.

abundant. It also comes so naturally to people and brings parents, grandparents and siblings so much joy, that they find it difficult to believe that it could be wrong, at least in the absence of special conditions.

However, we should not put too much store on these intuitions, for they are *unreflective* intuitions formed under the influence of well-demonstrated biases. Once we begin to think about it, there should be nothing counter-intuitive about a view that, if acted upon, would eliminate all (human) suffering. Life contains lots of suffering. Even if one believes that vast portions of life are good, it is hard to deny that any child one creates will thereby become vulnerable to unspeakably horrible fates. Nor are the chances of actually succumbing to these fates remote. If we consider the cumulative risks, the chance of escaping all serious harms is very small. (If we include death as a serious harm, then the chance of escaping is reduced to zero.)

Anti-natalism might run up against unreflective intuitions, but it is not at all inconsistent with a more considered view. If more people saw this, they would feel less need to avoid the basic asymmetry. They would also be less alarmed by the implications of the quality-of-life argument – and more alarmed by procreation itself.

In memory of Asha Barron (5 April 199  25 anuary 2012) who died on the day this paper was completed.

# Index

Page numbers in **bold** refer to tables and those in *italic* refer to figures.

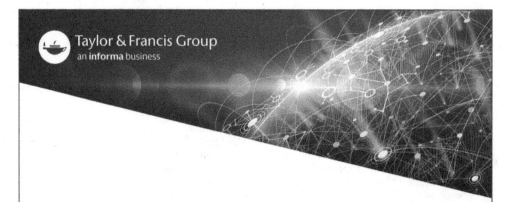